The Mt. Pleasant Public Library
PLEASANTVILLE, NEW YORK

MOOSEWOOD RESTAURANT COOKS FOR A CROWD

Other Books from MOOSEWOOD RESTAURANT

New Recipes from Moosewood Restaurant

Sundays at Moosewood Restaurant

The Moosewood Restaurant Kitchen Garden

Moosewood Restaurant Cooks at Home

The Moosewood Restaurant Low-Fat Cookbook

(to be released Fall 1996)

MOOSEWOOD RESTAURANT COOKS FOR A CROWD

Recipes
with a Vegetarian Emphasis
for 24 or More

The Moosewood Collective

John Wiley & Sons, Inc.

New York • Chichester • Brisbane • Toronto • Singapore

Photography by J. Gerard Smith

Library of Congress Cataloging in Publication Data:
Moosewood Restaurant cooks for a crowd : recipes with a vegetarian
    emphasis for 24 or more / the Moosewood Collective.
        p.   cm.
    Includes index.
    ISBN 0-471-12017-0 (alk. paper)
    1. Moosewood Restaurant.   2. Vegetarian cookery.   3. Quantity
cookery.   4. Cookery (Natural foods)   I. Moosewood Collective.
    TX837.M6743   1996   95-41512
    641.5'636—dc20

Printed in the United States of America

10 9 8 7 6 5 4 3 2 1

Contributors to This Book

Moosewood Restaurant is owned and managed by a group of 20 people. We work at a variety of tasks related to the business, from shifts at the restaurant to writing cookbooks. We strive to foster a spirit of cooperation and generosity, as well as friendship and creativity. Restaurant work is often pressured and challenging, but group ownership works to distribute the responsibilities.

All of these recipes were created at Moosewood Restaurant. Some of these dishes are old favorites, developed by departed, but still appreciated, collective members. Others are newcomers to the scene. The recipes in this book reflect what we actually do in the restaurant—quantity cooking. For our previously published cookbooks, we adapted our restaurant recipes to accommodate the needs of home cooks. Many of those dishes appear here in the ingredient/procedure format we follow at the restaurant. We hope this book will be helpful to cooks already converting our small-scale recipes to a larger scale.

Testers for the recipes in this book include Joan Adler, Tony Del Plato, Dave Dietrich, David Hirsch, Maggie Pitkin, Sara Robbins, and Tom Walls. The dessert chapter was authored by Susan Harville and edited by Nancy Lazarus. Project coordination and recipe selection, conceptualization and writing were accomplished by Joan Adler, David Hirsch, and Wynelle Stein.

Contents

Stuffed Vegetables

Desserts

Guide to Ingredients

Appendices   477

Index   487

Preface

Moosewood Restaurant has been offering an innovative whole foods cuisine since 1973. During that time, we have both witnessed and been a part of the changing face of the American diet. Our clientele has shifted through the years from a young counterculture audience in the early 1970s to a more inclusive, across-the-board population at the present time. One striking aspect of that change is the increasing number of people, vegetarian or not, who readily embrace the idea of meatless meals. We suspect that this phenomenon is the result of a few factors—a greater awareness of the connection between our health and the foods we eat, a greater appreciation of the diverse traditional vegetarian cuisines of the world, and a concern for the sustainability of life on our planet. In addition to the problems of erosion and deforestation caused by the overgrazing of livestock, it takes 9 pounds of grain to produce 1 pound of meat.

We have developed an extensive repertoire of vegetarian recipes, plus some fish and seafood dishes. Our recipes feature the full spectrum of vegetables, herbs, grains, beans, nuts, and soy and dairy products, with an avoidance of foods that are heavily processed or have chemical additives.

It has been very gratifying for us to have our reputation enhanced by the popularity of the Moosewood Restaurant cookbooks. As a result of this exposure, we have been invited to conduct a number of classes and seminars on vegetarian cooking. In these classes and in conversations with professionals in the field, requests have been made for us to write a book that offers flavorful, satisfying dishes with a vegetarian emphasis that can be prepared in volume. We hope that this book will prove that healthful and delicious institutional food need not be an oxymoron. Our aim is to present recipes and related information that will be useful to foodservices of all sizes—from a small catering firm to a large institutional facility.

At the present time, there is only one Moosewood Restaurant, at the original location in Ithaca, New York. We are modestly sized, seating 70 people from fall through spring, expanding to 100 in the summer, thanks to an outdoor patio. The fact that our kitchen is small has necessitated developing recipes that do not require complicated equipment. Our kitchen contains two ranges, two ovens plus a convection oven, a small microwave, a food processor, a blender, a mixer, conventional stainless steel pots and pans, steam tables, and counter space. We cook from "scratch" and use fresh vegetables, herbs, and authentic ethnic ingredients to create a quality food product. What defines our style as "Moosewood" is an eclectic menu influenced by international and American regional cooking that reflects a diversity of flavors and tastes. Any discussion of a Moosewood style has to include the knowledge, talent, and enthusiasm brought to the restaurant during the last 20-plus years by the many fine chefs who have each contributed to the continuing adventure.

An informal survey we conducted with foodservice professionals yielded an interest in recipes to serve 24. All of the recipes in this book have been tested at the restaurant for that amount (except soups, which were tested for 50 servings), and many also have been succesfully halved, doubled, or tripled. In addition to over 250 recipes, each with a nutritional analysis, this book contains a Menu Planning section, a Guide to Ingredients, and other appendices. The section "Menu Planning" reflects the important considerations of nutrition and balance, esthetics, and labor and cost factors, and the desire to generate an exciting, appealing cuisine. "The Guide to Ingredients" at the end of the book is a resource for information that may be unfamiliar to foodservice people who have limited experience in vegetarian or specific ethnic cuisines. Each section of recipes is preceded by introductory material offering specific information and tips. Many of the recipes also contain serving or menu suggestions.

These recipes are presented in a clear, easy-to-read-and-follow format, using basic techniques and equipment. The procedures describe what we do at the restaurant. We expect that experienced chefs will adjust the procedures to make best use of their own equipment. Similarly, the ingredients listed are ones we would use at Moosewood Restaurant. Budgetary constraints may restrict some facilities in their use of fresh ingredients. However, an eye to seasonings and cooking techniques may help to enliven prepackaged foods.

We offer a range of dishes that balance the need for lower-fat foods with the desire for an occasional "richer" selection. So some of these recipes represent restaurant fare that may be an occasional indulgence. However, we understand the need to address dietary concerns for low-fat and lower-fat foods. Here are some suggestions that will not substantially affect the workability of these recipes, or hinder the good taste of our food:

- Substitute low-fat milk or cheeses in soups and dairy entrées.
- Sweat, rather than sauté, vegetables in stock, water, juice, or wine.
- When excluding fats and oils, increase herbs and seasonings for flavor.
- Use nonstick pots and pans.
- Omit higher-fat toppings, such as nuts or sour cream. Substitute low-fat cheeses, salsas, or a mixture of chopped fresh herbs.
- If possible, substitute canola and olive oils for oils that are lower in monounsaturates, such as soy, peanut, or cottonseed oils.

Our cooking method involves time allowance for such preparation tasks as peeling, chopping, grating, and measuring ingredients. While labor is needed for this work, it is fairly simple hand work and easy to learn. We think that hand cutting, which results in somewhat uneven pieces, yields a more pleasing, home-style, human-scale quality than the manufactured "perfection" of machine-sliced foods. Of course, appearance is more important in dishes such as stir-fries or stews than in fillings or casseroles in which the vegetables are not "on display" and can be cut in the most expedient manner.

Ingredient measurements are given in both volume and weight, with some exceptions when only one type of measure seemed appropriate. For example, 1 level

teaspoon of a dried spice is easier to measure by volume than by weight. Bulky foods, such as sliced rounds of eggplant and zucchini, are difficult to measure in volume; we give weight measurements only. For most ingredients, weight gives a more consistently accurate measure than volume, because containers of cut foods can be more or less densely packed. See page 479 for the volume/weight equivalents of basic ingredients used in this book. Note that the measurements given in all recipes are for prepped (peeled, sliced, chopped, grated, etc.) ingredients. Appendix 1 on page 477 provides information on the percentage of food volume or weight usually trimmed or pared off in the preparation for cooking. This chart is useful for determining how much of a specific whole vegetable is needed to complete a recipe.

Dishes such as pasta, stir-fries, steamed vegetables, and some seafood are generally cooked to order at Moosewood, but most of the recipes in this book are geared for steam table service. This can be a distinct advantage for the many kinds of facilities in which dishes usually are not cooked to order, but are held for serving.

Through the years, we have served countless portions of many of the recipes here. Because our menu items change from day to day and from season to season, it would be impossible to estimate how many portions have been served. We have enjoyed learning from each other and reflecting on the variety of cultures that influence our lives. It is always gratifying to learn of others' appreciation of our work. We hope that these recipes—our customers' favorites—will generate enthusiasm in a wider arena for high-quality, fresh, wholesome food.

Acknowledgments

For over 20 years, Moosewood Restaurant has been a collective experience, from the management of the business to the food that is brought to the table. Our recipes are truly the product of all of the talented chefs who have contributed their effort and creativity; we thank you. We would especially like to thank our present-day coworkers for their support and patience during this project.

Thanks to our agents, Arnold and Elise Goodman, our editor, Claire Thompson, and production editor, Donna Conte, for their excellent advice and enthusiastic encouragement. We appreciate the careful eye, attentive organization, and good humor of our typist, Michael Aman, and the professional expertise of the The CBORD Group, Inc., which provided the nutritional analyses, especially Laura Winter Falk M.S., R.D. and Laura Ryan.

We are grateful to all of the Moosewood Restaurant fans; your support and appreciation keeps us going.

Moosewood Restaurant offers direct consultation to the foodservice industry in the following areas: planning meatless menus; using vegetarian protein sources in eclectic or traditional ethnic cuisines; preparing quick and easy meals; low-fat cooking; and cooking with fresh vegetables, herbs, and natural food products.

For more information, phone or fax (607) 273-5327, or write to the attention of David Hirsch, Moosewood Restaurant, 215 N. Cayuga Street, Ithaca, NY 14850.

MOOSEWOOD RESTAURANT COOKS FOR A CROWD

Menu Planning

The challenge of planning menus that feature whole foods, natural ingredients, and vegetarian cuisine can be a creative, adventuresome experience. Our style of menus at Moosewood Restaurant offers dishes that are influenced by both international and regional cuisines. By reflecting in our menus the diversity of flavors and fresh ingredients from around the world, we are able to create interesting menus that avoid a narrow definition of a healthful cuisine.

The success of the menus is based on three important components: the quality and availability of the ingredients, careful planning for preparation to ensure that the dishes are fresh tasting and visually appealing, and the balance and variety of dishes that comprise the menus.

INGREDIENTS AND THE PANTRY

Fresh Produce

Any food establishment or service that uses predominantly natural ingredients or offers vegetarian dishes will need frequent restocking of fresh vegetables, fruits, and herbs.

At Moosewood Restaurant, our menu changes every day, so we keep on hand, through daily ordering, a large variety of produce that is in peak condition. We are constantly monitoring our stock of basic ingredients such as onions, garlic, potatoes, carrots, and tomatoes, as well as ordering items that may need time to ripen such as avocadoes, bananas, mangoes, peaches, and other fresh fruit. The quantity and variety of our produce are also influenced by what has come into season and by what we plan to serve, especially when we need a large quantity of specific items for certain recipes.

We use and recommend that you also use produce that is locally, or at least regionally, produced, whenever possible. In season we buy from local growers and organic farmers and rely on our produce vendor for our daily stocking. He buys from our region and keeps a personal eye on quality and cost. In this manner, we avoid using produce that is bred primarily for yield and shipping rather than for freshness and taste.

The following recommendation for stocking fresh produce, of course, reflects our geographic location in central New York State. Use it as a guide to be modified or expanded upon depending on your location and the season.

Fresh Vegetables, Fruits, and Herbs: Inventory

Apples
Artichokes
Asparagus
Avocados
Bananas
Beets
Blueberries
Broccoli
Brussels sprouts
Cabbage: green and red, napa or bok choy
Carrots
Celery
Chile peppers
Cucumbers
Garlic: whole or fresh peeled
Ginger
Grapefruit
Grapes
Greens: kale, Swiss chard, watercress
Green beans
Herbs: basil, chives, cilantro, dill, marjoram, mint, oregano, rosemary, sage, tarragon, thyme
Kiwis
Leeks
Lemons

Lettuce: Boston, iceberg, red and green looseleaf, romaine
Limes
Mangoes
Melons: cantaloupe, honeydew, watermelon
Onions: red, Spanish, Vidalia
Oranges
Parsley
Parsnips
Peaches
Pears
Peppers: sweet; green, red, yellow
Pineapples
Plums
Potatoes: baking, chef's, red, sweet
Raspberries
Scallions
Shallots
Snow peas or sugar snap peas
Spinach
Strawberries
Squash: summer, zucchini
Squash: winter; acorn, butternut, delicata
Tomatoes: beefsteak, cherry, plum
Turnips

The Pantry

The range of ingredients that are stocked in a whole foods pantry will be an eclectic mix of domestic, imported, and ethnic ingredients. We consciously avoid using products that are heavily processed or have chemical additives. Many excellent suppliers, whose product lines feature natural, gourmet, and specialty foods in bulk, now exist in most regions. Searching out these suppliers is worthwhile so that you can benefit from these superior ingredients, which will enhance the dishes on your menus. We again recommend using as many locally or regionally produced products as possible. For example, tofu, tempeh, seitan, cheeses and dairy products, fresh pasta, honey, maple syrup, eggs, and juices will all be fresher and better tasting when you obtain them closer to the source. If any ingredients in the following lists are unfamiliar, refer to the *Guide to Ingredients* on page 467 for a detailed description.

Pantry Ingredients: Nonperishable Inventory

Beans: dried, canned if necessary

Black turtle
Black-eyed peas
Chick-peas (garbanzos)
Cannellini (white kidney)
Great Northern
Lentils, green and red
Limas
Pintos
Navy or pea beans
Red kidney
Split peas, green and yellow
Soy beans

Canned Goods

Artichoke hearts
Baby corn
Coconut milk, unsweetened
Fruits, unsweetened, in juice
Grape leaves
Olives: black, calamata, Spanish

Oils: olive (cold pressed and extra-virgin), peanut, pure soy
Pimientos
Pepperoncini
Roasted red peppers
Tomato products: juice, paste, plum, purée
Water chestnuts

Condiments, Dried Herbs, Flavorings, and Spices

Allspice
Annatto
Basil
Bay leaf
Black pepper
Cardamom
Cayenne
Chesapeake Bay seasoning
Chili oil and paste
Chinese fermented black beans
Coriander

(continued)

Cinnamon
Cloves
Cumin
Curry paste and powder
Dill
Dijon mustard
Fennel
Fish sauce
Five-spice powder
Fruit spreads: apricot, blueberry, raspberry, strawberry
Garam masala
Hoisin sauce
Horseradish
Lemon grass
Marjoram
Mint
Mustard seed
Nutmeg
Oregano
Paprika: hot and Hungarian sweet
Rosemary
Saffron
Sage
Sea salt
Sesame oil
Soy sauce or tamari
Tabasco or hot sauce
Tarragon
Thyme
Turmeric

Grains

Barley
Buckwheat groats (kasha)
Bulghur
Couscous
Cornmeal

Flour: pastry, unbleached white, whole wheat
Millet
Rice: basmati (brown and white), brown (short and long grain)

Pasta

Asian style: rice, soba, udon noodles
Flavored: egg noodles, fettuccine, specialty, tri-colored
Italian style: a variety of shapes including: fettucine, lasagna, linguini, orrechetti, orzo, ravioli, shells, ziti
Whole grain

Miscellaneous

Baking basics: baking powder and soda, chocolate naps (semisweet and unsweetened), cornstarch, flours, extracts, oats, pure vanilla
Breads (preferably whole grain): baguettes, Italian, rye, whole wheat
Crackers: sesame, whole wheat
Dried mushrooms: shiitake
Juices: apple and cider, concord grape, orange, peach, pear
Sun-dried tomatoes
Sweeteners: honey, maple syrup, molasses, sugar (brown, confectioners', white)
Tortilla chips: stone ground corn

Wines and Liqueurs

Chinese rice wine
Dry red and white wine
Liqueurs (amaretto, coffee, Grand Marnier)
Marsala
Mirin
Sherry

Pantry Ingredients: Perishable Inventory

Breads

Whole wheat pita

Cheeses

Brie
Cheddar
Cream
Cottage
Danish bleu
Finnish Swiss
Fontina
Fresh mozzarella
Gruyere
Havarti
Jarlsberg
Monterey Jack
Mozzarella
Neufchâtel
Parmesan
Provolone
Ricotta
Smoked Cheddar

Dairy

Butter
Buttermilk
Half-and-half
Heavy cream
Milk: skim, 1%, whole
Soy margarine
Yogurt: low-fat, nonfat

Eggs

Organic, if possible

Fish

Fresh white fillets
Shrimp and other seafood

Frozen Foods

Berries
Black-eyed peas
Cut corn
Lima beans
Okra
Green peas
Spinach
Tortillas: corn and whole wheat

Fruits, Dried

Apricots (unsulfured)
Currants
Dates
Figs
Pears
Prunes
Raisins

Filo Pastry

Miso

White and dark

Nuts and Seeds

Almonds
Cashews
Hazelnuts
Peanuts
Peanut butter (unsalted organic)
Pinenuts
Poppy seeds

(continued)

Sesame seeds	***Tempeh***
Tahini	
	Tofu
Seitan	Plain and seasoned
Plain and flavored	

PLANNING FOR PREPARATION

In a whole foods cuisine, the appealing texture, flavor, and presentation of the dishes is maintained through careful preparation.

Because this style of cooking can be labor-intensive, the menu planner must consider the tasks that can be accomplished ahead of time to ease preparation. At Moosewood, the menu planner informs the prep cooks about the vegetables to prepare for the daily menus, which fresh herbs and other ingredients are in stock, and which components of the dishes on the menu can be precooked. For example, because we prefer the texture and taste of dried beans cooked from scratch, fresh vegetables, fruits, and sauces that have a home-style flavor, we guide our cooks in the timing of their advance preparation. They prepare a fresh vegetable stock, grate cheeses, make dressings, salsas, and chutneys, and prepare basic vegetables such as onions, garlic, carrots, and peppers to be used in the next meal.

Because vegetables are the key player in our recipes, they require the most attention. We plan for the advance baking, braising, and marinating of specific vegetables. Hand-cut vegetables are important when they are prominent in the look of a dish, for example, a stew, sauté, or main dish salad. We save time and effort with machine-cut vegetables when they will be blended into a filling, soup, or sauce. Our chefs are careful not to overcook vegetables, and often green beans, sweet peas, spinach, asparagus, and broccoli are steamed in separate batches and then added to the dish right before serving.

It is also the menu planner's job to guide the judicious use of leftovers, which we view as a creative resource. For example, a peanut, tomato, cheese, or hot sauce can be reused to prepare stews, soups, and casseroles. Leftover steamed and roasted vegetables in good condition or cooked beans and grains can become the base for frittatas or casseroles or can be mixed in a side dish or main dish salad. Refer to our chapter introductions and individual recipes for additional information.

Finally, although garnishing our dishes takes little effort, it is a consideration for the menu planner. We plan to have chopped herbs, parsley, scallions, nuts, minced colorful peppers, and sliced fruits that will beautifully enhance the dishes that we serve with pride.

BALANCE AND VARIETY IN THE MENU

Our menu planners consider the cost of ingredients when planning the daily menus by balancing dishes that use expensive ingredients such as artichoke hearts and red peppers with those that use less expensive items like beans and grains. When planning menus, they also consider ease of preparation so that only a few selections will be labor-intensive, like our filled pastries or vegetable sautés, whereas the others will be simpler to prepare, like stove-top stews or simmering bean dishes.

It is also important to vary and balance the tastes within a selection. Side dishes and toppings can simultaneously complement the main dish, refresh the palate from a more dominant taste, and enhance the interest of the dish. Thus, we often serve our curries with toasted cashews, a cooling side of yogurt, and a sweet and pungent chutney. Similarly, simple dishes like Caribbean Black Beans become a gorgeous and intriguing entrée when served on Golden Spanish Rice with a crimson Mango Salsa.

A varied and balanced dish also influences the nutritional value of the meal. For example, just as bean protein is completed by grains, the fruits, vegetables, nuts, and dairy in toppings and side dishes contribute important vitamins, minerals, carbohydrates, and fiber to the meal. Use the vegetarian food pyramid that is found in Appendix 3 as a guide for preparing meatless meals that will satisfy the nutritional needs of your dining population. Also, with each recipe in this book, we offer serving suggestions and side dishes that can provide extra nutrition and balance. On many recipe headnotes, we indicate the featured "ethnic" flavors to help you coordinate the other dishes on your menu.

RECIPES AND SAMPLE MENUS

When using the recipes in this book for planning menus, we advise you to consider the season and the dietary concerns of your customers. Specific recommendations for menu planning, serving suggestions, and presentation appear on each recipe.

Offer a wide range of dishes through a season to spark the enthusiasm of your chefs and capture the interest of your diners.

In the following sample menus, we have outlined seasonal selections that also address ease of preparation and dietary preferences. You will find a wealth of other recipes in this book to use to create comparable menus. In addition, we include some ethnic menus for a special meal or occasion when the dishes celebrate the cusine of a specific culture or part of the world. It is always fun and challenging to plan these special meals, because we experiment with exotic ingredients and create innovative dishes. We encourage you to choose from these, our favorite recipes, to plan your own exciting repertoire of menus.

SPRING

In the spring, we rejoice at the return of tender lettuces to use in beautiful salads. We take advantage of the abundance of iron-rich greens such as spinach, chard, escarole, and kale to mix with sharp cheeses in casseroles or to use in lighter pasta dishes. We also add these flavorful greens to soups and stews where they provide bright color and texture. The refreshing flavor of young asparagus and the sweet bite of fresh peas and baby summer squash accent a number of main dish salads, entrées, and soups. Our desserts are now resplendent with ripe fresh strawberries, rhubarb, cherries, and apricots.

Lunch

Entrées
Thai Noodle Salad with cup of soup	Main dish salad, nondairy, vegan
Mexican Vegetables on Cornbread	Stew, quick and easy
Frittata Espinaca with Carrot Salad	Casserole, hearty

Soups
Cream of Asparagus	Festive
Portuguese Kale and White Bean	Nondairy, vegan, low fat

Sandwiches

Tofu Burgers	Nondairy, vegan
Garden Vegetable–Feta Pita	Quick and easy

Dinner

Entrées

Spanakopita with Artichoke Heart–Tomato Salad	Filled pastry, festive
Pasta Primavera with cup of soup	Main dish salad, nondairy, vegan
Dolmas with Tzatziki	Stuffed vegetable, nondairy, festive
Fresh Baked Fish with Asian Marinade and Snow Peas	Quick and easy, low fat

Soups

Curried Sweet Pea	Festive, low fat
Tomato Garlic	Quick and easy, low fat

Desserts

Fruit Ricotta Mousse	Quick and easy
Sarah's Fresh Apple Cake	Home-style
Apricot Almond Baklava	Festive

SUMMER

The bounty of summer is a menu planner's dream. Inspired by a lavish array of vegetables and fruits, we create dishes that honor their fresh flavors. The inherent beauty of vegetarian meals is evident in the stews, sautés, and sauces that are brimming with multicolored peppers, succulent tomatoes, and aromatic fresh herbs. We offer a variety of refreshing chilled soups and salads, and our desserts capture the best of summer's goodness with ripe melons, plums, peaches, and berries.

(continued)

Lunch

Entrées

Sweet Pepper and Cheese Strata	Casserole, hearty
Tabouli Salad Plate with Hummus and Grape Leaves	Main dish salad, nondairy, vegan
Pasta with Very Fresh Tomato–Basil Sauce	Quick and easy, low fat, nondairy, vegan

Soups

Chilled Gazpacho	Quick and easy, low fat, nondairy, vegan
Vegetable Chowder	Hearty, quick and easy

Sandwiches

Monterey Pita	Festive
Tempeh Reuben	Hearty

Dinner

Entrées

Pissaladiere (Tomato–Basil Pie)	Filled pastry, hearty, festive
Caribbean Vegetable Stew	Nondairy, vegan, low fat
Vegetable–Tofu Almondine with Asian Cabbage Slaw	Main dish salad, nondairy, vegan
Greek-Style Zucchini Casserole	Hearty

Soups

Chilled Buttermilk Borscht	Low fat
West African Peanut	Nondairy, vegan, low fat

Desserts

Tropical Fruit Salad	Low fat, nondairy, vegan
Gingered Plum Sauce on frozen yogurt	Quick and easy, low fat
Peach Parfait with Amaretto Cream	Festive

FALL/WINTER

At harvest time, a cornucopia of vegetables, fruits, beans, and grains are represented on our home-style menus. We offer hearty stews and gingery or spicy vegetable sautés. Our soups, salads, and casseroles feature nutritious beets, potatoes, parsnips, cabbage, and a variety of winter squashes. We create savory pastries and festive stuffed vegetables for holiday celebrations and present an assortment of delicious desserts, emphasizing fresh apples, pears, grapes, citrus, cranberries, and dried fruits.

Lunch

Entrées

Russian Salad with cup of soup	Nondairy, low fat
Rumpledethumps	Casserole, hearty
Winter Vegetable Stew with bread and cheese	Quick and easy, hearty, low fat

Soups

Autumn Gold	Nondairy, vegan, low fat
Creamy Onion with croutons	Hearty, quick and easy

Sandwiches

Herbed Ricotta Spread	Quick and easy
Floating Cloud Pita	Nondairy, vegan

Dinner

Entrées

Caribbean Black Beans with Mango Salsa	Nondairy, vegan, quick and easy, low fat
Ukrainian Vegetable Strudel with baked apple	Hearty, festive

(continued)

Spinach Lasagna Putanesca   Festive
Holiday Stuffed Squash with Orange   Nondairy, vegan, festive, low fat
     Ginger Sauce

Soups
Apple   Low fat
Parsnip Cheddar   Hearty, low fat

Desserts
Cranberry Apple Crisp   Home-style
Pumpkin Pear Pie   Festive
Scandinavian Dried Fruit Pudding   Low fat, nondairy, vegan

ETHNIC MENUS
∾

Greek and Middle Eastern

Soups
Lebanese Vegetable   Nondairy, vegan, low fat
Turkish Spinach–Lentil   Nondairy, vegan, low fat

Entrées
Fish Santorini with Greek Roasted   Festive
     Potatoes and Easy Artichoke
Greek-Style Cannellini and Vegeta-   Stew, low fat, nondairy, vegan
     bles with orzo
Vegetable Moussaka   Casserole, hearty
Spinach–Tofu Borekas with Carrot   Nondairy, vegan
     Salad

Desserts
Apricot Almond Baklava   Festive
Lemon Yogurt Grapes   Quick and easy, low fat

Mexican

Soups

Sopa de Lima — Nondairy, vegan, low fat

Crema de Elote — Hearty, festive

Entrées

Pompano Tampico on rice with green beans — Nondairy, festive

Chilaquile Casserole with Golden Spanish Rice — Hearty

Mole de Olla with cornbread — Nondairy, low fat

Black Bean–Sweet Potato Burritos on rice with Citrus Salsa — Nondairy, vegan, low fat

Desserts

Fresh Orange Compote — Quick and easy, low fat, vegan, nondairy

Coconut Pound Cake — Festive

African

Soups

North African Split Pea — Nondairy, vegan, low fat

West African Peanut — Nondairy, vegan

Entrées

Eggplant Marrakech with Fassoulia — Stuffed vegetable, nondairy, vegan, low fat

Fish West African Style on Coconut Rice with Sara's Greens — Nondairy, low fat

Creole Beans and Rice with Cucumber Tomato Salsa — Nondairy, vegan

Vegetable Tajine on couscous with grated feta cheese — Stew, low fat, hearty

Desserts

LD's Mango–Yogurt Dessert — Quick and easy, low fat

Butter Almond Pound Cake — Festive

(continued)

Menu Planning ∽ ∽ ∽ **13**

Eastern European

Soups

Budapest Vegetable	Nondairy, vegan, low fat
Finnish Golden Split Pea	Nondairy, vegan, low fat

Entrées

Balkan Moussaka	Hearty, pasta casserole
Vegetable Piroshki with Sweet and Sour Red Cabbage	Hearty, filled pastry
Bulgarian Stew with rye bread	Low fat, vegan, nondairy
Potato Kugel with applesauce and Kasha with Mushrooms	Nondairy

Desserts

Sour Cream Raisin Pound Cake	Festive
Triple Pear Crisp	Home-style

SOUPS

That this chapter is the longest in the book is a reflection of the universal popularity of soup. Soup is deeply associated with the concepts of nourishment and nurturing, both of which are more fully realized with a higher quality soup made with fresh ingredients.

All the recipes are scaled to serve fifty 6-ounce cups of soup, a standard size that might precede a larger meal. At Moosewood we also serve 8-ounce bowls that we frequently combine with bread and a salad to make a light meal. Heartier soups that lend themselves to this treatment include:

- Black Bean
- Budapest Vegetable
- Creamy Cauliflower Cheese
- Lebanese Vegetable
- Davina Stein's Vegetable
- North African Split Pea
- Portuguese Kale and White Bean
- Santa Fe Chowder
- Turkish Spinach–Lentil
- Vegetable Chowder

Leftover stews, bean dishes, and sauces that are in good condition may more effectively "reincarnate" on the next meal's menu as soups than in their original form. When converting a leftover to soup, use creativity in deciding what to add besides stock or water. For example, leftover Caribbean Black Beans, thinned with stock, orange juice, and a small amount of Hot Sauce, makes an excellent soup. The bean mixture from Pasta e Fagioli, thinned with tomato juice and stock and served with Parmesan cheese, becomes minestrone. We frequently serve Eggplant–Spinach Curry with a Lentil Dhal; combine both with stock for a spicy curried lentil–vegetable soup. Thin the spinach sauce from Fettucine Toscana with milk and stock, adjust the seasonings, and you have a cream of spinach soup.

Apple

50 6-oz. Servings

Delicately sweet and spiced, this soup brightens chilly fall or winter meals or is refreshing chilled for warmer seasons.

Equipment:	2½-gallon stockpot, 6-oz. ladle
Preparation Time:	30 minutes
Cooking Time:	30 minutes

Ingredients	Volume	Weight
Vegetable oil	¼ cup	
Onions, chopped	1⅓ qts.	1 lb. 5 oz.
Apples, cored, peeled, cut in chunks	7 qts.	8 lbs. 5 oz.
Apple juice or Vegetable Stock (p. 63)	1 gal.	
Cinnamon	2 tsp.	
Cloves, ground	1 tsp.	
Nutmeg, ground	½ tsp.	
Milk (or part half-and-half)	1 qt.	
Maple syrup (optional)	¼ to ½ cup	
Salt and black pepper to taste		

Garnishes

Yogurt, sour cream, or whipped cream (optional)
Cinnamon (optional)

Procedure

1. Sauté the onions in oil until they are softened.
2. Add the apples and juice or stock and simmer until the apples are tender.
3. Purée with the remaining ingredients until smooth.
4. Serve warm or chilled.
5. If desired, top with yogurt, sour cream or whipped cream, and a sprinkling of cinnamon.

Servings	Calories	Protein (g)	Fat (g)	Cholesterol (mg)	Carbohydrates (g)	Fiber (g)	Sodium (mg)
1	99	0.9	1.8	1	20.8	2.0	15

Autumn Gold

50 6-oz. Servings

This soothing soup has a rich flavor and gorgeous color.

Equipment:	2½-gallon stockpot, 6-oz. ladle
Preparation Time:	30 minutes (if squash precooked) to 1 hour
Cooking Time:	1 hour

Ingredients	Volume	Weight
Winter squash, cooked pulp	3 qts.	6 lbs.
Onions, chopped	2½ qts.	2 lbs. 8 oz.
Vegetable oil	½ cup	
Thyme, dried	1 tsp.	
Nutmeg, ground	1 tsp.	
Cinnamon, ground	1 tsp.	
Bay leaves	8	
Carrots, chopped	1 qt.	1 lb. 4 oz.
Celery, chopped	2 qts.	2 lbs.
Vegetable Stock (p. 63) or water	3 qts.	
Tomato juice	1½ qts.	
Apple juice	1 qt.	
Orange juice	1 qt.	
Salt and black pepper to taste		

Garnishes

Whipped cream, sour cream, or yogurt (optional)

Procedure

1. If cooking squash, bake seeded halves, covered with foil, in a 400° oven for about 1 hour, or until softened.
2. Sauté the onions in oil for a couple of minutes.
3. Add the spices and bay leaves and continue sautéing until the onions are translucent.
4. Add the carrots, celery, and stock or water. Bring to a boil; then simmer, covered, until the vegetables are tender. Remove the bay leaves.
5. In a blender, purée the squash, vegetables, and juices in batches until smooth. Taste for salt and pepper.
6. Reheat gently.
7. Garnish with a dollop of whipped heavy cream, sour cream, or yogurt if desired.

Servings	Calories	Protein (g)	Fat (g)	Cholesterol (mg)	Carbohydrates (g)	Fiber (g)	Sodium (mg)
1	67	2.0	2.7	0	15.4	3.2	134

Black Bean

50 6-oz. Servings

This Latin American classic is very popular at the restaurant.

Equipment:	2½-gallon stockpot, 6-oz. ladle
Preparation Time:	20 minutes (with precooked beans)
Cooking Time:	30 minutes

Ingredients	Volume	Weight
Black beans, dried	2 qts.	3 lbs. 4 oz.
or cooked, drained	5 qts.	7 lbs. 8 oz.
Vegetable oil	½ cup	
Onions, chopped	2½ qts.	2 lbs. 8 oz.
Garlic, pressed or minced	12 cloves or	
	¼ cup	
Coriander seed, ground	2 Tbsp.	
Cumin, ground	3 Tbsp.	
Cayenne	¼ to 1 tsp.	
Mustard, dry	1 Tbsp.	
Carrots, diced	1½ qts.	2 lbs.
Celery, diced	2 qts.	2 lbs.
Green or red peppers, diced	1½ qts.	1 lb. 8 oz.
Water or Vegetable Stock (p. 63)	3 qts.	
Dry sherry	1 cup	
Salt	2 Tbsp.	
Orange juice	1 qt.	
Lemon juice	2 Tbsp.	

Garnish

Sour cream or yogurt (optional)	1 cup	

Procedure

1. If using dried beans, soak the beans in water to cover overnight, or for at least 3 hours; or bring to a boil, remove from heat, and let soak for 1 hour. After soaking, drain and cook the beans in 1½ gallons of water until tender, for 30 to 45 minutes. Drain and set aside.
2. Sauté the onions and garlic in oil until the onions are softened.
3. Add the spices and sauté for 3 to 4 minutes, stirring often to prevent burning.
4. Add the vegetables, water or stock, and sherry and simmer until the vegetables are tender.
5. Stir in the cooked beans and orange and lemon juice. For a thicker soup, blend or process one-third of the soup and then remix with the remaining soup.
6. Reheat gently to prevent scorching.
7. Serve with a dollop of sour cream or yogurt if desired.

Servings	Calories	Protein (g)	Fat (g)	Cholesterol (mg)	Carbohydrates (g)	Fiber (g)	Sodium (mg)
1	147	7.0	2.9	0	23.9	7.3	315

Budapest Vegetable

50 6-oz. Servings

This wonderfully seasoned soup is substantial enough to be a meal, accompanied by a hearty bread and green salad.

Equipment:	2½-gallon stockpot, 6-oz. ladle	
Preparation Time:	30 minutes	
Cooking Time:	1 hour	

Ingredients	Volume	Weight
Vegetable oil	½ cup	
Onions, chopped	2½ qts.	2 lbs. 8 oz.
Garlic, minced or pressed	10 cloves or 3 Tbsp.	
Hungarian paprika	3 Tbsp.	
Marjoram, dried	1 Tbsp.	
Carrots, chopped	1 qt.	1 lb. 4 oz.
Cabbage, thinly sliced	1½ qts.	1 lb. 4 oz.
Green beans, cut in 1-in. pieces	3 cups	12 oz.
Green peppers, chopped	3 cups	12 oz.
Zucchini, halved lengthwise, cut in half-moons	3 cups	1 lb.
Mushrooms, sliced	1½ qts.	1 lb.
Tomatoes, canned with juice, crushed	1½ qts.	3 lb.
Salt	1 Tbsp.	
Vegetable Stock (p. 63) or water	5 qts.	
Red wine, dry	1 cup	
Tomato juice	1½ qts.	
Soy sauce	¼ cup	
Dill, dried	¼ cup	
Additional salt and black pepper to taste		

Procedure

1. Sauté the onions and garlic in oil until the onions are translucent.
2. Add the paprika, marjoram, carrots, and cabbage and sauté on low heat, stirring occasionally, for 10 minutes.
3. Add the remaining vegetables and salt, reduce heat, cover, and cook for 10 minutes, stirring occasionally.
4. Add the liquids and seasonings and simmer until all vegetables are tender, for about 20 minutes.

Servings	Calories	Protein (g)	Fat (g)	Cholesterol (mg)	Carbohydrates (g)	Fiber (g)	Sodium (mg)
1	80	2.0	2.6	0	13.1	2.5	366

Soups

Buttermilk Borscht

50 6-oz. Servings

Our version of a traditional Eastern European recipe includes the creamy and tangy qualities of buttermilk in a vivid magenta soup.

Equipment:	2½-gallon stockpot, 6-oz. ladle
Preparation Time:	30 minutes (with precooked beets)
Chilling Time:	2 hours

Ingredients	Volume	Weight
Beets, cooked, peeled, julienned or grated		6 lbs.
Vegetable Stock (p. 63)	1 gal.	
Cucumbers, peeled, seeded, diced	3 qts.	3 lbs. 8 oz.
Dill, fresh, chopped	3 Tbsp.	
Scallions, green and white parts, chopped	1½ cups	4 oz.
Dill pickle, chopped	1½ cups	8 oz.
Buttermilk	2 qts.	
Yogurt, plain, low-fat or nonfat	1 qt.	
Sour cream	1 qt.	
Salt and black pepper to taste		

Garnish

	Volume
Chives or parsley, chopped	2 cups

Procedure

1. Combine the beets, vegetable stock, cucumbers, dill, scallions, and dill pickle. Whisk in the yogurt and sour cream until smooth.
2. Chill.
3. Garnish with chives or parsley.

Servings	Calories	Protein (g)	Fat (g)	Cholesterol (mg)	Carbohydrates (g)	Fiber (g)	Sodium (mg)
1	114	4.4	4.4	2	15.6	2.0	183

Cream of Broccoli
or Asparagus

50 6-oz. Servings

These are two of Moosewood's most popular soups. They are a wonderful complement to a main dish salad or a warming first course to an elegant dinner.

Equipment:	2½-gallon stockpot, 6-oz. ladle
Preparation Time:	30 minutes
Cooking Time:	40 minutes

Ingredients	Volume	Weight
Onions, coarsely chopped	2½ qts.	2 lbs. 8 oz.
Vegetable oil	½ cup	
Salt	2 Tbsp.	
Dill, dried	1 Tbsp.	
or Basil, dried	1 Tbsp.	
or Thyme, dried	2 tsp.	
Carrots, coarsely chopped	1 qt.	1⅓ lbs.
Water	3 qts.	
Potatoes, unpeeled if desired	3 qts.	3 lbs.
Broccoli, stems peeled and chopped and florets (each in separate containers)	5 qts. (total)	3 lbs. 12 oz.
or Asparagus, snapped, coarsely chopped (reserving 4 cups of asparagus tips)	4 qts. (total)	4 lbs. 12 oz.
Milk*	1 qt.	
Additional salt and black pepper to taste		

Procedure

1. Sauté the onions in oil with salt and one or two of the herbs until the onions are translucent.
2. Stir in the carrots and continue to sauté until they brighten.
3. Add the water and potatoes. Bring to a boil, reduce to a simmer, and cook until the potatoes are tender, but not overcooked.

(continued)

4. Set aside half of the broccoli florets. Add the remaining florets and stems (or coarsely chopped asparagus) and resume simmering until the broccoli (or asparagus) is bright green and tender.
5. Purée the soup with milk, in batches, in a commercial blender or food processor.
6. Reheat gently; adjust salt and pepper.
5. Steam or blanch the reserved broccoli florets or the asparagus tips. Stir vegetables into the soup immediately before serving.

*Use 2% milk for a lighter soup or substitute 1 cup of heavy cream for 1 cup of milk for a richer one.

Servings	Calories	Protein (g)	Fat (g)	Cholesterol (mg)	Carbohydrates (g)	Fiber (g)	Sodium (mg)
1	97	2.7	2.8	1	16.3	2.4	316

Creamy Cauliflower Cheddar

50 6-oz. Servings

Full flavored and satisfying, this warming soup is for cold-weather menus.

Equipment:	2½-gallon stockpot, 6-oz. ladle
Preparation Time:	30 minutes
Cooking Time:	1 hour

Ingredients	Volume	Weight
Vegetable oil	½ cup	
Garlic, minced or pressed	10 cloves or 3 Tbsp.	
Onions, chopped	2½ qts.	2 lbs. 8 oz.
Salt	2 Tbsp.	
Dill, dried	2 tsp.	
or fresh	3 Tbsp.	
Carrots, coarsely chopped	1¼ qts.	1 lb. 10 oz.
Cauliflower, cut in florets	3 qts.	4 lbs. 10 oz.
Potatoes, coarsely chopped	2 qts.	2 lbs.
Water	1 gal.	
Cheddar cheese, grated	3 qts.	2 lbs. 4 oz.
Dijon mustard	1 Tbsp.	
Milk	1 qt.	
Salt and black pepper to taste		

Procedure

1. Sauté the garlic and onions in oil. Add the salt and dill and continue to sauté until the onion is translucent, for about 10 minutes.
2. Add the carrots, cauliflower, potatoes, and water and bring to a boil. Reduce

(continued)

heat and simmer until the potatoes are easily pierced with a fork. Remove from the heat.

3. Stir in the cheese, mustard, and milk. Cool for 15 minutes.
4. Purée in batches in a blender until smooth. Add more salt and pepper to taste.
5. Reheat gently; do not boil.

Servings	Calories	Protein (g)	Fat (g)	Cholesterol (mg)	Carbohydrates (g)	Fiber (g)	Sodium (mg)
1	151	7.1	9.6	23	9.8	2.0	445

Creamy Onion

50 6-oz. Servings

Top this simple yet elegant soup with croutons.

Equipment:	2½-gallon stockpot, 6-oz. ladle
Preparation Time:	30 minutes
Cooking Time:	45 minutes

Ingredients	Volume	Weight
Potatoes, coarsely chopped	1 gal.	4 lbs.
Water or Vegetable Stock (p. 63)	1¼ gals.	
Vegetable oil	½ cup	
Onions, coarsely chopped	1¼ gals.	5 lbs.
Dry white wine	2 cups	
Neufchâtel or cream cheese, cubed	1½ qts.	1 lb. 8 oz.
Milk	1 qt.	
Salt	2 Tbsp.	
Black pepper	1 tsp.	
Dill weed, dried	1 Tbsp.	
Thyme, dried	1 tsp.	

Croutons for garnish

Procedure

1. Boil the potatoes in water or stock until soft. Drain and reserve the liquid.
2. Sauté the onions in oil until the onions are translucent.
3. Add wine and simmer until the onions have softened.
4. In a blender, purée the onions, potatoes with their cooking liquid, cheese, milk, and seasonings in batches until smooth.
5. Reheat gently.
6. Garnish with croutons if desired.

Servings	Calories	Protein (g)	Fat (g)	Cholesterol (mg)	Carbohydrates (g)	Fiber (g)	Sodium (mg)
1	119	3.1	5.9	12	12.7	1.2	353

Crema Andaluz
50 6-oz. Servings

Tomatoes and cayenne add zest to a humble, creamy potato soup.

Equipment:	2½-gallon stockpot, 6-oz. ladle
Preparation Time:	20 minutes
Cooking Time:	40 minutes

Ingredients	Volume	Weight
Olive oil	½ cup	
Onions, coarsely chopped	2½ qts.	2 lbs. 8 oz.
Salt	1 Tbsp.	
Tomatoes, canned, whole with juice	2¼ qts.	4 lbs. 8 oz.
Vegetable Stock (p. 63) or water	1 qt.	
Potatoes, coarsely chopped	5 qts.	5 lbs.
Tarragon, dried	3 Tbsp.	
Cayenne	⅛ tsp.	
Milk	1 qt.	
Half-and-half (or use additional milk)	1 qt.	

Procedure

1. Sauté the salted onions in oil until the onions are translucent.
2. Add the tomatoes, stock or water, potatoes, tarragon, and cayenne. Bring to a boil; then simmer until the potatoes are soft.
3. In a blender, purée the soup in batches with the milk and the half-and-half until smooth.
4. Reheat gently; do not boil.

Servings	Calories	Protein (g)	Fat (g)	Cholesterol (mg)	Carbohydrates (g)	Fiber (g)	Sodium (mg)
1	115	2.8	5.0	8	15.9	1.7	169

Crema de Elote
50 6 oz. Servings

Redolent with aromatic spices, this creamy, yet piquant soup is an appropriate starter course for Mexican or other Latin meals.

Equipment:	2½-gallon stockpot, 6-oz. ladle
Preparation Time:	30 minutes
Cooking Time:	45 minutes

Ingredients	Volume	Weight
Vegetable oil	½ cup	
Garlic, minced or pressed	10 cloves or 3 Tbsp.	
Onions, chopped	3 qts.	3 lbs.
Coriander seed, ground	2 Tbsp.	
Cumin seed, ground	2 Tbsp.	
Chile peppers, fresh, minced	¼ cup (or to taste)	1½ oz.
Tomatoes, fresh, chopped	1½ qts.	2 lbs. 4 oz.
Potatoes, diced	1¼ qts.	1 lb. 4 oz.
Green and red peppers (a mix is nice)	2½ qts.	2 lbs. 8 oz.
Vegetable Stock (p. 63) or water	2½ qts.	
Corn, cut fresh or frozen	2½ qts.	5 lbs.
Milk	3 cups	
Monterey Jack cheese, grated	5⅓ cups	1 lb.
Salt and black pepper to taste		

Procedure

1. Sauté the onions and garlic in oil on low heat until the onions are soft.
2. Add the coriander, cumin, and chiles and sauté for a few minutes.
3. Add the chopped tomatoes and cook until they are juicy.

(continued)

4. Add the potatoes, peppers, and stock or water. Bring to a boil, cover, and simmer until the potatoes are tender, about 10 minutes.
5. Add the corn and cook until heated through.
6. Purée half of the soup in a blender with the milk and cheese until smooth.
7. Combine with the rest of the soup; adjust salt and pepper.
8. Heat the soup gently; do not boil.

Servings	Calories	Protein (g)	Fat (g)	Cholesterol (mg)	Carbohydrates (g)	Fiber (g)	Sodium (mg)
1	151	5.4	6.1	9	21.5	2.7	76

Curried Sweet Pea
50 6-oz. Servings

Curry provides a light seasoning for this velvety smooth soup.

Equipment:	2½-gallon stockpot, 6-oz. ladle
Preparation Time:	30 minutes
Cooking Time:	40 minutes

Ingredients	Volume	Weight
Vegetable oil	½ cup	
Onions, chopped	2½ qts.	2 lbs. 8 oz.
Garlic, minced or pressed	8 cloves or 2¾ Tbsp.	
Potatoes, sliced	2 qts.	2 lbs.
Carrots, chopped	5 cups	1 lb. 11 oz.
Turmeric	1 Tbsp.	
Curry powder	3 Tbsp.	
Vegetable Stock (p. 63) or water	3¼ qts.	
Green peas, frozen or fresh	2 qts.	2 lbs. 8 oz.
Milk or half-and-half	2 qts.	
Salt and black pepper to taste		

Procedure

1. Sauté the onions and garlic in oil until the onions are golden.
2. Add the rest of the ingredients except the peas and milk. Bring to a boil and then simmer until the vegetables are tender, for about 20 minutes.
3. Add the peas and simmer: frozen peas for 10 minutes; fresh peas for 5 minutes.
4. Purée the soup in a blender, in batches, with the milk or half-and-half. Add salt and pepper to taste.
5. Reheat gently; do not boil.

Servings	Calories	Protein (g)	Fat (g)	Cholesterol (mg)	Carbohydrates (g)	Fiber (g)	Sodium (mg)
1	86	3.0	3.2	3	12.0	2.3	50

Davina Stein's Vegetable

50 6-oz. Servings

This generous, full-bodied soup is an excellent starter course for cold-weather menus, or it can be served in larger portions as a meal with dark bread and salad.

Equipment:	2½-gallon stockpot, 6-oz. ladle
Preparation Time:	45 minutes
Cooking Time:	2 hours

Ingredients	Volume	Weight
Water	1¾ gals.	
Lima beans, soaked overnight	1½ cups	10 oz.
Barley, uncooked	1½ cups	12 oz.
Rice, uncooked	1 cup	6.4 oz.
Garlic	10 cloves or 3 Tbsp.	
Dill, dried	2 Tbsp.	
Bay leaves	4	
Vegetable oil	½ cup	
Onions, chopped	3 cups	12 oz.
Celery, chopped	1 qt.	1 lb.
Paprika, sweet Hungarian	2 Tbsp.	
Potatoes, chopped	2½ cups	12 oz.
Carrots, chopped	2½ cups	12 oz.
Green beans, cut in 1-in. lengths	2 cups	12 oz.
Tomatoes, fresh, chopped	2½ cups	15 oz.
Salt	3 Tbsp.	
Salt and black pepper to taste		

Procedure

1. Soak lima beans overnight or for at least 4 hours.
2. Combine soaked and drained lima beans with the water, barley, rice, garlic, dill, and bay leaves and bring to a boil. Lower the heat and simmer for 1 hour. Add more water if needed.
3. In another pot, sauté the onions and celery in oil for a few minutes.
4. Sprinkle in the paprika and add the potatoes and carrots. Cook, covered, for a few minutes.
5. Stir in the green beans and continue to cook for 5 minutes more. Set aside until the grains and beans are tender.
6. Add the vegetables and tomatoes to the cooked grains and beans and simmer covered, on very low heat (use a flame tamer if possible) for 1 to 1½ hours. Stir occasionally. Adjust salt and pepper to taste.

Note: If reheating leftover soup, it may be necessary to thin with water or vegetable stock.

Servings	Calories	Protein (g)	Fat (g)	Cholesterol (mg)	Carbohydrates (g)	Fiber (g)	Sodium (mg)
1	75	1.8	2.5	0	12.0	2.4	444

Finnish Golden Split Pea

50 6-oz. Servings

The generous use of sweet root vegetables helps to create a comforting and subtly seasoned soup.

Equipment:	2½-gallon stockpot, 6-oz. ladle
Preparation Time:	30 minutes
Cooking Time:	1 hour

Ingredients	Volume	Weight
Yellow split peas, dried	1½ qts.	3 lbs.
Vegetable Stock (p. 63) or water	1½ gals.	
Potatoes, coarsely chopped	3 qts.	3 lbs.
Carrots, coarsely chopped	3 cups	1 lb.
Celery, coarsely chopped	1½ qts.	1 lb. 8 oz.
Onions, coarsely chopped	2 qts.	2 lbs.
Turnips, coarsely chopped	3 cups	1 lb. 8 oz.
Parsnips, coarsely chopped	3 cups	1 lb. 8 oz.
Dried mustard	2 Tbsp. or more to taste	
Allspice	1 tsp.	
Cumin, ground	1 Tbsp.	
Marjoram, dried	1 Tbsp.	
Thyme, dried	1 Tbsp.	
Salt	2 Tbsp.	
Black pepper to taste		

Garnishes

Yogurt (optional)	1½ pints
Croutons (optional)	3 qts.

Procedure

1. Rinse the split peas. Bring the peas and the stock or water to a boil.
2. At the boil, add the chopped vegetables, reduce the heat, and simmer for 45 minutes to 1 hour, or until the split peas are very soft and almost disintegrating. Use a heat diffuser to prevent scorching.
3. Purée the soup in a blender or food processor until it is quite smooth. It will be very thick.
4. Add the herbs, spices, and salt and pepper and reheat gently.
5. If desired, serve this soup steaming hot with a dollop of yogurt and/or croutons.

Servings	Calories	Protein (g)	Fat (g)	Cholesterol (mg)	Carbohydrates (g)	Fiber (g)	Sodium (mg)
1	108	4.1	0.5	0	23.1	5.2	326

Gazpacho

50 6-oz. Servings

This vibrant, refreshing soup evokes the flavors of a summer garden.

Equipment:	2½-gallon stockpot, 6-oz. ladle
Preparation Time:	30 minutes
Chilling Time:	1 hour or more

Ingredients	Volume	Weight
Tomato juice, chilled	1½ gals.	
Tomatoes, fresh, chopped	2 qts.	3 lbs.
Cucumbers, peeled, seeded, chopped	1½ qts.	2 lbs.
Red and green peppers, chopped	1½ qts.	1 lb. 8 oz.
Red onion, diced	2 cups	11 oz.
Cumin, ground	1 Tbsp.	
Tabasco, splash or to taste		
Garlic, pressed	6 med. cloves or 2 Tbsp.	
Parsley, fresh, chopped	½ cup	
Red wine or balsamic vinegar	¼ cup	
Lemon juice, fresh	1 Tbsp.	
Salt and black pepper to taste		

Procedure

1. Chill the tomato juice the night before or for 3 hours in a freezer.
2. Add the rest of the ingredients.
3. Can be served as is but will improve with further chilling time to allow flavors to meld.

Variations
- Add fresh cilantro.
- Add cooked corn kernels and cubed avocado.

Servings	Calories	Protein (g)	Fat (g)	Cholesterol (mg)	Carbohydrates (g)	Fiber (g)	Sodium (mg)
1	34	1.4	0.2	0	8.0	1.3	400

Lebanese Vegetable

50 6-oz. Servings

Tangy and hearty, this soup nicely accompanies Baba Ganoush (p. 71) or Garden Vegetable–Feta Pita (p. 76).

Equipment:	2½-gallon stockpot, 6-oz. ladle
Preparation Time:	30 minutes (with precooked chick-peas)
Cooking Time:	45 minutes

Ingredients	Volume	Weight
Onions, chopped	2½ qts.	2 lbs. 8 oz.
Olive oil	½ cup	
Carrots, chopped	1½ qts.	2 lbs.
Cayenne pepper	¼–½ tsp.	
Coriander seeds, ground	1 Tbsp.	
Garlic, minced or pressed	10 cloves or 3 Tbsp.	
Potatoes, chopped	2 qts.	2 lbs.
Salt	1 Tbsp.	
Stock (see note)	5 qts. plus 1 cup	
Tomatoes, fresh, chopped	1 3/4 qts.	2 lbs. 8 oz.
Artichoke hearts, cut into eighths	1 qt.	1 lb. 4 oz.
Chick-peas, cooked, drained	5 cups	2 lbs.
Lemon juice	½ cup	
Parsley, fresh, chopped	½ cup	
Salt and black pepper to taste		

Procedure

1. Sauté the onions in olive oil for 5 minutes.
2. Add the carrots, cayenne, coriander, and garlic. Cover and cook for 5 minutes.
3. Add the potatoes, salt, and stock. Cover and bring to a boil; then simmer until the potatoes are tender, being careful not to overcook the potatoes.

(continued)

4. Stir in the tomatoes, artichoke hearts, and chick-peas. Add the lemon juice, parsley, and salt and pepper and gently simmer to heat the soup. Cooking on a high boil will adversely affect the texture and appearance of the soup.

Note: For stock, use chick-pea cooking water, Vegetable Stock (p. 63), artichoke heart brine from canned, drained artichokes, or a combination of all three.

Servings	Calories	Protein (g)	Fat (g)	Cholesterol (mg)	Carbohydrates (g)	Fiber (g)	Sodium (mg)
1	108	2.8	2.7	0	19.5	3.8	237

Miso Vegetable
50 6-oz. Servings

Move over, chicken soup. Miso makes an excellent nutritious broth; it is enhanced here with vegetables and the smoky flavor of shiitake mushrooms.

Equipment:	2½-gallon stockpot, 6-oz. ladle
Preparation Time:	20 minutes
Cooking Time:	40 minutes

Ingredients	Volume	Weight
Shiitake mushrooms		2 oz.
Hot water	1 qt.	
Vegetable oil	½ cup	
Onions, thinly sliced	3 qts.	3 lbs.
Ginger root, fresh, grated	¼ cup	
Carrots, sliced in half moons	2¼ qts.	3 lbs.
Cabbage, chopped	3½ qts.	2 lbs. 8 oz.
Water or Vegetable Stock (p. 63)	1 gal. plus 1¾ qts.	
Soy sauce	1 cup	
Honey (optional)	¼ cup	
Miso (p. 472)	1½ cups	
Tofu, cut into small cubes		1 lb. 8 oz.

Garnishes

Scallions, thinly sliced	2 bunches	
Sesame seeds	½ cup	

Procedure

1. In a small bowl, soak the shiitake mushrooms in the hot water for 20 minutes. After they are soft, remove and discard the stems and slice the caps into ¼-in. strips. Reserve the soaking liquid.

(continued)

2. Sauté the onions and ginger in oil until the onions are translucent.
3. Add the carrots and sauté 5 minutes more.
4. Add the cabbage and water or vegetable stock. Bring to a boil and then simmer for 10 minutes.
5. Add the rest of the ingredients, the shiitake mushrooms, and the soaking liquid and simmer until the vegetables are just tender. Avoid cooking the soup at a full boil to retain the nutritious enzymes in the miso.
6. Serve piping hot with a sprinkling of scallions and sesame seeds.

Servings	Calories	Protein (g)	Fat (g)	Cholesterol (mg)	Carbohydrates (g)	Fiber (g)	Sodium (mg)
1	104	3.1	3.9	0	15.6	3.0	536

Mulligatawny

50 6-oz. Servings

This multicolored soup has the bouquet and savor of tropical India.

Equipment:	2½-gallon stockpot, 6-oz. ladle
Preparation Time:	30 minutes
Cooking Time:	40 minutes

Ingredients	Volume	Weight
Vegetable oil	½ cup	
Onions, chopped	2½ qts.	2 lbs. 8 oz.
Celery, chopped	1 qt.	1 lb.
Chile peppers, seeded, chopped	5 small	3 oz.
or Cayenne	¼ tsp.	
Turmeric	2 Tbsp.	
Coriander seed, ground	¼ cup	
Water or Vegetable Stock (p. 63)	1 gal.	
Salt	1 Tbsp.	
Carrots, chopped	1½ qts.	2 lbs.
Potatoes, cut in small cubes	1½ qts.	3 lbs.
Red and/or green peppers, chopped	1 qt.	1 lb.
Tomatoes, fresh, chopped	5½ cups	2 lbs.
Coconut, unsweetened, grated	1 cup	4 oz.
Coconut milk (p.470)	2 cups	14 oz.
Lemon or lime juice	½ to 1 cup	
Cilantro, fresh, chopped	3 Tbsp.	

Procedure

1. Sauté the onions and celery in oil until the onions are translucent.
2. Add chiles or cayenne, turmeric, and coriander and sauté for 2–3 minutes, stirring continuously to prevent burning.

(continued)

3. Add stock or water, salt, carrots, and potatoes. Bring to a boil, reduce to a simmer, and cook, covered, for 20 minutes.
4. Add the peppers, tomatoes, coconut, and coconut milk. Simmer for another 10 to 15 minutes or until the vegetables are tender.
5. Add lemon or lime juice to taste and cilantro.

Servings	Calories	Protein (g)	Fat (g)	Cholesterol (mg)	Carbohydrates (g)	Fiber (g)	Sodium (mg)
1	89	1.4	4.0	0	12.8	2.0	172

North African Split Pea

50 6-oz. Servings

Simple to prepare, this rewarding soup has the aromatic presence of a spice bazaar.

Equipment:	2½-gallon stockpot, 6-oz. ladle
Preparation Time:	10 minutes
Cooking Time:	1 hour and 20 minutes, including cooking the split peas

Ingredients	Volume	Weight
Green split peas	2 qts.	4 lbs.
Water	1 gal.	
Onions, chopped	2 qts.	2 lbs.
Garlic, minced or pressed	10 cloves or 3 Tbsp.	
Vegetable oil	½ cup	
Bay leaves	8	
Cumin, ground	2 Tbsp.	
Cinnamon, ground	2 tsp.	
Cayenne	½ tsp.	
Cardamom, ground	1 Tbsp.	
Vegetable Stock (p. 63) or water	2 qts.	
Lemon juice, fresh	¼ cup	
Brown rice, cooked	1 qt.	1 lb. 10 oz.
Salt and black pepper to taste		

Procedure

1. Rinse the split peas and combine with the water; boil, then simmer, covered, for 45 minutes to 1 hour.
2. Meanwhile, in another pot, sauté the onion and garlic until the onion is translucent.

(continued)

3. Mix in the spices and sauté for 5 minutes more, stirring frequently to prevent burning. Set aside.
4. When the split peas are cooked, stir in the onion mixture and the remaining ingredients. Remove the bay leaves.
5. Reheat gently if necessary.

Servings	Calories	Protein (g)	Fat (g)	Cholesterol (mg)	Carbohydrates (g)	Fiber (g)	Sodium (mg)
1	98	3.9	2.7	0	15.3	3.7	10

Parsnip Cheddar

50 6-oz. Servings

Parsnips add a distinctive sweetness to this creamy-smooth soup that can warm the brisk days of fall and winter.

Equipment:	2½-gallon stockpot, 6-oz. ladle
Preparation Time:	30 minutes
Cooking Time:	1 hour

Ingredients	Volume	Weight
Onions, chopped	2½ qts.	2 lb. 8 oz.
Vegetable oil	½ cup	
Salt	2 Tbsp.	
Caraway seeds	2 Tbsp.	
Parsnips, peeled and chopped	3 qts.	4 lbs.
Potatoes, peeled and chopped	1 gal.	4 lbs.
Water	1 gal.	
Fennel seed, ground	1 Tbsp.	
Cheddar cheese, sharp, grated	3 qts.	2 lbs. 4 oz.
Milk	1 qt.	
Black pepper to taste		

Garnish

Dill or parsley sprigs

Procedure

1. Sprinkle the onions with the salt and sauté in oil until the onions are translucent.
2. Stir in the caraway seeds and parsnips and sauté briefly.
3. Add the potatoes and water, bring to a boil; then reduce to a simmer and cook, covered, until the potatoes are soft.

(continued)

4. Stir in the fennel, cheese, milk, and black pepper. Purée in a blender until smooth.
5. Reheat gently; do not boil.
6. Garnish with a sprig of dill or parsley.

Servings	Calories	Protein (g)	Fat (g)	Cholesterol (mg)	Carbohydrates (g)	Fiber (g)	Sodium (mg)
1	182	7.2	9.6	23	17.7	2.5	428

Portuguese Kale and White Bean

50 6-oz. Servings

Nutritious and satisfying, this is a harmonious blend of vegetables and spices. Traditionally made with sausage, we find that the sun-dried tomatoes add a similar texture and savory flavor.

Equipment:	2½-gallon stockpot, 6-oz. ladle
Preparation Time:	30 minutes
Cooking Time:	40 minutes (if using precooked beans)

Ingredients	Volume	Weight
White beans (navy, pea, or Great Northern), dry	3¼ cups	1 lb. 6 oz.
or cooked and drained	2¼ qts.	3 lbs. 4 oz.
Onions, chopped	2½ qts.	2 lbs. 8 oz.
Olive oil	½ cup	
Garlic, minced or pressed	10 cloves or 3 Tbsp.	
Fennel seeds, ground	2 Tbsp.	
Oregano, dried	1 Tbsp.	
Bay leaves	8	
Sun-dried tomatoes, soaked, drained, chopped	1 cup	
Carrots, chopped	1¼ qts.	1 lb. 8 oz.
Potatoes, chopped	1½ qts.	1 lb. 8 oz.
Vegetable Stock (p. 63) or water	1 gal. plus 3 cups	
Kale, chopped		2 lbs.
Tomatoes, fresh or canned, chopped	3¼ cups	1 lb. 4 oz.
Lemon juice	¼ cup	
Salt and black pepper to taste		

(continued)

Procedure

1. If using dried beans, soak the beans in water to cover overnight, or for at least 3 hours; or bring to a boil, remove from heat, and let soak for 1 hour. After soaking, drain and cook the beans until tender in 2½ quarts of water for 30 to 45 minutes. Drain and set aside.
2. Sauté the onions, garlic, fennel, oregano, and bay leaves in olive oil until the onions soften.
3. Soak the sun-dried tomatoes in boiling water to cover and set aside.
4. Add the carrots and potatoes to the onions, sauté briefly.
5. Add the stock, cover, bring to a boil, and then simmer, covered, until the potatoes are barely tender.
6. Add the kale and the fresh and sun-dried tomatoes and simmer until the kale is tender.
7. Add the cooked beans and lemon juice and salt and pepper to taste.
8. Heat gently.

Note: If cooking white beans, the bean liquid could be used as part of the stock. This soup improves as it sits when the flavors have "married."

Servings	Calories	Protein (g)	Fat (g)	Cholesterol (mg)	Carbohydrates (g)	Fiber (g)	Sodium (mg)
1	130	4.9	2.9	0	22.9	2.8	124

Potage Georgette

50 6-oz. Servings

Appealing to young and old alike, this naturally sweet soup is enlivened by the addition of fresh ginger. Garnish each serving with a circle of thinly sliced lemon. Serve as a first course or as the significant other to a tangy sandwich such as Antipasto Pita (p. 69) or Roasted Eggplant-Pepper Salad (p. 83).

Equipment:	2½-gallon stockpot, 6-oz. ladle
Preparation Time:	20 minutes
Cooking Time:	40 minutes

Ingredients	Volume	Weight
Vegetable oil	½ cup	
Onions, chopped	1 gal.	4 lbs.
Celery, chopped	1 qt.	1 lb.
Ginger root, fresh, grated	3 Tbsp.	3 oz.
Sweet potatoes, peeled, coarsely chopped	2 gal.	8 lbs.
Vegetable Stock (p. 63) or water	1 gal.	
Bay leaves	4	
Salt	2 Tbsp.	
Milk	1 qt.	
Heavy cream	1 pt.	
Black pepper to taste		

Procedure

1. Sauté the onions in oil until the onions are translucent.
2. Stir in the celery and ginger root and continue to sauté until the onions begin to brown.
3. Add the sweet potatoes, water or stock, bay leaves, and salt. Cover the pot, bring

(continued)

to a boil, and reduce to a simmer for 15–20 minutes, or until the potatoes are soft.

4. Remove the bay leaves. In a blender, purée the soup mixture in batches, with the milk and cream until smooth.

5. Adjust the salt, add black pepper, and reheat gently.

Servings	Calories	Protein (g)	Fat (g)	Cholesterol (mg)	Carbohydrates (g)	Fiber (g)	Sodium (mg)
1	189	3.0	8.6	14	26.2	3.2	332

Santa Fe Chowder

50 6-oz. Servings

This rich and fragrant soup is brightened by the piquant seasonings of the Southwest.

Equipment:	2½-gallon stockpot, 6-oz. ladle
Preparation Time:	25 minutes
Cooking Time:	40 minutes

Ingredients	Volume	Weight
Vegetable oil	½ cup	
Chile peppers, minced	3 small	4 oz.
Onions, chopped	3 qts.	3 lbs.
Cumin, ground	1 Tbsp.	
Coriander	1 Tbsp.	
Oregano	2 tsp.	
Carrots, diced	2 cups	1 lb.
Sweet potatoes, peeled, cubed	2½ qts.	2 lbs. 8 oz.
White potatoes, cubed	2 qts.	2 lbs.
Vegetable Stock (p. 63) or water	3 qts.	
Frozen corn	1¼ qts.	2 lbs. 8 oz.
Green and/or red peppers, chopped	1 qt.	1 lb.
Tomatoes, fresh, chopped	1 qt.	1 lb. 8 oz.
Zucchini, diced	2 cups	10 oz.
Cream or Neufchâtel Cheese		8 oz.
Cheddar cheese, grated	2 cups	6 oz.
Cilantro, fresh	3 Tbsp.	
Salt and black pepper to taste		

Procedure

1. Sauté the chile peppers and onions in oil with the cumin, coriander, and oregano until the onions are translucent.
2. Add the carrots, sweet and white potatoes, and stock or water and simmer for 10 minutes.

(continued)

3. Add the corn, peppers, tomatoes, and zucchini and cook until all the vegetables are tender.
4. Remove 12 cups of the soup and purée with the cream and Cheddar cheeses. Return to the pot.
5. Stir in the cilantro and salt and pepper.
6. Reheat gently; do not boil.

Servings	Calories	Protein (g)	Fat (g)	Cholesterol (mg)	Carbohydrates (g)	Fiber (g)	Sodium (mg)
1	148	3.7	5.6	9	23.1	3.1	60

Savannah Bisque

50 6-oz. Servings

This lush, smooth soup evokes the popular Southern duet of pimientos and Cheddar.

Equipment:	2½-gallon stockpot, 6-oz. ladle
Preparation Time:	30 minutes
Cooking Time:	40 minutes

Ingredients	Volume	Weight
Celery, sliced	1¼ qts.	1 lb. 4 oz.
Onions, coarsely chopped	1 qt.	1 lb.
Vegetable oil	¼ cup	
Sweet potatoes, peeled, cubed	2 qts.	2 lbs.
White potatoes, peeled, cubed	2 qts.	2 lbs.
Vegetable Stock (p. 63) or water	3 qts.	
Cheddar cheese, grated	1 qt.	12 oz.
Cream or Neufchâtel cheese, cubed	1½ cups	12 oz.
Pimientos		8 oz.
Salt and black pepper to taste		

Procedure

1. Sauté the celery and onions in vegetable oil until the onions are translucent, for about 10 minutes.
2. Add the potatoes and stock or water and simmer, covered, until the vegetables are soft, about 20 minutes.
3. Remove from the heat, stir in the cheeses and pimientos, and purée in a blender, in batches, until smooth.
4. Add salt and pepper to taste. Reheat gently.

Servings	Calories	Protein (g)	Fat (g)	Cholesterol (mg)	Carbohydrates (g)	Fiber (g)	Sodium (mg)
1	116	3.4	5.9	15	12.9	1.6	86

Sopa de Lima

50 6-oz. Servings

Our vegetarian version of a classic soup from the Yucatan region of Mexico is easy to prepare.

Equipment:	2½-gallon stockpot, 6-oz. ladle
Preparation Time:	20 minutes
Cooking Time:	35 minutes

Ingredients	Volume	Weight
Vegetable oil	½ cup	
Onions, chopped	2½ qts.	2 lbs. 8 oz.
Garlic, minced or pressed	10 cloves or 3 Tbsp.	
Chili peppers, fresh, minced	¼ cup (or to taste)	1.5 oz.
Cumin seed, ground	2 Tbsp.	
Oregano, dried	2 Tbsp.	
Tomatoes, fresh, chopped	1¼ gals.	7 lbs. 8 oz.
Vegetable Stock (p. 63) or water	1¼ qts.	
Lime juice, fresh	1½ cups	
Salt to taste		

Garnishes

Grated Monterey Jack cheese	1 qt.	12 oz.
Crumbled tortilla chips		
Chopped fresh cilantro (optional)	½ cup	

Procedure

1. Sauté the onions and garlic in oil until the onions are translucent.
2. Add the chilies, cumin, and oregano and sauté for an additional 5 minutes.
3. Add the chopped tomatoes and sprinkle with a little salt. Cover and simmer gently until the tomatoes begin to release their juices. Stir occasionally.
4. Add stock and simmer, covered, for about 20 minutes.
5. Add lime juice and additional salt if desired.
6. Serve topped with grated cheese, tortilla chips, and chopped cilantro if desired.

Servings	Calories	Protein (g)	Fat (g)	Cholesterol (mg)	Carbohydrates (g)	Fiber (g)	Sodium (mg)
1	99	3.5	5.9	8	9.7	1.8	63

Tomato–Garlic

50 6-oz. Servings

Although this soup is practically instant and perfect for busy, rushed occasions, we like it so much that it frequently appears on our menus. Garlicky croutons are a key ingredient in this soup.

Equipment:	2½-gallon stockpot, 6-oz. ladle
Preparation Time:	5 minutes
Cooking Time:	15 minutes

Ingredients	Volume	Weight
Olive oil	¾ cup	
Garlic, minced or pressed	25–30 cloves, or ½ cup	
Tomato juice	6 46-oz. cans	
Hungarian paprika	4 Tbsp.	
Dry sherry	1½ cups	
Vegetable Stock (p. 63)	1 qt.	

Garnishes

	Volume	Weight
Croutons	3 qts.	
Grated Parmesan	1½ cups	6 oz.

Procedure

1. Briefly sauté the garlic in olive oil. Do not allow it to brown.
2. Add the tomato juice, paprika, sherry, and stock. Bring to a boil; then simmer, covered, for 10 minutes.
3. Serve topped with croutons and cheese.

Note: For croutons, toss oven-toasted bread cubes in pressed or minced garlic heated in olive oil or butter; then retoast briefly.

Servings	Calories	Protein (g)	Fat (g)	Cholesterol (mg)	Carbohydrates (g)	Fiber (g)	Sodium (mg)
1	85	2.9	4.6	3	8.7	1.0	631

Turkish Spinach–Lentil

50 6-oz. Servings

This innovative medley of ingredients makes a tasty, protein-balanced soup substantial enough to serve as a main dish.

Equipment:	2½-gallon stockpot, 6-oz. ladle
Preparation Time:	20 minutes
Cooking Time:	1 hour and 15 minutes

Ingredients	Volume	Weight
Lentils, dried	2 qts.	3 lbs. 4 oz.
Salt	2 Tbsp.	
Vegetable Stock (p. 63) or water	2 gals.	
Olive oil	½ cup	
Onions, chopped	2 qts.	2 lbs.
Garlic, minced or pressed	8 cloves or 2¾ Tbsp.	
Cayenne	¼ tsp.	
Bay leaves	8	
Bulghur, raw (p. 468)	2 cups	11 oz.
Parsley, fresh, chopped	1 cup	
Tomatoes, fresh, chopped	6½ cups	2 lbs. 8 oz.
Tomato paste	¾ cup	
Salt	1 tsp.	
Rosemary, dried or fresh	1 tsp.	
Black pepper to taste		
Spinach, fresh, coarsely chopped		20 oz. (2 10-oz. bags)

Procedure

1. Rinse the lentils. In a stockpot, bring them to a boil in salted water or vegetable stock, reduce the heat, cover the pot, and simmer for 40 minutes, or until the lentils are soft.
2. In the second pot, sauté the onions and garlic in the olive oil until the onions are translucent.

(continued)

3. Add the cayenne, bay leaves, and bulghur. Stir over medium heat until the bulghur and onions are lightly browned.
4. Stir in the parsley, tomatoes, tomato paste, and salt. Turn off the heat.
5. When the lentils are cooked, add them and their cooking liquid to the onion–bulghur mixture. Add the rosemary and simmer for 15 minutes.
6. Adjust for salt and pepper.
7. Stir in the fresh spinach just before serving, allowing it to wilt in the hot soup.

Servings	Calories	Protein (g)	Fat (g)	Cholesterol (mg)	Carbohydrates (g)	Fiber (g)	Sodium (mg)
1	135	5.4	2.8	0	24.1	6.1	390

Vegetable Chowder

50 6-oz. Servings

This vegetable chowder is nutritious "comfort food." Compose a tasty and balanced lunch with a bowl of chowder, a crisp tossed salad, and whole grain bread. Or create a new soup with the addition of fish, seafood, or Cheddar cheese.

Equipment:	2¹/₂-gallon stockpot, 6-oz. ladle
Preparation Time:	30 minutes
Cooking Time:	40 minutes

Ingredients	Volume	Weight
Vegetable oil	¹/₂ cup	
Onions, chopped	2¹/₂ qts.	2 lbs. 8 oz.
Celery, chopped	3 cups	12 oz.
Basil, dried	1 Tbsp.	
Dill weed, dried	1 Tbsp.	
Thyme, dried	¹/₂ tsp.	
Potatoes, coarsely chopped	6¹/₂ cups	1 lb. 10 oz.
Water	6¹/₂ cups	
Carrots, diced	1¹/₂ qts.	2 lbs.
Corn, fresh or frozen	3 cups	1 lb. 8 oz.
Zucchini, diced	1¹/₂ qts.	2 lbs.
Mushrooms, sliced	1 qt.	12 oz.
Milk	6¹/₂ cups	
Salt and black pepper to taste		

Procedure

1. Sauté the onions, celery, and herbs in oil until the onions are translucent.
2. At the same time, in a smaller pot, combine the potatoes and water, bring to a boil, lower the heat, and simmer until the potatoes are soft. Set aside.

(continued)

3. Returning to the onion mixture, add the carrots and corn. Continue sautéing until the vegetables are tender but still colorful.
4. Stir in the zucchini and mushrooms. Sauté until the zucchini softens and the mushrooms begin to sweat. Turn off the heat.
5. Purée the potatoes and water, in batches, in a blender. Use some milk if more liquid is needed for puréeing. The purée should be smooth.
6. Pour each batch and the remaining milk into the sautéed vegetables. Adjust for salt and black pepper.
7. Reheat gently.

Servings	Calories	Protein (g)	Fat (g)	Cholesterol (mg)	Carbohydrates (g)	Fiber (g)	Sodium (mg)
1	86	2.5	3.2	2	13.4	2.1	41

Vegetable Stock

Yields 2 gallons

We make fresh vegetable stock every evening to use for the next day's soup. This simple, basic recipe makes a versatile, mildly flavored stock. The optional additions listed can be used in place of, or along with, the ingredients of the basic recipe.

Equipment:	4- or 5-gallon stockpot
Preparation Time:	20 minutes
Cooking Time:	1 hour

Ingredients	Volume	Weight
Potatoes, coarsely chopped	2 qts.	2 lbs.
Onions, coarsely chopped	2 qts.	2 lbs.
Carrots, coarsely chopped	1½ qts.	2 lbs.
Celery, coarsely chopped	2 cups	8 oz.
Apples or pears, quartered and cored	2 cups	8 oz.
Bay leaves	8	
Black peppercorns	2 Tbsp.	
Water	2½ gals.	

Optional Additions

Garlic cloves
Leeks, including tough green parts
Parsnips
Sweet potatoes
Winter squash
Zucchini or summer squash

Procedure

1. Combine all the ingredients and bring to a boil in a covered pot. Simmer for 1 hour or more.

(continued)

2. Strain the stock and discard the vegetables. The stock will keep refrigerated for 3 to 4 days or frozen indefinitely.

Variation

- For an Asian-style soup stock, add a few slices of fresh ginger root and/or the soaking liquid from dried shiitake mushrooms.

Servings	Calories	Protein (g)	Fat (g)	Cholesterol (mg)	Carbohydrates (g)	Fiber (g)	Sodium (mg)
1	53	1.2	0.2	0	12.5	2.2	26

West African Peanut Soup

50 6-oz. Servings

This exotic menu addition features a staple protein in African cuisine.

Equipment:	2½-gallon stockpot
Preparation Time:	25 minutes
Cooking Time:	40 minutes

Ingredients	Volume	Weight
Onions, chopped	2 qts.	2 lbs. 8 oz.
Vegetable oil	½ cup	
Cayenne or ground, dried chili peppers	½ to 1 tsp.	
Ginger root, fresh, grated	2 Tbsp.	
Carrots, chopped	1 qt.	1¼ lbs.
Sweet potatoes, chopped (white potatoes can be substituted for up to half the quantity)	1 gal.	4 lbs.
Salt	1 Tbsp.	
Vegetable Stock (p. 63) or water	1 gal.	
Tomato juice	1½ qts.	# 5 can
Peanut butter	1 qt.	
Sugar (optional)	2 to 4 Tbsp.	

Garnish

Scallions or chives, chopped	3 cups

Procedure

1. Sauté the onions in oil until the onions are translucent.
2. Stir in the cayenne, ginger, and carrots and sauté for a few minutes more.
3. Add the sweet potatoes, salt, and stock or water. Bring to a boil, reduce to a simmer, cover, and cook until the vegetables are tender.

(continued)

4. Purée the soup with the tomato juice and peanut butter in a blender until smooth. Add sugar, if needed, to enhance the flavor.
5. Reheat gently, on a flame tamer if available.
6. Serve with a generous garnish of scallions or chives.

Servings	Calories	Protein (g)	Fat (g)	Cholesterol (mg)	Carbohydrates (g)	Fiber (g)	Sodium (mg)
1	205	6.4	11.6	0	21.9	3.4	349

SANDWICHES AND DIPS

Pita sandwiches are a staple lunch item at the restaurant. Juicy fillings are better contained in pita bread pockets than in conventional sliced-bread sandwiches. Served with a cup or bowl of soup, a pita sandwich makes a balanced, light meal of vegetables, protein, and carbohydrates. Besides filling sandwiches, all the recipes in this section can perform double duty as dips, salads, appetizers, and/or side dishes or can be served side by side to create a combination platter. A few combinations that we recommend include

- Baba Ganoush, Hummus, and Herbed Ricotta Spread
- Roasted Eggplant–Pepper Salad and White Bean Dip
- Olivada and Marinated Vegetables (p. 333)
- Greek Salad and Tzatziki (p. 344)

Serve any of these with pita bread, cut into wedges and toasted lightly. Pita is an excellent, firm bread for dipping.

Antipasto Pita

24 6-oz. Servings

This marvelous sandwich cleverly features the components of the time-honored antipasto salad.

Preparation Time: 20 minutes

Ingredients	Volume	Weight
Provolone cheese, cubed	5½ cups	1 lb. 6 oz.
Pepperoncini (Italian-style pickled peppers), sliced	1½ cups	
Bell pepper, red and green, diced	2 cups	8 oz.
Celery, diced	1 qt.	1 lb.
Tomato, fresh, diced	1¼ qts.	1 lb. 9 oz.
Red onion, diced	1 cup	5 oz.
Black olives, pitted, halved	2 cups	12 oz.

Dressing

Vegetable oil	1 cup	
Olive oil	½ cup	
Cider or red wine vinegar	⅔ cup	
Garlic, minced or pressed	4 med. cloves or 1 heaping Tbsp.	
Salt	½ tsp.	
Dijon mustard	2 Tbsp.	
Black pepper	½ tsp.	
Parsley, fresh, chopped	2 Tbsp.	
Basil, oregano, marjoram (in any combination or alone), fresh, chopped	¼ cup	
or dried	1⅓ Tbsp.	
Leaf or romaine lettuce leaves		
Pita bread, halved, lightly toasted	12 whole	2 oz. each

(continued)

Procedure

1. Combine the cheese and vegetables in a large bowl.
2. Whisk together the dressing ingredients and toss with the vegetable–cheese mixture.
3. Assemble the sandwich by lining each warmed pita pocket with a lettuce leaf and 5 oz. of filling.

Variation
- Mix fresh mozzarella cheese with provolone to total 5½ cups.

Servings	Calories	Protein (g)	Fat (g)	Cholesterol (mg)	Carbohydrates (g)	Fiber (g)	Sodium (mg)
1	368	10.9	27.5	18	22.8	1.1	1137

Baba Ganoush
24 6-oz. Servings

With a smoky eggplant flavor and a texture creamy with lemon and tahini, this classic paté serves as a sandwich filling or dip with crudités. Prepare as a side dish for a Middle Eastern Combo Plate with Hummus (p. 79) or White Bean Dip (p. 87), and Carrot Salad (p. 321).

Preparation Time: 15 minutes
Baking Time: 40 minutes

Ingredients	Volume	Weight
Eggplants, whole		9 lbs. 8 oz.
Lemon juice, fresh	2 cups	
Tahini (p. 474)	2 cups	
Garlic, pressed	12 med. cloves or 4 Tbsp. or more to taste	
Parsley, fresh, finely chopped	1 cup	
Salt	1 Tbsp.	
Leaf lettuce		
Pita bread, halved, lightly toasted	12 whole	2 oz. each
Feta cheese, grated	3 qts.	3 lbs.

Procedure

1. Pierce the skins of the eggplants several times and place them on a baking sheet. Bake at 400° for 40 minutes to 1 hour, or until the outsides crinkle and the insides become very soft.
2. When the eggplants are cool enough to handle, scoop out the insides.

(continued)

3. Using a food processor, purée the pulp with the lemon juice, tahini, garlic, parsley, and salt until smooth. Cool to room temperature.
4. Line a warmed pita pocket with leaf lettuce, spoon in the baba, and serve as is, or, if desired, top with a sprinkling of feta cheese.

Variations

*   For a nondairy alternative, top with chopped fresh tomatoes, chopped black olives, and alfalfa sprouts.

Servings	Calories	Protein (g)	Fat (g)	Cholesterol (mg)	Carbohydrates (g)	Fiber (g)	Sodium (mg)
1	247	8.2	11.3	0	33.5	5.7	496

Creamy Italian Pita

24 5-oz. Servings

The smooth cheeses and crunchy vegetables blend wonderfully to use as a filling for sandwiches or baked stuffed peppers or as a dip with colorful raw vegetables.

Preparation Time: 20 minutes

Ingredients	Volume	Weight
Ricotta cheese	2½ qts.	5 lbs.
Parmesan cheese, finely grated	1 qt.	12 oz.
Celery, finely chopped	1 qt.	1 lb.
Tomatoes, fresh, cubed	2½ cups	1 lb.
Basil, fresh, chopped	¼ cup	
or dried	1½ Tbsp.	
Black pepper to taste		
Romaine or leaf lettuce		
Pita bread, halved, lightly toasted	12 whole	2 oz. each

Procedure

1. In the bowl of a food processor, whirl the ricotta cheese with the Parmesan until whipped and blended.
2. Stir in the chopped celery, tomatoes, and seasoning.
3. Assemble the sandwich by lining each warmed pita pocket with a lettuce leaf and 4 oz. of filling.

Servings	Calories	Protein (g)	Fat (g)	Cholesterol (mg)	Carbohydrates (g)	Fiber (g)	Sodium (mg)
1	284	20.1	12.8	40	23.3	0.7	550

Delancey St. Pita

24 9.5-oz. Servings

This is our vegetarian version of a New York deli sandwich. To be authentic, serve with a kosher dill pickle and a frosty egg cream, or with a cup of Buttermilk Borscht (p. 24).

Preparation Time: 10 minutes (45 minutes if preparing tofu)

Ingredients	Volume	Weight
Seasoned Tofu, sliced (p. 220) (2½ × recipe)		3¾ lbs.
Sauerkraut		3 lbs.
Tomatoes, fresh, sliced		3 lbs.
Lemon-Tahini Dressing (p. 119)	1½ qts.	
or Russian dressing	1½ qts.	
Romaine or leaf lettuce		
Pita bread, halved, lightly toasted	12 whole	2 oz. each

Procedure

1. To assemble, fill each pita pocket with
   - a leaf of lettuce
   - 2.5 oz. tofu
   - 2 oz. sauerkraut
   - 2 oz. sliced tomato

   and top with 2 oz. of Lemon-Tahini Dressing or Russian Dressing.

Servings	Calories	Protein (g)	Fat (g)	Cholesterol (mg)	Carbohydrates (g)	Fiber (g)	Sodium (mg)
1	291	10.7	12.9	0	38.1	4.3	903

Floating Cloud Pita

24 7-oz. Servings

This wholesome, Moosewood-style sandwich is featured on our menu practically every week. Our customers love it for lunch with Miso Vegetable Soup (p. 41).

Preparation Time: 10 minutes using prepared tofu, 45 minutes if preparing tofu; 10 minutes for the dressing

Ingredients	Volume	Weight
Seasoned Tofu (p. 220)		1 lb. 8 oz.
Carrot, grated		3 lbs.
Cucumber, sliced		1 lb. 8 oz.
Spinach leaves or leaf lettuce		1 lb. 8 oz.
Miso-Ginger Dressing (p. 41)	1 qt.	
Pita bread, halved, lightly toasted	12 whole	2 oz. each
Alfalfa or mung sprouts (optional)		

Procedure

1. To assemble, fill each pita pocket with
    - 1 oz. spinach or a leaf of lettuce
    - 1 oz. tofu
    - 2 oz. grated carrot
    - 1 oz. sliced cucumber

    and dress with 1 oz. Miso-Ginger Dressing.
2. Top with sprouts if desired.

Servings	Calories	Protein (g)	Fat (g)	Cholesterol (mg)	Carbohydrates (g)	Fiber (g)	Sodium (mg)
1	321	6.2	21.6	0	28.9	3.0	481

Garden Vegetable–
Feta Pita

24 9-oz. Servings

We enjoy this easy-to-prepare, colorful salad in a pita. The nutty Middle-Eastern-style dressing enhances the flavor.

Preparation Time: 20 minutes; 10 minutes for the dressing

Ingredients	Volume	Weight
Bell peppers, red, green, or gold, alone or mixed, diced	1 qt.	1 lb.
Cucumbers, peeled, seeded, diced	1 qt.	1 lb. 4 oz.
Carrots, grated	1 qt.	1 lb. 6 oz.
Tomatoes, fresh, diced	1 qt.	1 lb. 4 oz.
Romaine or leaf lettuce		
Pita bread, halved, lightly toasted		
Lemon-Tahini Dressing (see p. 119)	1½ qts.	
Feta cheese, grated	3 qts.	3 lbs.

Procedure

1. Combine the vegetables.
2. Assemble the sandwich by lining each warm pita pocket with green or red romaine or looseleaf lettuce, and 4 oz. of filling.
3. For each half pita, use 2-oz. ladle of Lemon-Tahini Dressing and 2 oz. of grated feta as a topping.

Servings	Calories	Protein (g)	Fat (g)	Cholesterol (mg)	Carbohydrates (g)	Fiber (g)	Sodium (mg)
1	426	17.3	27.1	50	33.9	4.6	832

Greek Salad

24 5-oz. Servings

This traditional favorite makes a fine sandwich and is an inspired combination with Turkish Spinach–Lentil Soup (p. 59).

Preparation Time: 30 minutes

Ingredients	Volume	Weight
Artichoke hearts, canned, drained, cut into quarters	1½ qts.	2 lb.
Roasted red peppers, drained, chopped	¾ cup	3 oz.
or Red bell pepper, chopped	¾ cup	3 oz.
Celery, chopped	1 qt.	1 lb.
Tomatoes, fresh, chopped	2 cups	12 oz.
Garlic, minced or pressed	3 cloves or 1 Tbsp.	
Olive oil	⅓ cup	
Lemon juice, fresh	3 Tbsp.	
Dill, fresh, chopped	3 Tbsp.	
or dried	1 Tbsp.	
Parsley, fresh, chopped	⅓ cup	
Feta cheese, grated or cubed	2 cups	10 oz.
Calamata olives, pitted, sliced (optional)	1 cup	6 oz.
Romaine or leaf lettuce		
Pita bread, halved, lightly toasted	12 whole	2 oz. each

Procedure

1. Combine all ingredients in a large bowl, or set aside the feta and garnish with it.
2. Assemble the sandwich by lining each warmed pita pocket with a lettuce leaf and 4 oz. of filling.

Servings	Calories	Protein (g)	Fat (g)	Cholesterol (mg)	Carbohydrates (g)	Fiber (g)	Sodium (mg)
1	86	3.4	5.8	11	6.6	2.6	186

Herbed Ricotta Spread

24 5-oz. Servings

Create this spread in an instant for a satisfying topping on toast, in pita bread, or with crackers. It can be dressed up with roasted red peppers or capers. You can easily incorporate any leftovers into Spanakopita (p. 295) or Frittata Espinaca (p. 137).

Preparation Time: 10 minutes
Chilling Time: 30 minutes

Ingredients

Ingredients	Volume	Weight
Ricotta cheese	2½ qts.	5 lbs.
Feta cheese, grated	2¼ qts.	2 lb. 4 oz.
Olive oil	⅓ cup	
Parsley, chopped	1 cup	
Scallion, green and white parts, chopped	½ cup	1.25 oz.
Dill, fresh, chopped	¼ cup	

Procedure

1. Mix all the ingredients in the bowl of a food processor or with an electric mixer until smooth.
2. Chill for 30 minutes to allow the flavors to blend.

Servings	Calories	Protein (g)	Fat (g)	Cholesterol (mg)	Carbohydrates (g)	Fiber (g)	Sodium (mg)
1	275	17.1	19.9	68	7.0	0.1	608

Hummus

24 5-oz. Servings

We prepare this internationally known specialty with lots of lemon, garlic, and parsley. Serve as a pita filling with tomato slices, lettuce, and sprouts if you wish or present as a spread with toasted pita triangles or use alongside Couscous with Artichoke Hearts and Walnuts (p. 95) or Salat Morocain (p. 102).

Preparation Time: 15 minutes (using precooked garbanzo beans)

Ingredients	Volume	Weight
Garbanzo beans, dried	1 qt.	1 lb. 12 oz.
or well cooked, drained, liquid reserved	3 qts. or 1 #10 can	4 lbs. 4 oz.
Garbanzo bean cooking liquid or water	1 qt.	
Lemon juice, fresh	1 cup	
Tahini (see p. 474)	2 cups	
Garlic, minced or pressed	10 cloves or 3 Tbsp.	
Parsley, fresh, chopped	1 cup	
Cayenne (optional)	½ tsp.	
Salt	1¼ Tbsp.	

Procedure

This recipe must be prepared in batches using a food processor or blender.

1. If using dried beans, rinse and soak overnight in water to cover or bring to a boil, remove from the heat, and soak for 1–2 hours. After the beans have soaked, drain and cook until tender in 1 gallon of water for 1½ hours. Drain.
2. Reserve 1 cup of the cooking liquid or water.
3. In a food processor or blender, purée all the ingredients until the hummus is creamy, but not completely smooth.
4. Add as much of the reserved liquid as needed to get desired consistency.

Note: For dip, prepare a thinner mixture with more liquid.

Servings	Calories	Protein (g)	Fat (g)	Cholesterol (mg)	Carbohydrates (g)	Fiber (g)	Sodium (mg)
1	263	9.8	10.5	0	34.8	7.4	762

Mockamole

24 5-oz. Servings

Our protein-filled adaptation of the traditional guacamole has a creamy, light texture and the added spark of hot pepper and cumin. Serve as a sandwich filling or use to garnish a Mexican-style entrée such as Chilaquile Casserole (p. 133), Black Bean–Sweet Potato Burritos (p. 273), or Pepper Cheese Enchiladas (p. 288).

Preparation Time: 15 minutes

Ingredients	Volume	Weight
Haas avocados, ripe (p. 471)	6	
Tofu		3 lbs. 12 oz.
Lemon juice, fresh	1¼ cups	
Garlic, pressed	5 med. cloves or 1½ Tbsp.	
Salt	2 tsp.	
Black pepper	2 tsp.	
Hot pepper sauce	1 Tbsp.	
Cumin seed, ground	2 tsp.	

Procedure

Prepare in two batches.
1. Halve the avocados, discard the pits, and scoop out the flesh.
2. Place half the pulp in a commercial food processor or blender. Crumble in half the tofu and half the remaining ingredients. Process until smooth and creamy. A few tablespoons of water may be necessary for smooth processing.
3. Correct for salt and hot pepper sauce.
4. Repeat with the rest of the ingredients.

Note: To prevent discoloration, make an airtight seal with plastic wrap lightly pressed onto the top of the Mockamole.

Servings	Calories	Protein (g)	Fat (g)	Cholesterol (mg)	Carbohydrates (g)	Fiber (g)	Sodium (mg)
1	146	3.5	9.4	0	14.5	3.3	218

Monterey Pita
25 5-oz. Servings

The bright, summery tastes in this delicious sandwich will satisfy everyone all year long. Try serving with Santa Fe Chowder (p. 53) or Sopa de Lima (p. 56) for a delightful Southwestern combination.

Preparation Time: 20 minutes

Ingredients	Volume	Weight
Avocado, cubed	2 qts.	4 lbs.
Tomatoes, fresh, diced	1 qt.	1 lb. 4 oz.
Cucumbers, peeled, seeded, diced	1 qt.	1 lb. 2 oz.
Black olives, halved or sliced	1 cup	6 oz.
Garlic, pressed	8 cloves or 2½ Tbsp.	
Lemon juice, fresh	¾ cup	
Salt and black pepper to taste		
Romaine or leaf lettuce leaves		
Pita bread, halved, lightly toasted	12 whole	2 oz. each
Alfalfa sprouts for topping		
Monterey Jack cheese, grated (optional)	1 qt.	12 oz.

Procedure

1. Combine the vegetables and cheese in a large bowl.
2. Add garlic and lemon juice. Stir gently with a wooden spoon to preserve the shape of the avocado as much as possible. Correct for salt and pepper.
3. Line the pita pockets with lettuce and fill with the mixture. Top with cheese, if desired, and sprouts.

Servings	Calories	Protein (g)	Fat (g)	Cholesterol (mg)	Carbohydrates (g)	Fiber (g)	Sodium (mg)
1	225	5.2	11.2	19	26.8	4	342

Olivada

24 2- to 3-oz. Servings

This versatile, richly flavored spread can be served with tomato slices or Fresh Mozzarella and Sun-dried Tomatoes (p. 327) on toasted Italian bread or in a pita. It is a luscious pasta or pizza topping with greens sautéed in garlic. For a version that highlights the essence of the Mediterranean, substitute pitted Greek or Italian olives for the milder California black olives.

Preparation Time: 10 minutes

Ingredients	Volume	Weight
Black olives, pitted, drained	2¹/₂ qts.	2 lbs. 8 oz.
Garlic, minced or pressed	5 cloves or 1¹/₂ Tbsp.	
Pine nuts	¹/₃ cup	1¹/₃ oz.
Olive oil	¹/₄–¹/₂ cup	

Procedure

1. Coarsely chop half the olives and set aside.
2. In the bowl of a food processor or in a blender, whirl the remaining olives with the garlic, pine nuts, and ¹/₄ cup of olive oil until the mixture is somewhat smooth. If it is too stiff, add the additional ¹/₄ cup of oil.
3. Stir in the chopped olives.

Note: Covered and refrigerated, Olivada will keep for about a week. It is best served at room temperature.

Servings	Calories	Protein (g)	Fat (g)	Cholesterol (mg)	Carbohydrates (g)	Fiber (g)	Sodium (mg)
1	197	1.5	20.8	0	4.7	0.1	1554

Roasted Eggplant–
Pepper Salad
24 6-oz. Servings

Roasting the eggplant and peppers creates an authentic Mediterranean flavor for this dish, which is then enlivened with capers, garlic, and wine vinegar. It is excellent served in or with pita bread, or as a dip with crudités. Try it alongside Fish Algiers (p. 168) or on a salad plate with Tabouli (p. 104).

Preparation Time: 10 minutes
Baking Time: 1 hour

Ingredients	Volume	Weight
Eggplant, whole		8 lbs.
Peppers, red and green, whole		2 lbs. 12 oz.
Celery, chopped	1½ cups	6 oz.
Tomatoes, fresh, chopped	1¼ qts.	1 lb. 12 oz.
Capers, drained	¼ cup	
Parsley, fresh, chopped	¼ cup	
Wine vinegar	¼ cup	
Garlic, minced or pressed	8 cloves or 2½ Tbsp.	

Salt and black or cayenne pepper to taste

Procedure

1. Preheat oven to 400°.
2. Pierce the eggplant skins several times with a fork.
3. Bake the whole eggplants and peppers on a foil-lined tray. Turn peppers three or four times during 30 minutes of baking, after which time they should be softened. Remove to cool.

(continued)

4. Eggplant will need an hour or more to soften. Remove to cool.
5. Peel, seed, and chop the peppers. Scoop the eggplant pulp from their skins and chop. Discard the skins.
6. Combine the roasted vegetables with the remaining ingredients. The flavor will improve with at least 2 hours of chilling, overnight is ideal.

Servings	Calories	Protein (g)	Fat (g)	Cholesterol (mg)	Carbohydrates (g)	Fiber (g)	Sodium (mg)
1	66	2.2	0.6	0	15.6	4.8	60

Scandinavian Pita

24 5-oz. Servings

This popular sandwich combines the pleasant taste of Jarlsberg cheese with the bite of red onion and a tangy dill mayonnaise.

Preparation Time: 20 minutes

Ingredients	Volume	Weight
Jarlsberg cheese, cubed	1¼ qts.	1 lb. 4 oz.
Cucumbers, peeled, seeded, cubed	1¼ qts.	1 lb. 8 oz.
Tomatoes, fresh, cut into small cubes	1¼ qts.	1 lb. 14 oz.
Red onion, sliced paper-thin	2 cups	11 oz.
Dill weed, fresh, chopped	½ cup	
or dill weed, dried	1½ Tbsp.	
White horseradish	½ cup	
Mayonnaise (commercial or homemade)	2 cups	
Romaine or leaf lettuce		
Pita bread, halved, lightly toasted	12 whole	2 oz. each

Procedure

1. Combine cheese and vegetables in a large bowl.
2. Add dill and horseradish and stir in the mayonnaise.
3. Assemble the sandwich by lining each warmed pita pocket with a lettuce leaf and 4 oz. of filling. Serve upright in a bowl.

Servings	Calories	Protein (g)	Fat (g)	Cholesterol (mg)	Carbohydrates (g)	Fiber (g)	Sodium (mg)
1	260	10.7	14.0	27	25.0	0.7	356

Tempeh Reuben

24 Open-Face Sandwiches

This new-age version of the popular Jewish deli sandwich is extremely tasty. It is the Moosewood staff's favorite.

Equipment:	large skillet
Preparation Time:	10 minutes
Cooking Time:	20 minutes

Ingredients	Volume	Weight
Vegetable oil	1 cup	
Onions, chopped	3 qts.	3 lbs.
Garlic, minced or pressed	8 cloves or 2 Tbsp.	
Fennel seed, ground	1 Tbsp.	
Tempeh (see p. 474), cubed		4 lbs.
Soy sauce	3/4 cup	
Rye bread, toasted	24 slices	

Toppings

Russian dressing	3 cups	
Sauerkraut, drained, warmed	1½ qts.	3 lbs.
Swiss cheese, grated	2 qts.	2 lbs.

Procedure

1. In a heavy skillet, sauté the onions, garlic, and ground fennel for about 5 minutes.
2. Add the tempeh, sauté on low heat, stirring often, for about 20 minutes, until the tempeh starts to brown. Add soy sauce, remove from heat.
3. Layer the sandwiches as follows: rye toast, 4 oz. tempeh mixture, 1 oz. Russian Dressing, ¼ cup sauerkraut, and ⅓ cup grated Swiss cheese. Broil until the cheese is melted. Serve hot.

Servings	Calories	Protein (g)	Fat (g)	Cholesterol (mg)	Carbohydrates (g)	Fiber (g)	Sodium (mg)
1	628	29.6	41.2	40	39.3	3.9	1318

White Bean Dip

24 3-oz. Servings

This is an interesting, lighter twist on Hummus (p. 79). Serve as a dip or in pita bread as a flavorful, healthful sandwich, garnished with capers, roasted red peppers, and chopped black olives.

Preparation Time: 15 minutes if using prepared beans

Ingredients	Volume	Weight
Dried white beans (navy or pea), cooked	3 qts.	4 lbs. 12 oz.
or dry	4½ cups	2 lbs.
Olive oil, extra-virgin	¾ cup	
Lemon juice, fresh	1 cup	
Garlic, pressed	6 med. cloves or 2 Tbsp.	
Cumin seed, ground	2 tsp.	
Hungarian paprika	2 tsp.	
Salt	1 tsp. or more to taste	
Pita bread	12 whole	2 oz. each

Garnishes

Capers (optional)
Pimientos (optional)
Calamata or California olives (optional)

Procedure

1. If using dried beans, soak overnight in water to cover or bring to a boil. Remove from the heat and soak for 1–2 hours. After the beans have soaked, drain and cook in 1 gal. of water for 45 minutes. Drain.

(continued)

2. In a food processor or blender, purée the beans a quart at a time emptying each batch into a large mixing bowl.
3. Stir in the olive oil, lemon juice, garlic, and spices.
4. To serve as a dip, toast pita bread and cut into triangular wedges.

Servings	Calories	Protein (g)	Fat (g)	Cholesterol (mg)	Carbohydrates (g)	Fiber (g)	Sodium (mg)
1	281	11.6	8.8	0	41.4	0.1	255

Sandwiches and Dips

MAIN DISH SALADS

Salads made from a selection of vegetables, legumes, grains, or pasta are substantial enough to be the centerpiece of a meal. We usually complement main dish salads with soup and bread for a balance of taste and nutrition. A main dish salad can be served in smaller portions than we suggest as the starter course for a larger meal. Although these salads are a popular lunch menu item the year around, we tend to serve them in larger portions than indicated here for dinners when warm weather influences our customers to choose lighter fare.

All foodservice benefits from attractive presentation; salad plates in particular lend themselves to the artful arrangement of elements. You can make fanciful "beds" for salads with red leaf or ruffled looseleaf lettuce and choose garnishes for both visual and taste appeal. For example, a Tabouli salad is both delicious and appealing topped with a little "snowcap" of grated feta cheese and chopped parsley. White Bean and Tomato Salad is accented and enhanced by sharp and salty Greek olives, and Thai Noodle Salad is given textural interest and added protein when topped with roasted peanuts.

Main dish salads offer a response to the growing demand for healthful, lighter meals. They also may simply help satisfy those diners who want to leave room for dessert.

Aegean Potato Salad

24 8-oz. Servings

Creamy and lively, this salad was inspired by a love of potatoes, feta cheese, and garlic. Served in smaller portions, it can also enhance a Greek combination platter with stuffed grape leaves, Easy Artichokes (p. 324), or our Artichoke Heart–Tomato Salad (p. 313).

Equipment:	2-gallon stockpot
Preparation Time:	20 minutes
Cooking Time:	30 minutes

Ingredients	Volume	Weight
Potatoes, red or white, peeled, cubed	9 qts.	9 lbs.
Feta cheese, freshly grated	2 cups	8 oz.
Parmesan cheese, freshly grated	1 cup	3 oz.
Ricotta cheese	2 cups	1 lb.
Garlic, pressed	12 cloves, or 4 Tbsp.	
Scallion greens or chives, chopped	1½ cups	4 oz.
Olive oil	1½ cups	
Cider vinegar	1 cup + 2 Tbsp.	
Dill weed, fresh, chopped	¼ cup	
or dried	4 tsp.	
Black pepper to taste		

Garnishes

	Volume	Weight
Greek olives (optional)		
Tomato wedges (optional)	4 whole	9 oz.

Procedure

1. Cook the potatoes in boiling, unsalted water until just tender.
2. While the potatoes cook, combine the remaining ingredients.

(continued)

3. Drain the potatoes and, while still hot, gently fold them into the cheese mixture.
4. Serve on a bed of greens with Greek olives and tomato wedges.

Note: Aegean Potato Salad can be served warm but improves with chilling.

Servings	Calories	Protein (g)	Fat (g)	Cholesterol (mg)	Carbohydrates (g)	Fiber (g)	Sodium (mg)
1	163	3.5	9.1	7	17.7	1.6	114

Main Dish Salads

Black Bean and Rice Salad

24 9-oz. Servings

Borrowed from the cuisine of Mexico's Yucatan, this salad is plentiful with tastes and textural surprises. The combination of beans and rice makes this a complete protein entrée. Serve chilled or at room temperature.

Preparation Time: 20 minutes
Cooking Time: beans, 1½ hours
rice, 45 minutes

Ingredients	Volume	Weight
Black beans, dried	2½ cups	1 lb.
or cooked, drained	2 qts.	3 lbs.
Brown rice, raw	1 qt.	1 lb. 10 oz.
or cooked	3 qts.	5 lbs.
Celery, finely chopped	1¼ qts.	1 lb. 4 oz.
Spanish olives, sliced	1 cup	6 oz.

Dressing

Orange juice	2¼ cups
Olive oil	¾ cup
Cider vinegar	⅓ cup
Scallion, chopped	1½ cups
Parsley, fresh, chopped	½ cup
Cilantro, fresh, chopped	½ cup
Coriander seed, ground	2 Tbsp.
Cumin, ground	2 Tbsp.
Orange peel, grated	3 Tbsp.
Cinnamon	1 Tbsp.
Salt and black pepper to taste	

Garnishes

Walnuts, toasted and chopped (optional)	2 cups	8 oz.
Cilantro or parsley sprigs		

(continued)

Procedure

1. If using dried beans, soak the beans overnight in water to cover; or bring to a boil, remove from the heat and let soak for 1 to 2 hours and drain. After soaking, cook the beans until tender in 2 qts. of water for 1 to 1½ hours. Avoid overcooking. Drain and chill beans for a few hours or overnight.
2. Cook the brown rice in 7 cups of water (p. 468).
3. Combine the cooked beans with the rice, olives, and celery.
4. Whisk together the dressing ingredients.
5. Combine dressing with rice and bean mixture.
6. Top servings with toasted walnuts, if desired, and herb sprigs. Serve chilled or at room temperature.

Note: This is the perfect dish for using leftover rice. It also provides a good filling for tomato shells or avocado halves.

Servings	Calories	Protein (g)	Fat (g)	Cholesterol (mg)	Carbohydrates (g)	Fiber (g)	Sodium (mg)
1	251	6.5	9.2	0	36.7	1.3	422

Main Dish Salads

Couscous with Artichoke Hearts and Walnuts

25 8-oz. Servings

The light, fluffy grains of couscous are perfect vehicles for fresh herbs, smoky walnuts, and the meaty, tangy quality of artichoke hearts. At room temperature or chilled, this elegant salad can be served alone, beside grilled fish, or in combination with Tzatziki (p. 344) and a Carrot Salad (p. 321).

Preparation Time: 15 minutes

Ingredients	Volume	Weight
Water, boiling	2 qts.	
Couscous, dry	1½ qts.	2 lbs. 7 oz.
Olive oil	2 Tbsp.	
Salt	½ tsp.	
24 whole artichoke hearts, quartered	2 qts.	2 lbs. 8 oz.
Scallions, minced	2 cups	5 oz.
Garlic, pressed	4 lg. cloves or 1½ Tbsp.	
Parsley, fresh, chopped	2 cups	
Dill, fresh, chopped	¼ cup	
Tarragon, fresh, chopped	¼ cup	
or Mint, fresh, chopped	¼ cup	
Olive oil	¾ cup	
Lemon juice, fresh	½ cup	
Walnuts, toasted, chopped	2 cups	8 oz.
Salt	1 Tbsp.	
Black pepper to taste		

Garnish

Feta cheese, grated (optional)	3 cups	12 oz.
Hard-boiled eggs, quartered (optional)	1 dozen	1 lb. 5 oz.

(continued)

Main Dish Salads

Procedure

1. In a large bowl, cover the couscous with boiling water. Stir in the oil and salt with a fork, cover tightly with foil, and set aside for 10 minutes. Fluff with a fork.
2. Mix the remaining ingredients into the cooked couscous. Adjust for salt and pepper.
3. Serve chilled or at room temperature, garnished with feta cheese or hard-boiled eggs.

Note: In place of each ¼ cup of fresh herbs, use 1 Tbsp. of dried herbs. If dried mint is unavailable, use the contents of a packet of herbal mint tea.

Servings	Calories	Protein (g)	Fat (g)	Cholesterol (mg)	Carbohydrates (g)	Fiber (g)	Sodium (mg)
1	322	8.8	14	0	42	5.4	389

Pasta Primavera

24 10-oz. Servings

The sautéed mushrooms and sun-dried tomatoes distinguish this pasta salad from many. Serve on a bed of curly leaf lettuce with a favorite minestrone, Tomato–Garlic Soup (p. 58), or Crema Andaluz (p. 30).

Preparation and Cooking Time: 40 minutes

Ingredients	Volume	Weight
Pasta, medium shells or short tubes		4 lbs.
Olive oil, mixture of ½ extra-virgin and ½ regular	½ cup	
Lemon juice, fresh	½ cup	
Basil, fresh, chopped	1 cup	
or dried	3 Tbsp.	
Olive oil	¼ cup	
Garlic, pressed	10 cloves or 3 Tbsp.	
Mushrooms, sliced	1½ qts.	1 lb. 4 oz.
Asparagus, cut in 1-in. pieces	2 qts.	2 lbs.
or Green beans cut in 1-in. pieces	2 qts.	2 lbs. 4 oz.
Green peas	1 qt.	1 lb. 4 oz.
Tomatoes, fresh, chopped	1¾ qts.	2 lbs. 10 oz.
Parsley, fresh, chopped	1 cup	
Sun-dried tomatoes, soaked, drained, thinly sliced (optional) (p. 474)	1 cup	3 oz.
Parmesan cheese, freshly grated	1 cup	4 oz.
Salt and black pepper to taste		

Garnish

Parmesan cheese, freshly grated (optional)	3 cups	12 oz.

(continued)

Main Dish Salads

Procedure

1. Cook the pasta until al dente. Drain and rinse with cold water, drain again.
2. Toss pasta with ½ cup olive oil, lemon juice, and basil.
3. Sauté the garlic in olive oil for 1 minute. Add the mushrooms and cook on medium heat until just tender. Remove from heat.
4. Steam the asparagus or green beans and peas until tender.
5. Toss the vegetables, pasta, and remaining ingredients.
6. Serve chilled or at room temperature, with additional grated Parmesan if desired.

Servings	Calories	Protein (g)	Fat (g)	Cholesterol (mg)	Carbohydrates (g)	Fiber (g)	Sodium (mg)
1	445	15.9	10.5	4	72.6	6.3	197

Main Dish Salads

Rice Salad Provençal

24 10-oz. Servings

A quick, colorful salad with flavor and flair. The taste and texture of each vegetable is preserved through the rapid blanching process. Garnish with feta cheese, tomato wedges, and Mediterranean olives, like calamata or niçoise.

Preparation Time: 20 minutes
Cooking Time: 40 minutes

Ingredients	Volume	Weight
Basmati brown rice, raw	1 qt.	1 lb. 6 oz.
or cooked (p. 468)	3 qts.	5 lbs.
Carrots, diced	1 qt.	2 lbs.
Green and/or red peppers, diced	1 qt.	1 lb.
Mushrooms, sliced	1¼ qts.	1 lb.
Green peas, frozen or fresh cut	1 qt.	1 lb. 4 oz.
Celery, thinly sliced	2 cups	8 oz.
Parsley, fresh, chopped	1/2 cup	
Salt	1 Tbsp. or more to taste	
Black pepper to taste		

Marinade

Olive oil	1 cup	
Vegetable oil	1 cup	
Lemon juice, fresh	1 cup or more to taste	
Garlic, pressed	4 med. cloves or 1 heaping Tbsp.	
Herbs: tarragon, basil, dill, marjoram (choose 1 or 2), fresh	4 Tbsp.	
or dried	4 tsp.	

Garnish

Feta cheese, grated (optional)	3 cups	12 oz.

(continued)

Procedure

1. Cook the rice in 7 cups of water and cool to room temperature.
2. Steam or blanch each of the vegetables, except for the celery, until tender but firm.
3. Transfer the rice to a large bowl and fold in the cooked vegetables, celery, and parsley. Season with salt and pepper.
4. Whisk the marinade ingredients together and pour over the vegetable–rice mixture. Toss gently and adjust for salt and pepper.
5. Refrigerate until well chilled, stirring occasionally until the marinade flavors the rice.

Note: This is an excellent dish for using leftover rice.

Servings	Calories	Protein (g)	Fat (g)	Cholesterol (mg)	Carbohydrates (g)	Fiber (g)	Sodium (mg)
1	332	4.7	20	0	34.8	3.2	354

Main Dish Salads

Russian Salad

24 10-oz. Servings

When was the last time you ate a pink salad you could trust? Trust us—you won't be disappointed. Serve Russian Salad on a bed of greens with wedges of hard-boiled eggs and a fan of sesame crackers. Or, like our Russian grandmothers, bring out the pumpernickel and pickled herring.

Preparation and Cooking Time: 30 minutes

Ingredients	Volume	Weight
Potatoes, peeled, diced	2 qts.	2 lbs.
Carrots, peeled, diced	3 qts.	4 lbs.
Beets, peeled, diced	3 qts.	4 lbs.
Green peas, frozen, thawed	1 qt.	1 lb. 4 oz.
Red onion, minced	1 cup	4 oz.
Dill pickle, chopped	2 cups	10 oz.
Mayonnaise	3 cups	
Lemon juice, fresh	1/3 cup	
Salt and black pepper to taste		

Garnish

Capers (optional)

Procedure

1. Cook the potatoes in boiling water until tender. Drain and remove to a large mixing bowl.
2. In separate batches, cook the carrots and the beets until tender.
3. Add the carrots to the mixing bowl but do not add the beets. Set them aside and chill.
4. Add the remaining ingredients to the potatoes and carrots and stir gently. Chill.
5. Fold the beets into the salad just before serving so the salad will be a light pink color. (Adding any earlier will give you a color nearer to bubble gum.) As an accent, garnish with a sprinkling of capers.

Servings	Calories	Protein (g)	Fat (g)	Cholesterol (mg)	Carbohydrates (g)	Fiber (g)	Sodium (mg)
1	231	4.3	9.9	7	33.7	5.8	487

Salat Morocain

24 8-oz. Servings

Salat Morocain is lovely served on a bed of leaf lettuce surrounded by tomato wedges, hard-boiled eggs, and glossy calamata olives. It is also a fine addition to a Mediterranean Combo Plate with Baba Ganoush (p. 71) and Tzatziki (p. 344). When served with Turkish Spinach–Lentil Soup (p. 59) or North African Split Pea Soup (p. 45), it provides both good cultural companionship and complete protein.

Preparation and Cooking Time: 45 minutes

Ingredients	Volume	Weight
Couscous, dry (p. 470)	1½ qts.	2 lbs. 7 oz.
Salt	2 tsp.	
Saffron threads (optional)	2 pinches	
Boiling water	1¼ qts.	
Carrots, diced	1½ qts.	2 lbs.
Peppers, diced (a mixture of red, green, and yellow is nice)	1 qt.	1 lb.
Green or wax beans, stemmed, cut in 1-in. pieces	1 qt.	1 lb. 4 oz.
Red onion (or scallions), finely sliced	1 cup	6 oz.
Currants	1⅓ cups	6 oz.
Almonds, toasted, and chopped	2 cups	8 oz.

Marinade

Vegetable or olive oil	1 cup	
Lemon juice, fresh	1 cup	
Salt	2 tsp. or more to taste	
Cinnamon	1 tsp.	
Orange juice	¾ cup	
Parsley, fresh, chopped	1 cup	
Spearmint, fresh, chopped	¼ cup	
or Mint, dried	2 tsp.	
Cayenne	⅛ tsp.	

Garnish

Hard-boiled eggs (optional)	1 dozen	1 lb. 5 oz.

Procedure

1. Combine the couscous, salt, and optional saffron in a large mixing bowl; stir in the boiling water. Cover with aluminum foil for 15 minutes; fluff after 10 minutes and recover.
2. Concurrently, steam or blanch the carrots, peppers, and beans separately. As soon as each vegetable is barely tender, add it to the couscous.
3. Stir in the onion or scallions, currants, and almonds.
4. Whisk together the marinade ingredients.
5. Toss the marinade with the couscous mixture and chill for at least 1 hour. Correct for salt.
6. Garnish each serving with half a hard-boiled egg.

Servings	Calories	Protein (g)	Fat (g)	Cholesterol (mg)	Carbohydrates (g)	Fiber (g)	Sodium (mg)
1	370	9.3	14.9	0	51.8	6.2	427

Tabouli

24 8-oz. Servings

This popular Middle Eastern grain salad is traditionally made with parsley, lemon, bulghur, and olive oil. Additional ingredients mark the creativity of cooks the world over; this is our tabouli. Serve on greens topped with tomatoes, chopped or cut into wedges, and feta cheese. Create a Middle Eastern Combo Plate with Tabouli, Hummus (p. 79), and Baba Ganoush (p. 71).

Preparation and Cooking Time: 30 minutes

Ingredients	Volume	Weight
Bulghur, dry (p. 468)	2 qts.	2 lbs. 12 oz.
Salt	1 Tbsp.	
Boiling water	3 qts.	
Spearmint, dried (or the contents of 2 herbal tea bags)	4 tsp.	
or Mint, fresh, chopped	¼ cup	

Dressing

Olive oil	2 cups	
Lemon juice, fresh	2 cups	
Garlic, pressed	12 cloves or 3½ Tbsp.	
Scallions, chopped	1 qt.	10 oz.
Parsley, fresh, chopped	1½ qts.	8 oz.
Cucumbers, peeled, seeded, diced	3 qts.	3 lbs. 8 oz.
Almonds, toasted and coarsely chopped	3 cups	12 oz.

Garnish

Feta cheese, grated (optional)	3 cups	12 oz.

Procedure

1. Place the bulghur, salt, boiling water, and mint in a large bowl. Cover and let sit for 20 to 30 minutes. After 15 minutes, stir to fluff and recover.
2. Whisk together the dressing ingredients.
3. Add the dressing, vegetables, and nuts to the bulghur.
4. Chill for an hour or more, stirring occasionally.
5. Garnish each serving with ½ oz. of feta cheese.

Servings	Calories	Protein (g)	Fat (g)	Cholesterol (mg)	Carbohydrates (g)	Fiber (g)	Sodium (mg)
1	469	11	27.3	0	51.6	13.2	1214

Thai Noodle Salad

24 7- to 8-oz. Servings

It is traditional to garnish this salad. So, at the very least, decorate each plate with a wedge of lime and a sprinkling of roasted peanuts. Mung sprouts and tofu boost the protein and cilantro assures the authenticity of the dish.

Preparation and Cooking Time: 1 hour

Ingredients	Volume	Weight
Linguine		3 lbs.

Sauce

Basil, fresh, minced	¾ cup	
Cilantro, fresh, minced	¾ cup	
Spearmint, fresh	¾ cup	
or dried	1 Tbsp.	
Ginger root, fresh, grated	⅓ cup	
Garlic, pressed	8 med. cloves or 2 Tbsp.	
Salt	1 Tbsp.	
Chili peppers, fresh, minced	2–3 Tbsp.	
or Chili paste (p. 469)	1–2 Tbsp.	
Scallions, green and white parts, chopped	1 cup	
Lime juice, fresh	½ cup	2.5 oz.
Coconut milk, unsweetened (p. 470)		28 oz.
Sesame oil, dark (p. 473)	¾ cup	

Vegetables

Choose at least three or four of any of the following to total 1½ gallons:

Carrots, julienned
Red, green, or yellow peppers, thinly
   sliced
Snow or snap peas, stemmed
Green peas, fresh or frozen
Mung bean sprouts
Water chestnuts, sliced

Garnishes

Peanuts, roasted, coarsely chopped	2 cups	10 oz.
Lime wedges	4 limes	
Cilantro, fresh, chopped	1½ cups	
Seasoned tofu (p. 220)		1 lb. 8 oz.
Mung bean sprouts		8 oz.

Procedure

1. Cook the linguine until al dente. Drain and toss with 3–4 Tbsp. of vegetable or dark sesame oil to keep the pasta from sticking together. Chill well.
2. Whisk together the sauce ingredients and set aside.
3. Blanch your choice of vegetables (excluding the water chestnuts) until barely tender. Plunge each vegetable immediately into cold water and drain. Add the water chestnuts to the other vegetables now, if you wish.
4. Combine the noodles, sauce, and vegetables. Refrigerate until cool and serve promptly to prevent the noodles from overly absorbing the seasonings and diluting the flavor. Adjust seasonings if necessary. Garnish each plate with one or more of the optional toppings.

Servings	Calories	Protein (g)	Fat (g)	Cholesterol (mg)	Carbohydrates (g)	Fiber (g)	Sodium (mg)
1	225	5.2	11.2	19	26.8	4.0	339

Udon Noodles and Vegetables

24 10-oz. Servings

The warm, robust, and complex peanut sauce in this dish is a blend of Chinese and Southeast Asian cuisines. Serve this salad on a bed of fresh spinach topped with the suggested garnishes. The baked tofu in the recipe can be mixed directly into the dish or served as a garnish.

Preparation and Cooking Time: 1 hour

Ingredients	Volume	Weight
Udon noodles (see p. 475) or linguine		3 lbs.

Sauce

Ingredients	Volume	Weight
Peanut butter, smooth, unsweetened	2 cups	1 lb. 2 oz.
Chinese Rice vinegar (p. 469)	2 cups	
Soy sauce	1½ cups	
Water, warm	2 cups	
Sesame oil, dark (p. 473)	1½ cups	
Chili pepper, fresh, minced	3 Tbsp.	
Fennel seed, ground	1 Tbsp.	
Basil, fresh, chopped	1 cup	
or dried	3 Tbsp.	
Garlic, pressed	6 cloves, or 2 Tbsp.	
Scallion, green and white parts, chopped	2½ cups	7 oz.
Seasoned tofu (p. 220), cubed		1 lb. 8 oz.
Cucumbers, peeled, seeded, diced	1 qt.	1 lb. 4 oz.

Garnishes

Ingredients	Volume	Weight
Carrots, grated	1½ cups	8 oz.
or Mung bean sprouts		8 oz.

Procedure

1. Cook the pasta until tender. Rinse with cold water and drain.
2. While the pasta cooks, combine the sauce ingredients and prepare the vegetables and tofu.
3. Toss all the ingredients together.
4. Garnish servings with grated carrot or mung bean sprouts.

Servings	Calories	Protein (g)	Fat (g)	Cholesterol (mg)	Carbohydrates (g)	Fiber (g)	Sodium (mg)
1	503	15.0	27.8	49	50.7	3.7	1113

Main Dish Salads

Vegetable-Tofu Almondine

25 9-oz. Servings

This Asian-style marinated salad is exotically seasoned and makes a beautiful presentation. Serve on a bed of fresh spinach with a wedge of melon or other fruit slices. Garnish with bean sprouts.

Preparation and Cooking Time: 1 hour

Ingredients	Volume	Weight
Tofu, pressed (p. 474)		6 lbs. (unpressed weight)
Sesame oil, dark (p. 473)	¾ cup	
Soy sauce	1 cup	
Whole almonds	1½ cups	8 oz.
Green beans, stemmed, snapped	1¾ qts.	2 lbs.
Carrots, julienned or sliced diagonally into half-moons	1¾ qts.	2 lbs. 6 oz.
Snow peas, stemmed	2 cups	8 oz.
Mushrooms, thickly sliced	2 cups	10 oz.
Scallions, sliced diagonally	1½ cups	3 oz.

Marinade

Vegetable oil	¾ cup	
Sesame oil, dark	⅓ cup	
Chinese Rice vinegar (p. 469)	1 cup	
Ginger root, fresh, grated	⅓ cup	
Anise, ground (p. 467)	2 tsp.	
Coriander seed, ground	1⅓ Tbsp.	
Honey or brown sugar	⅛–¼ cup	
Salt	2 tsp.	

Garnish

Mung bean sprouts		8 oz.

Procedure

1. Preheat the oven to 350°. Use a convection oven, if available, for crisper, firmer tofu.
2. Cut the tofu into 1-in. cubes and arrange in single layers in two long, shallow insert or baking pans.
3. Whisk together the sesame oil and soy sauce and pour over the tofu.
4. Bake for 30 minutes, turning the tofu every 10–15 minutes so that all the surfaces can brown. Use a rubber spatula to prevent breaking the tofu.
5. Meanwhile, set a timer for 5 minutes, spread the almonds on a baking sheet, and toast at 350° until brown and aromatic.
6. Blanch each of the vegetables, except for the scallions, until just tender but still firm.
7. Transfer the baked tofu, toasted almonds, cooked vegetables, and scallions to a large bowl.
8. Whisk together the marinade ingredients and toss gently with the tofu–vegetable mixture.
9. Chill or serve at once, garnished with bean sprouts.

Servings	Calories	Protein (g)	Fat (g)	Cholesterol (mg)	Carbohydrates (g)	Fiber (g)	Sodium (mg)
1	372	9.7	23.6	0	33.6	5.5	751

Main Dish Salads

White Bean and Tomato

24 9.5-oz. Servings

Once the beans are cooked, this salad is quick and rewarding. It is a tribute to the award-winning trio of ripe tomatoes, garlic, and a fine olive oil. Serve with crusty Italian bread, medallions of fresh mozzarella cheese, and olives.

Preparation Time: 20 minutes
Cooking Time: 45 minutes (if cooking beans)

Ingredients	Volume	Weight
Navy or pea beans, dried	2¼ qts.	3 lbs. 8 oz.
or cooked, drained	1½ gals.	9 lbs. 4 oz.
Garlic, pressed	10 cloves or 3 Tbsp.	
Red onion, minced	1½ cups	8 oz.
Celery, thinly sliced crosswise	2 qts.	2 lbs.
Tomatoes, fresh, cut in ½-in. cubes	3⅓ qts.	5 lbs.
Basil or mint, fresh, chopped	½ cup	
or dried	3 Tbsp.	
Lemon juice, fresh	¾ cup	
Extra-virgin olive oil	¾ cup	
Salt and black pepper to taste		

Garnish

Calamata olives (optional)		9 oz.

Procedure

1. If using dried beans, soak the beans overnight in water to cover; or bring to a boil, remove from the heat, let soak for 1–2 hours, and then drain. After soaking, cook beans until tender in a gallon of water for 30–45 minutes. Avoid overcooking. Drain and chill beans for a few hours or overnight.
2. Combine all the ingredients, stirring gently.
3. Serve chilled or at room temperature, as a main dish, side salad, or appetizer.

Servings	Calories	Protein (g)	Fat (g)	Cholesterol (mg)	Carbohydrates (g)	Fiber (g)	Sodium (mg)
1	346	17.1	8.6	0	53.1	1.9	51

DRESSINGS

Our salad dressings offer variety with flavors that range from the smooth and mellow Moosewood Restaurant's House Dressing to the bright and pungent Japanese Dressing. All have more vitality and personality than the conventional mayonnaise-based and package-mix dressings currently available commercially. At Moosewood, we most often use these dressings on tossed green salads. However, many are more versatile and can be used with pita sandwich fillings or to dress raw or cooked vegetables.

Nondairy dressings include

- Honey–Mustard Vinaigrette
- Japanese Dressing
- Lemon–Tahini Dressing
- Miso–Ginger Dressing
- Roasted Garlic Dressing
- Tofu–Basil Dressing
- Vinaigrette Salad Dressing

Dairy dressings include

- Bleu Cheese Dressing
- Feta–Garlic Dressing
- Low-Fat Garlic Dressing
- Moosewood Restaurant's House Dressing

Bleu Cheese Dressing

2 quarts

A rich, versatile dressing that works on spinach and other green salads as well as in pita sandwiches. Try bleu cheese dressing substituted for the recommended dressings in the Garden Vegetable–Feta Pita (p. 76) and Floating Cloud Pita (p. 75).

Preparation Time: 10 minutes

Ingredients	Volume	Weight
Bleu cheese, crumbled	5¼ cups	1 lb. 8 oz.
Sour cream	2 cups	1 lb.
Low-fat or nonfat yogurt	2 cups	1 lb.
Garlic, pressed	6 cloves or 2 Tbsp.	
Lemon juice, fresh	6 Tbsp.	
Milk	1 cup	

Procedure

Prepare the dressing in two batches.
1. Set aside ½ lb. of the bleu cheese.
2. Blend half of the ingredients and half of the remaining bleu cheese in a commercial food processor or blender until smooth and creamy. Repeat.
3. Add the reserved bleu cheese to the dressing.

Note: Covered and refrigerated, this dressing will keep for 4–5 days.

Servings	Calories	Protein (g)	Fat (g)	Cholesterol (mg)	Carbohydrates (g)	Fiber (g)	Sodium (mg)
1	60	3.0	4.7	12	1.5	0	159

Feta-Garlic Dressing

2 quarts

Rich, creamy, and assertively seasoned, this dressing is fast becoming one of Moosewood's most popular.

Preparation Time: 10 minutes

Ingredients	Volume	Weight
Olive oil	3 cups	
Cider or white vinegar	¼ cup	
Garlic, pressed or chopped	6 cloves or 2 Tbsp.	
Dill weed, dried	1 Tbsp.	
Feta cheese, grated	1 qt.	1 lb.
Milk	3 cups	
Black pepper, freshly ground, to taste		

Procedure

Prepare the dressing in two batches.
1. In a commercial blender, whirl half of all the ingredients, except the milk, for 1 minute.
2. With the machine running, slowly pour in half the milk. Turn off the machine as soon as the dressing is thick and creamy. Overblending will cause separation.
3. Repeat.

Note: Refrigerated and tightly covered, this dressing will stay fresh for 4–5 days. If separation occurs, reblend.

Servings	Calories	Protein (g)	Fat (g)	Cholesterol (mg)	Carbohydrates (g)	Fiber (g)	Sodium (mg)
1	119	1.4	12.3	7	1.0	0	85

Honey–Mustard Vinaigrette

2 quarts

Simple and sassy, this dressing doubles as a marinade for baked or grilled fish.

Preparation Time: 10 minutes

Ingredients	Volume	Weight
Cider vinegar	1 1/3 cups	
Dijon mustard	1 1/3 cups	
Honey	1 1/3 cups	
Vegetable oil	1 qt.	
Salt to taste		

Procedure

1. In a mixing bowl, whisk together the vinegar and mustard. If a less tart dressing is desired, slightly reduce the vinegar and increase the mustard.
2. Whisk in the honey and then the oil, drizzling both in until well blended. Add salt to taste.

This recipe can also be made in batches in a commercial food processor or Hobart mixer.

Note: Covered and refrigerated, this dressing will keep indefinitely.

Servings	Calories	Protein (g)	Fat (g)	Cholesterol (mg)	Carbohydrates (g)	Fiber (g)	Sodium (mg)
1	151	0.2	14.4	0	6.4	0	62

Japanese Dressing

2 quarts

This pungent, nondairy dressing is excellent on salads and steamed vegetables that accompany Asian-style dishes.

Preparation Time: 10 minutes

Ingredients	Volume	Weight
Garlic, minced or pressed	4 cloves or 1½ Tbsp.	
Onion, minced	¾ cup	4 oz.
Carrot, grated	2 cups	10 oz.
Ginger root, fresh, grated	⅔ cup	
Mustard, powdered	2 tsp.	
Soy sauce	½ cup	
Unsweetened apple juice	½ cup	
Sesame oil, dark (p. 473)	4 tsp.	
Rice vinegar	2 cups	
Vegetable oil	1 qt.	
Black pepper to taste		

Procedure

Prepare the dressing in two batches.
1. In a commercial blender, combine half of all the ingredients except the vegetable oil.
2. Slowly add half the vegetable oil until the dressing is smooth and thickened.
3. Repeat.

Note: This dressing will keep for up to 1 week refrigerated in a tightly covered container.

Servings	Calories	Protein (g)	Fat (g)	Cholesterol (mg)	Carbohydrates (g)	Fiber (g)	Sodium (mg)
1	136	0.2	14.5	0	1.4	0.2	108

Lemon–Tahini Dressing

1 quart

This Middle-Eastern-style dressing has the nutty flavor of sesame seeds and a creamy, smooth texture. Traditionally used to season baba ganoush, hummus, and falafels, Lemon–Tahini Dressing is also wonderful on tossed salads.

Preparation Time: 10 minutes

Ingredients	Volume	Weight
Tahini (p. 474)	2 cups	
Water, cool	1½ cups	
Lemon juice, fresh	1 cup	
Garlic, pressed	3 cloves or 1 Tbsp.	
Parsley, fresh, chopped	3 Tbsp.	
Cumin, ground	1 tsp.	
Cayenne pepper	pinch	
Salt to taste		

Procedure

1. Pour the tahini into a large mixing bowl. Gradually whisk in the water and lemon juice until smooth and creamy.
2. Whisk in the rest of the ingredients and salt to taste. Add additional water, if necessary, to achieve the consistency of heavy cream.

Note: This dressing will keep indefinitely, covered and refrigerated.

Servings	Calories	Protein (g)	Fat (g)	Cholesterol (mg)	Carbohydrates (g)	Fiber (g)	Sodium (mg)
1	64	2.0	5.2	0	3.6	1.1	14

Low- (or No) Fat Garlic Dressing

2 quarts

A healthful, calcium-rich choice, this recipe can be made fat-free by using nonfat cottage cheese.

Preparation Time: 10 minutes

Ingredients	Volume	Weight
Low-fat or nonfat cottage cheese	1³/₄ qts.	3 lbs. 8 oz.
Dijon mustard	2 Tbsp.	
Vinegar	1/2 cup	
Garlic, pressed	10 med. cloves or 3 Tbsp.	
Scallions, chopped	3 cups	7¹/₂ oz.
Parsley, fresh, chopped	1 cup	
Salt	1 Tbsp. or to taste	
Black pepper to taste		

Procedure

Prepare the dressing in two batches.

1. In a commercial blender or food processor, whirl half of all the ingredients. If the dressing is not blending easily, add 3–5 Tbsp. of water (some cottage cheeses are drier than others).
2. Repeat.

Note: Refrigerated and tightly covered, this dressing will keep for about 1 week.

Servings	Calories	Protein (g)	Fat (g)	Cholesterol (mg)	Carbohydrates (g)	Fiber (g)	Sodium (mg)
1	25	3.6	0.5	2	1.6	0.1	219

Miso–Ginger Dressing

2 quarts

This dressing is one of our most frequently requested recipes. Its zesty, exotic flavor enlivens green salads of all types.

Preparation Time: 10 minutes

Ingredients	Volume	Weight
Miso, light (p. 472)	³/₄–⁷/₈ cup	
Ginger root, fresh, grated	¹/₂ cup	
Cider vinegar	²/₃ cup	
Sesame oil, dark (p. 473)	²/₃ cup	
Vegetable oil	3¹/₂ cups	
Water	2 cups	

Procedure

Prepare the dressing in two batches.
1. In a commercial blender, combine half the miso, ginger, vinegar, and sesame oil.
2. Slowly add half the vegetable oil until thoroughly blended.
3. Continue with the slow addition of half the water until the dressing is thick and creamy. Turn off at once; overblending may cause separation.
4. Repeat.

Note: Refrigerated and tightly covered, this dressing will stay fresh for 4–5 days. If separation occurs, reblend.

Servings	Calories	Protein (g)	Fat (g)	Cholesterol (mg)	Carbohydrates (g)	Fiber (g)	Sodium (mg)
1	138	0.4	14.9	0	1.2	0.2	113

Moosewood Restaurant's
House Dressing

5 quarts

This is our most highly prized dressing.

Preparation Time: 10 minutes

Ingredients	Volume	Weight
Vegetable oil	2 qts.	
Cider vinegar	1 cup	
Apple juice	1 cup	
Water	¼ cup	
Spinach leaves, fresh, loosely packed	1½ cups	2 oz.
Herb leaves, fresh: basil, dill, tarragon (2 or 3 in combination, loosely packed)	¾ cup	
or dried	3 Tbsp.	
Dijon mustard	2 Tbsp.	
Buttermilk	2 qts.	
Salt and black pepper to taste		

Procedure

Prepare the dressing in two batches.

1. In a commercial blender, whirl half of all the ingredients, except the buttermilk, for 1 minute.
2. With the machine running, slowly pour in half the milk. Turn off the machine as soon as the dressing thickens. Overblending will cause separation.
3. Repeat.
4. Add salt and pepper.

Note: Refrigerated and tightly covered, this dressing will keep for about a week. If the dressing separates, reblend.

Servings	Calories	Protein (g)	Fat (g)	Cholesterol (mg)	Carbohydrates (g)	Fiber (g)	Sodium (mg)
1	106	0.4	11.5	0	0.8	0	16

Roasted Garlic Dressing

2 quarts

Robust and full-flavored, this Mediterranean-style dressing is well paired with crisp greens and ripe tomatoes.

Preparation Time: 10 minutes
Baking Time: 1 hour

Ingredients	Volume	Weight
Garlic, unpeeled	30 cloves	4 oz.
Olive oil	1 qt.	
Balsamic vinegar	1⅓ cups	
Water	1⅓ cups	
Salt	4 tsp.	
Dijon mustard	4 Tbsp.	
Black pepper, ground	1 Tbsp.	

Procedure

Prepare the dressing in two batches.
1. Bake the garlic cloves in a lightly oiled, tightly covered pan at 350° for 1 hour, or until the cloves are soft and golden. Remove from oven and cool.
2. Squeeze the softened garlic from the skins. Discard skins.
3. In a commercial blender, purée half of the garlic with half of all the other ingredients until smooth.
4. Repeat.

Note: Covered and refrigerated, this dressing will keep for several weeks.

Servings	Calories	Protein (g)	Fat (g)	Cholesterol (mg)	Carbohydrates (g)	Fiber (g)	Sodium (mg)
1	130	0.2	14.2	0	0.8	0.1	161

Tofu Mayonnaise

1½ quarts

This dressing is an excellent choice for seasoning vegan dishes and salads.

Preparation Time: 10 minutes

Ingredients	Volume	Weight
Tofu (p. 474)		3 lbs. 4 oz.
Olive oil, may be part extra-virgin	1 cup	
Lemon juice, fresh	1 cup	
Dijon mustard	2 tsp.	
Salt	2 tsp.	
Black pepper or tabasco sauce	several dashes or splashes	
Garlic, pressed (optional)	4 cloves or 1½ Tbsp.	

Procedure

Prepare the dressing in two batches.

1. Place half of all the ingredients in a commercial blender or food processor and whirl until smooth. If a blender is used, add the liquid ingredients first and then the tofu, to avoid jamming the machinery. Blend in ¼ cup of water if the mayonnaise seems too thick.
2. Repeat.

Note: Covered and refrigerated, this dressing will keep for about 1 week.

Servings	Calories	Protein (g)	Fat (g)	Cholesterol (mg)	Carbohydrates (g)	Fiber (g)	Sodium (mg)
1	50	0.8	3.9	0	3.2	0	78

Tofu-Basil Dressing

2 quarts

A dairy-free dressing with a surprisingly creamy texture. Fresh basil is the key ingredient.

Preparation Time: 10 minutes

Ingredients	Volume	Weight
Tofu		2 lbs. 8 oz.
Cider vinegar	1 cup	
Unsweetened apple juice	1 cup	
Dijon mustard	1 Tbsp.	
Garlic, pressed	4 cloves or 1½ Tbsp.	
Basil, fresh, chopped	1 cup	
Salt	2 tsp.	

Procedure

Prepare the dressing in two batches.

1. Place half of all the ingredients in a commercial blender or food processor and purée until smooth. If using a blender, place liquids in first and then the tofu to avoid jamming the machine.
2. Repeat.

Note: Covered and refrigerated, this dressing will keep for about 1 week.

Servings	Calories	Protein (g)	Fat (g)	Cholesterol (mg)	Carbohydrates (g)	Fiber (g)	Sodium (mg)
1	17	0.6	0.3	0	3.0	0	79

Vinaigrette Salad Dressing
1 gallon

A wealth of herbs and seasonings create a marinade for cooked vegetables or a dressing for green salads. Herbs can be omitted to create a basic vinaigrette, or a variety can be added to create different flavors.

Preparation Time: 10 minutes

Ingredients	Volume	Weight
Vegetable oil	1¾ qts.	
Olive oil	1 qt.	
Cider or red wine vinegar	1¼ qts.	
Lemon juice, fresh	1 cup	
Garlic, pressed	10 cloves or 3 Tbsp.	
Salt	1⅓ Tbsp.	
Dijon mustard	½–¾ cup	
Black pepper	2 tsp.	
Parsley, fresh, chopped	2 cups	
Basil, marjoram, dill, chives, tarragon, in any combination, dried	¾ cup	
or fresh, chopped	2 cups	

Procedure

1. In a large bowl, whisk together all the ingredients.

Note: This dressing will keep indefinitely if refrigerated.

Servings	Calories	Protein (g)	Fat (g)	Cholesterol (mg)	Carbohydrates (g)	Fiber (g)	Sodium (mg)
1	176	0.1	19.6	0	1.1	0.1	92

CASSEROLES

Casseroles are substantial entrée selections that are easy introductions to meatless cuisine. They are often the selection our new customers choose, because casseroles have a long-standing niche in American home-style cooking. Most of the recipes in this section use familiar ingredients, some with a unique twist. For example, cornmeal "mush" becomes polenta, which is then breaded and baked as a vegetarian cutlet.

Because many of these casseroles are rich fare, they should be served with lighter side dishes or salads. Serving sizes suggested for each recipe are Moosewood Restaurant dinner portions. For example, while the Vegetable Moussaka recipe provides 6 servings from a half-size insert pan, 8 or 9 smaller servings from the same pan would certainly be adequate for lunch service. Most casseroles can be held in the steam table without problem, except for frittatas, which are at their best when served shortly after baking.

Artichoke Heart–
Cheese Frittata

24 8-oz. Servings

A basic frittata is made elegant by the addition of artichoke hearts. Serve with Gazpacho (p. 38) or Tomato–Garlic Soup (p. 58).

Equipment:	4 half-size insert pans, 4-in. deep
Preparation Time:	30 to 45 minutes
Baking Time:	40 minutes

Ingredients	Volume	Weight
Potatoes, sliced in ¼-in. rounds		6 lbs.
Vegetable oil	¼–½ cup	
Onions, chopped	2 qts.	2 lbs.
Garlic, minced or pressed	8 med. cloves or 2½ Tbsp.	
Dill weed, dried	4 tsp.	
Artichoke hearts, canned, drained, quartered	2¼ qts.	3 lbs.
Eggs	28 lg. or 1¾ qts.	3 lbs. 8 oz.
White flour	½ cup	
Salt	1 Tbsp.	
Black pepper to taste		
Sharp Cheddar cheese, grated	2 qts.	2 lbs.
Parmesan cheese, grated	1 qt.	1 lb.

Procedure

1. Boil the sliced potatoes until tender. Drain.
2. Sauté the onions and garlic in oil until the onions are golden. Remove from the heat.

(continued)

3. Stir the dill and artichoke hearts into the sautéed onions.
4. Beat the eggs with the flour, salt, and pepper.
5. Combine with the Cheddar and half of the Parmesan cheese.
6. Preheat the oven to 350°.
7. In four lightly oiled pans, dividing the ingredients equally between the pans, layer the potatoes, onion–artichoke heart mixture, and egg–cheese mixture. Sprinkle the reserved Parmesan on top.
8. Bake, covered, at 350° for 30 minutes. Uncover and bake for an additional 10 minutes until puffed and golden.
9. Cut each pan into 6 servings.

Servings	Calories	Protein (g)	Fat (g)	Cholesterol (mg)	Carbohydrates (g)	Fiber (g)	Sodium (mg)
1	528	31.0	29.3	363	36.2	5.6	1035

Caserola della Nonna

24 14-oz. Servings

This casserole is a grand production suitable for a generous feast or special occasion.

Equipment:	4 half-size insert pans, 4-in. deep
Preparation Time:	2 hours
Baking Time:	45 minutes

Ingredients	Volume	Weight
Eggplant, sliced in ½-in. rounds		6 lbs.
Potatoes, sliced in ¼-in. rounds		7 lbs.
Olive oil	½ cup	
Garlic, pressed	8 cloves or 2½ Tbsp.	
Onions, chopped	2½ qts.	2 lbs. 8 oz.
Zucchini, sliced in ¼-in. rounds		6 lbs.
Tomatoes, fresh or canned, chopped	3 qts.	5 lbs.
Basil, fresh	¾ cup	
or dried	¼ cup	
Mozzarella cheese, grated	1½ qts.	2 lbs.
Parmesan cheese, grated	1½ qts.	1 lb. 8 oz.
Bread crumbs	1 qt.	
Eggs, beaten	16 lg. (about 1 qt.)	2 lbs.

Procedure

1. Arrange the eggplant slices in lightly oiled pans. Cover tightly with aluminum foil and bake at 400° until tender, for approximately 45 minutes.
2. Boil the potatoes until just tender. Drain.
3. Sauté the garlic and onions in olive oil until the onions are translucent. If you are using dried basil, sauté it with the garlic and onions. If you are using fresh basil, it will be added later.

(*continued*)

4. Add the zucchini to the onions and sauté briefly until the zucchini is barely tender.
5. Mix the chopped tomatoes with the fresh basil.
6. Combine the grated cheeses.
7. Preheat the oven to 350°.
8. In four lightly oiled pans, layer each pan in the following order:
   - ¼ of the potato slices
   - ¼ of the eggplant slices
   - 2 cups of grated cheese
   - ¼ of the zucchini mixture
   - 3 cups of the tomatoes
   - 1 cup of the beaten eggs
   - 2 cups of grated cheese
   - 1 cup of the bread crumbs

   Bake at 350°, covered, for 30 minutes. Uncover and bake for an additional 15 minutes.
9. Cut each pan into 6 servings.

Servings	Calories	Protein (g)	Fat (g)	Cholesterol (mg)	Carbohydrates (g)	Fiber (g)	Sodium (mg)
1	585	33.4	25.5	220	58.0	8.5	940

Chilaquile Casserole

24 11-oz. Servings

So simple and hearty, this casserole is comfort food, à la Cuernavaca.

Equipment:	4 half-size insert pans, 4-in. deep	
Preparation Time:	30 minutes	
Cooking Time:	45 minutes to 1 hour	

Ingredients	Volume	Weight
Vegetable oil	¼ cup	
Onions, chopped	2 qts.	2 lbs.
Green peppers, chopped	2 qts.	2 lbs.
Corn, frozen, slightly thawed	1¼ qts.	2 lbs. 8 oz.
Tortilla chips		1 lb. 8 oz.
Refritos (p. 216)	1 gal.	
Spanish olives, chopped (optional)	1⅓ cups	8 oz.
Hot Sauce (p. 263)	2 qts.	
Sharp Cheddar cheese, grated	1½ qts.	1 lb. 2 oz.

Procedure

1. Sauté the onions in oil until they are translucent.
2. Add the peppers and continue sautéing until they begin to soften.
3. Stir in the corn and sauté a couple of minutes more.
4. Preheat oven to 375°.
5. Assemble the casseroles in lightly oiled pans by layering, per pan, in the following order:
   - tortilla chips (1/8th of total)
   - 1 qt. refried beans
   - ¼ of the onion–pepper–corn sauté
   - a sprinkling of Spanish olives, if desired
   - 2 cups hot sauce

(continued)

- tortilla chips (1/8th of total)
- 1½ cups grated Cheddar

6. Cover and bake at 375° for 30 minutes. Uncover and continue to bake for 10 minutes, until cheese is lightly browned.
7. Cut each pan into 6 servings.

Servings	Calories	Protein (g)	Fat (g)	Cholesterol (mg)	Carbohydrates (g)	Fiber (g)	Sodium (mg)
1	530	20.9	19.3	22	70.6	11.3	1072

Corn and Cheese Pudding

24 10-oz. Servings
with 1-oz. Hot Sauce

Creamy and satisfying, this casserole is popular with children from 8 to 80. Serve it with or without the Hot Sauce.

Equipment:	4 half-size insert pans, 2-in. deep
Preparation Time:	45 minutes
Baking Time:	35 minutes

Ingredients	Volume	Weight
Eggs	18 lg. or 4½ cups	2 lbs. 4 oz.
White flour	1 cup	
Milk	2¼ qts.	
Salt	1 Tbsp.	
Black pepper	1 tsp.	
Dill, dried	2 Tbsp.	
Corn, frozen or fresh	3 qts.	3 lbs. 8 oz.
Vegetable oil	½ cup	
Onions, finely chopped	3 qts	3 lbs.
Carrots, grated	2 qts.	2 lbs. 8 oz.
Peppers, green or red, finely chopped	2¼ qts.	2 lbs. 8 oz.
Cheddar cheese, sharp, grated	2 qts.	1 lb. 8 oz

Hot Sauce (p. 263)

Procedure

1. In several batches in a commercial blender, combine the eggs, flour, milk, seasonings, and half of the corn. Reserve the other half of the corn.
2. Sauté the onions in vegetable oil until they are translucent.

(continued)

3. Add the carrots and peppers and sauté until softened, for about 10 minutes.
4. Preheat the oven to 350°.
5. In a large bowl, combine the blended ingredients, the sautéed vegetables, the remaining corn, and the cheese.
6. Divide the mixture among four lightly oiled pans. Bake, uncovered, for about 35 minutes, until golden and firm.
7. Cut each pan into 6 servings and top with hot sauce if desired.

Servings	Calories	Protein (g)	Fat (g)	Cholesterol (mg)	Carbohydrates (g)	Fiber (g)	Sodium (mg)
1	422	20.3	22.3	234	38.7	4.7	646

Frittata Espinaca

24 10-oz. Servings

This puffed and crispy casserole is quick to prepare. At its best served soon after baking, Frittata Espinaca is suitable for brunch, lunch, or dinner. For use as a dinner entrée, pair with Bulghur Pilaf (p. 318), Carrot Salad (p. 321), or Fassoulia (p. 325).

Equipment:	4 half-size insert pans, 2-in. deep
Preparation Time:	45 minutes
Baking Time:	45–60 minutes

Ingredients	Volume	Weight
Spinach, fresh		5 lbs.
or frozen		7 lbs. 8 oz.
Bread crumbs, preferably fresh whole wheat	1 qt.	10 oz.
or Matzo meal (p. 471)		
Sharp Cheddar cheese, grated	3 qts.	2 lbs. 4 oz.
Cottage and feta cheese, mixed	2½ qts.	5 lbs.
Romano or Parmesan cheese, grated	1 qt.	1 lb.
Eggs, beaten	16 lg. or 1 qt.	2 lbs.
Nutmeg, freshly grated	1 tsp.	
Black pepper to taste		

Olive oil to coat pans

Procedure

1. If using fresh spinach, wash, and blanch or steam it until wilted. Drain, squeeze out the excess liquid, and chop. For frozen spinach, thaw and squeeze out the excess liquid.
2. Set aside half of the crumbs or matzo meal and 2 cups of Cheddar cheese.
3. Mix together the remaining ingredients and the spinach.

(continued)

4. Preheat the oven to 350°.
5. Dust the bottom of each oiled pan with the reserved bread crumbs or meal. Divide the spinach mixture evenly among the four pans. Sprinkle tops with the reserved Cheddar.
6. Bake at 350° for 45 minutes to 1 hour, or until golden brown and firm.
7. Cut each pan into 6 servings.

Servings	Calories	Protein (g)	Fat (g)	Cholesterol (mg)	Carbohydrates (g)	Fiber (g)	Sodium (mg)
1	572	40.4	39.5	285	15.4	3.7	1529

Greek-Style Zucchini Casserole

24 12-oz. Servings

This recipe is a Moosewood classic that has been on our menus for over 20 years. The bulghur pilaf, savory zucchini, and feta custard yield a dish that is both exotic and reassuring.

Equipment:	4 half-size insert pans, 4-in. deep
Preparation Time:	90 minutes
Baking Time:	1 hour, plus 15 minutes to set up

Ingredients	Volume	Weight
Bulghur (p. 468)	1 qt.	1 lb. 10 oz.
Boiling water	1 qt.	
Vegetable oil	½ cup	
Onions, thinly sliced	2½ qts.	2 lbs. 8 oz.
Garlic, pressed	10 med. cloves or 3 Tbsp.	
Zucchini, thinly sliced in rounds		7 lbs.
Oregano, dried	1 Tbsp.	
Basil, dried	1 Tbsp.	
Marjoram, dried	1 Tbsp.	
Black pepper	1 tsp.	
Eggs	12 lg. or 3 cups	1 lb. 8 oz.
Feta cheese, grated	2 qts.	2 lbs.
Cottage cheese	1½ qts.	3 lbs. 8 oz.
Parsley, fresh, chopped	1 qt.	6 oz.
Tomato paste	½ cup	
Soy sauce	½ cup	
Cheddar cheese, grated	1¾ qts.	1 lb. 6 oz.
Tomatoes, thinly sliced	8 med.	2 lbs. 4 oz.

(continued)

Procedure

1. Pour the boiling water over the bulghur, cover the bowl or pan, and let the bulghur sit until it becomes soft and the water has been absorbed.
2. Sauté the onions and garlic in oil until the onions are translucent.
3. Stir in the zucchini, herbs, and pepper and cook on medium heat until the zucchini are just tender.
4. In a separate bowl, beat the eggs.
5. Add the feta and cottage cheeses and mix well.
6. Flavor the softened bulghur by stirring in the parsley, tomato paste, and soy sauce.
7. Preheat the oven to 350°.
8. To assemble the casserole, divide the ingredients among four lightly oiled pans in the following order:
   - bulghur mixture
   - sautéed zucchini
   - feta mixture
   - grated Cheddar
   - tomato slices
9. Bake at 350°, covered, for 45 minutes, and for 15 minutes uncovered. Allow the casserole to sit for 10–15 minutes before serving.
10. Cut each pan into 6 servings.

Servings	Calories	Protein (g)	Fat (g)	Cholesterol (mg)	Carbohydrates (g)	Fiber (g)	Sodium (mg)
1	528	30.3	28.5	203	41.1	8.8	1218

Mediterranean Eggplant Casserole

24 12-oz. Servings

This casserole is distinguished by the addition of a North-African-style couscous pilaf. Serve with Tzatziki (p. 344).

Equipment:	4 half-size insert pans, 4-in. deep
Preparation Time:	90 minutes
Baking Time:	45 minutes

Ingredients	Volume	Weight
Eggplant, sliced in ½-in. thick rounds		6 lbs.

Pilaf

Ingredients	Volume	Weight
Couscous, dry	1 qt.	1 lb. 11 oz.
Water, boiling	1 qt.	
Onions, chopped	2 qts.	2 lbs.
Garlic, minced or pressed	8 cloves or 2 Tbsp.	
Vegetable oil	½ cup	
Carrots, diced	1 qt.	1 lb. 5 oz.
Currants, dried	1½ cups	
Almonds, toasted, chopped	1½ cups	6 oz.
Dill, marjoram, or basil, fresh *or* dried	3 Tbsp. 1 Tbsp.	
Lemon juice, fresh	5 Tbsp.	
Salt and black pepper to taste		

Topping

Ingredients	Volume	Weight
Eggs, beaten	10 lg. or 2½ cups	1 lb. 4 oz.
Cottage or ricotta cheese	1¾ qts.	3 lbs. 8 oz.
Feta cheese	1¼ qts.	1 lb. 4 oz.
Hungarian paprika	3 Tbsp.	
Tomato juice	1 qt.	

(continued)

Procedure

1. Lightly salt the eggplant slices and bake on oiled trays, tightly covered with aluminum foil, for approximately 45 minutes at 375°, until tender.
2. Pour the couscous in a mixing bowl and cover with an equal volume of boiling water and a pinch of salt. Cover bowl tightly and set aside.
3. Sauté the garlic and onions in oil until the onions are translucent.
4. Add the carrots and continue to sauté until the carrots are tender.
5. Add the remaining pilaf ingredients, except for the couscous, and remove from the heat.
6. Fluff the couscous with a fork to separate the grains and blend into the vegetable–herb mixture.
7. Combine the topping ingredients, except the paprika.
8. Preheat oven to 350°.
9. Dividing the ingredients among four lightly oiled pans, layer the casseroles in the following order:
   - Tomato juice
   - Pilaf
   - Baked eggplant slices
   - Topping dusted with paprika
10. Bake, covered, at 350° for 30 minutes. Uncover and bake for an additional 15 minutes, or until topping is firm.
11. Cut each pan into 6 servings.

Servings	Calories	Protein (g)	Fat (g)	Cholesterol (mg)	Carbohydrates (g)	Fiber (g)	Sodium (mg)
1	419	21.2	19.8	141	41.9	6.6	732

Mushroom–Leek Frittata

24 12-oz. Servings

Enjoy the sweet and smoky flavors of an elegant frittata.

Equipment:	4 half-size insert pans, 2-in. deep
Preparation Time:	1 hour
Baking Time:	50 minutes

Ingredients	Volume	Weight
Potatoes, thinly sliced		6 lbs.
Vegetable oil	¼ cup	
Garlic, minced or pressed	3 cloves or 1 Tbsp.	
Leeks, chopped	2 qts.	2 lbs. 8 oz.
Dill, dried	2 tsp.	
Marjoram, dried	2 tsp.	
Basil, dried	1½ Tbsp.	
Mushrooms, sliced	6 qts.	5 lbs.
Salt and ground black pepper to taste		
Neufchâtel cheese, cubed		1 lb. 8 oz.
Eggs	23 lg. or 5¾ cups	2 lbs. 14 oz.
Milk	2 qts.	
Sharp Cheddar cheese, grated	1½ qts.	1 lb. 2 oz.
Smoked Cheddar cheese, grated	3 cups	9 oz.

Procedure

1. Boil or steam the potatoes until tender, or place the potatoes on a lightly oiled baking sheet, brush with oil, and bake at 400° for 20 minutes. Turn the potatoes after 10 minutes.
2. Sauté the garlic, leeks, and herbs in oil until the leeks are tender.
3. Add the mushrooms and cook until juicy.

(continued)

4. Turn off the heat and stir in the Neufchâtel until creamy.
5. Beat the eggs and milk in a large mixing bowl. Fold in the Cheddars.
6. Preheat the oven to 350°.
7. In four lightly oiled pans, layer the potatoes, top with the creamy sautéed vegetables, and then finish with the cheese custard. Divide the ingredients equally among the four pans.
8. Bake at 350°, covered, for 40 minutes, and for 10–15 minutes more, uncovered, until the custard has set and is golden.
9. Cut each pan into 6 servings.

Servings	Calories	Protein (g)	Fat (g)	Cholesterol (mg)	Carbohydrates (g)	Fiber (g)	Sodium (mg)
1	545	27.9	31.5	325	39.5	4.7	513

Noodle Kugel

24 12-oz. Servings

Generations of Jewish cooks have created their own versions of this classic noodle dish. This is ours. Serve with applesauce or a baked apple half.

Equipment:	4 half-size insert pans, 4-in. deep
Preparation Time:	45 minutes
Baking Time:	35 minutes

Ingredients	Volume	Weight
Kugel		
Egg noodles, wide		2 lbs. 8 oz.
Eggs, lightly beaten	12 lg., 3 cups	1 lb. 8 oz.
Cottage cheese	4½ cups	2 lbs. 4 oz.
Neufchâtel cheese, softened	3 cups	1 lb. 8 oz.
Yogurt, plain, low-fat or nonfat	1 qt.	2 lbs.
Sour cream	2 cups	2 lbs. 6 oz.
Cinnamon	1 Tbsp.	
Raisins	2 cups	13 oz.
Maple syrup	½ cup	
Streusel Topping		
Walnuts, chopped	1 cup	5 oz.
Bread crumbs, unseasoned	1½ cups	2 oz.
Butter	4 Tbsp.	
Brown sugar	4 Tbsp.	

Procedure

1. Boil the noodles until tender. Do not overcook. Drain.
2. Combine the noodles with the rest of the ingredients in the kugel.
3. Preheat the oven to 350°.

(continued)

4. To make the streusel topping, combine and work the ingredients with your fingers to achieve a coarse crumble.
5. Pour the kugel evenly into four lightly oiled pans. Sprinkle on the streusel topping.
6. Bake at 350° for 20 minutes, covered, and for 10–15 minutes, uncovered.
7. Cut each pan into 6 servings.

Servings	Calories	Protein (g)	Fat (g)	Cholesterol (mg)	Carbohydrates (g)	Fiber (g)	Sodium (mg)
1	582	22.7	28.8	209	59.9	2.5	453

Polenta Cutlets

24 Servings
2 4-oz. cutlets each

These delectable vegetarian cutlets have a crisp coating and a creamy interior. Baked, not fried, they are at their best topped with your favorite tomato sauce and served at once. Serve with a stuffed pepper and escarole or similar greens sautéed with garlic and olive oil to create an Italian Combo Plate.

Equipment:	2 insert pans, 2-in. deep
Preparation Time:	1 hour to prepare and 2 hours to chill
Baking Time:	30 minutes

Ingredients	Volume	Weight
Polenta		
Boiling water	1¼ gal.	
Salt	1½ tsp.	
Cornmeal	2 qts.	
Olive oil	½ cup	
Garlic, pressed	8 cloves or 2½ Tbsp.	
Bread crumbs, fresh	2 qts.	
Parmesan cheese, finely grated	1 qt.	1 lb.
Parsley, chopped	3 cups	4 oz.
Basil, fresh, chopped	½ cup	
or dried	3 Tbsp.	
Salt and black pepper to taste		
White flour	1½ cups	
Eggs, lightly beaten	8 lg. or 2 cups	1 lb.

Procedure

1. Salt the boiling water. Using a whisk, slowly stir in the cornmeal. Lower the heat and simmer, stirring often, for about 20 minutes.

(continued)

2. Pour the cornmeal into lightly oiled baking pans, to a depth of just ½ in. Refrigerate for 2 hours or overnight.
3. In a large, heavy skillet, heat the olive oil. Add the garlic and sauté, being careful not to burn the garlic.
4. Add the bread crumbs and stir continuously for 3–4 minutes until the crumbs are toasted and browned.
5. Transfer to a bowl and add the Parmesan, parsley, basil, salt, and pepper. Stir.
6. Cut the chilled polenta into 48 triangles.
7. Preheat the oven to 350°.
8. Bread the cutlets as follows: Dredge in flour. Dip in eggs. Dredge in bread-crumb mixture.
9. Place the cutlets on oiled baking sheets and bake for 30 minutes until nicely browned.

Servings	Calories	Protein (g)	Fat (g)	Cholesterol (mg)	Carbohydrates (g)	Fiber (g)	Sodium (mg)
1	522	20.4	15.6	103	73.4	5.7	864

Potato Kugel

24 6.5-oz. Servings

This home-style dish combines all the elements of potato pancakes but in a simpler, lighter version that is baked, not fried. We serve it topped with a dollop of sour cream and a side of applesauce.

Equipment:	4 half-size insert pans, 2-in. deep
Preparation Time:	45 minutes
Baking Time:	30–40 minutes

Ingredients	Volume	Weight
Potatoes, peeled if skins are thick or scarred		4 lbs. 8 oz.
Onions, peeled		4 lbs.
Eggs	24 lg. or 1½ qts.	3 lbs.
Salt	2 Tbsp.	
Black pepper to taste		
Matzo meal (p. 471) or bread crumbs, fresh	1½ cups	4 oz.
Vegetable oil	1 cup	

Procedure

1. Coarsely grate the potatoes using the large-holed grater blade of a food processor or the large-holed side of a hand-held grater.
2. Transfer the potatoes to a colander and squeeze out as much water as possible.
3. Preheat the oven to 350°.
4. Grate the onions using the finer-holed blade of a food processor or hand-held grater. Squeeze out excess water.
5. Beat the eggs in a large bowl.
6. Add the potatoes, onions, salt, pepper, and matzo meal or bread crumbs. Mix well.

(continued)

7. Pour ¼ cup of oil into the bottom of each pan and place in the hot oven for 5 minutes.
8. Pour the batter into the hot pans. The hot oil will splash onto the sides of the pans and the surface of the batter. Spread the oil smoothly across the top of the batter with a spatula.
9. Bake, uncovered, for 30–40 minutes, or until crusty and golden.
10. Cut each pan into 6 servings.

Servings	Calories	Protein (g)	Fat (g)	Cholesterol (mg)	Carbohydrates (g)	Fiber (g)	Sodium (mg)
1	300	10.8	16.5	264	27.7	2.6	720

Rumpledethumps

24 11-oz. Servings

This hearty casserole is as much fun to eat as it is to say. It features vegetables high in beta-carotene, broccoli and cabbage.

Equipment:	3 half-size insert pans, 4-in. deep
Preparation Time:	1 hour
Baking Time:	35 minutes

Ingredients	Volume	Weight
Potatoes, chopped	2½ gals.	10 lbs.
Cabbage, chopped	3 qts.	2 lbs.
Broccoli, coarsely chopped	2 to 3 qts.	2 lbs.
Leeks, cleaned carefully, chopped *or* Onions, chopped	2 qts.	2 lbs.
Butter	1½ cups	12 oz.
Milk	3 cups	
Cheddar cheese, grated	1½ qts.	1 lb. 8 oz.
Nutmeg	1 tsp.	
Dijon mustard	1½ Tbsp.	
Prepared horseradish	1 tsp.	
Salt and black pepper to taste		

Procedure

1. Boil the potatoes in salted water until tender. Drain.
2. Steam or blanch each vegetable until barely tender. If using onions, lightly sauté or sweat them until translucent.
3. Preheat the oven to 350°.
4. Mash the potatoes with the butter, milk, and 2 cups of Cheddar cheese.
5. Stir in the vegetables and seasonings, adjusting for salt and pepper as needed.
6. Pour the filling evenly into three lightly oiled pans. Top with the remaining Cheddar.

(continued)

7. Bake at 350° for 20 minutes, covered, and for 10–15 minutes, uncovered.
8. Cut each pan into 8 servings.

Note: For a faster method, sauté the leeks or onions briskly in ¼ cup of oil. When translucent, add the cabbage and broccoli and cook until tender.

Servings	Calories	Protein (g)	Fat (g)	Cholesterol (mg)	Carbohydrates (g)	Fiber (g)	Sodium (mg)
1	436	13.6	22.0	63	48.7	6.0	359

Scarlett's Frittata

24 12-oz. Servings

The traditional pairing of Cheddar and pimiento give depth and zest to this baked omelet. Serve for brunch, lunch, or a light supper with Sara's Greens (p. 342).

Equipment:	4 half-size insert pans, 2-in. deep
Preparation Time:	45 minutes to 1 hour
Baking Time:	40 minutes

Ingredients	Volume	Weight
Sweet potatoes, peeled, thinly sliced		5 lbs.
Vegetable oil	¼ cup	
Onions, chopped	2 qts.	2 lbs.
Thyme, dried	2 tsp.	
Pimientos or roasted red peppers, drained, chopped	1½ cups	1 lb.
Neufchâtel cheese, cubed	3 cups	1 lb. 8 oz.
Sharp Cheddar cheese, grated	2 qts.	2 lbs.
Eggs	2 dozen lg. or 1½ qts.	3 lbs.
Milk	1¾ qts.	

Procedure

1. Boil sliced sweet potatoes until tender. Drain.
2. Sauté the onions and thyme in vegetable oil until the onions are softened.
3. Add the drained pimientos.
4. Stir the Neufchâtel cheese into the onions and pimientos, mixing to soften the cheese.
5. Add 6 cups of the sharp Cheddar.
6. Beat the eggs with the milk.
7. Preheat the oven to 350°.
8. Layer the oiled pans with one-fourth of the sweet potatoes, one-fourth of the

(continued)

onion–cheese mixture, and one-fourth of the egg–milk mixture. Top each frittata with ½ cup of the reserved Cheddar.

9. Bake, covered, at 350° for 30 minutes; uncover and bake for an additional 10 minutes or until the eggs have set.
10. Cut each pan into 6 servings.

Servings	Calories	Protein (g)	Fat (g)	Cholesterol (mg)	Carbohydrates (g)	Fiber (g)	Sodium (mg)
1	495	24.5	29.8	331	32.7	3.1	472

Sweet Pepper and Cheddar Strata

24 12-oz. Servings

A popular Moosewood dish, this casserole contrasts a creamy topping with savory Mexican-spiced peppers and a golden pilaf. For a festive meal, serve with the Avocado Salsa (p. 257) or Citrus Salsa (p. 259).

Equipment:	4 half-size insert pans, 4-in. deep
Preparation Time:	90 minutes
Baking Time:	45 minutes

Ingredients	Volume	Weight
Pilaf		
Vegetable oil	1 Tbsp.	
Brown rice, raw	3 cups	
Water	1½ qts.	
Turmeric	1 tsp.	
Cinnamon	½ tsp.	
Spanish olives, chopped or sliced (optional)	1 to 1½ cups	9 oz.
Onions, chopped	1½ qts.	1 lb. 8 oz.
Olive oil	¼–½ cup	
Garlic, pressed	12 med. cloves or 3½ Tbsp.	
Salt	1 Tbsp.	
Cumin, ground	1 Tbsp.	
Coriander, ground	1 Tbsp.	
Mustard, dry	2 tsp.	
Black pepper	1 tsp.	
Cayenne	½ tsp.	
Red and green peppers, sliced	1¼ gals.	5 lbs.
White flour	½ cup	
Hungarian paprika		

(continued)

Casseroles

Custard

Eggs	18 lg., 4½ cups	2 lbs. 4 oz.
Sour cream	1¼ qts.	
Yogurt, plain, low fat or nonfat	1¼ qts.	
Cheddar cheese, grated	2 qts.	2 lbs.

Procedure

1. Quickly sauté the brown rice in vegetable oil until the kernels begin to smell like popcorn. Stir often.
2. Add the water, turmeric, and cinnamon. Cover and bring to a boil. Reduce to a simmer and cook until done, about 50 minutes.
3. Remove from the heat and stir in the olives.
4. Sauté the onions, garlic, and spices in olive oil until the onions are translucent.
5. Add the peppers and sauté on low heat until the peppers soften.
6. Sprinkle in the flour and cook until it absorbs all the liquid. Stir often to avoid burning.
7. Whisk the custard ingredients together.
8. Preheat the oven to 350°.
9. Lightly oil four pans and layer as follows:
   - one-fourth of the pilaf (about 2¼ cups)
   - one-fourth of the vegetables
   - 2 cups of Cheddar
   - one-fourth of the custard (about 1¾ cups), dusted with paprika
10. Bake at 350° for 30 minutes, covered, and for 10–15 minutes, uncovered, until the custard is firm and golden.
11. Cut each pan into 6 servings.

Note: This dish can be simplified by using 9 cups of leftover brown rice or by substituting crumbled cornbread for the rice.

Servings	Calories	Protein (g)	Fat (g)	Cholesterol (mg)	Carbohydrates (g)	Fiber (g)	Sodium (mg)
1	515	22.2	32.1	241	35.5	1.7	676

Tofu "Meatloaf" with Mushroom Gravy

24 11-oz. Servings

This is the signature dish of our "Blue Plate Special." Serve with mashed potatoes, peas, carrots, and a nice piece of blueberry pie.

Equipment:	4 half-size insert pans, 2-in. deep
Preparation Time:	90 minutes
Baking Time:	30 minutes

Ingredients	Volume	Weight
Tofu (p. 474)		7 lbs. 8 oz. (unpressed weight)
Onions, chopped	3½ qts.	3 lbs. 8 oz.
Vegetable oil	¼ cup	
Carrots, grated	1½ qts.	1 lb. 10 oz.
Green peppers, chopped	1½ qts.	1 lb. 8 oz.
Dill, dried	1 Tbsp.	
Marjoram, dried	1 Tbsp.	
Walnuts, toasted, chopped	1¼ qts.	1 lb. 4 oz.
Tahini (p. 474)	2 cups	1 lb.
Soy sauce	½ cup	
Sesame oil, dark (p. 473)	¼ cup	
Dijon mustard	¼ cup	
Bread crumbs, fresh	1½ qts.	12 oz.

Gravy

Ingredients	Volume	Weight
Vegetable oil	¼ cup	
Mushrooms, sliced	5 qts.	4 lbs.
Soy sauce	½ cup	
Sherry, dry	1 cup	
Vegetable Stock (p. 63) or water	2½ qts.	
Salt and black pepper to taste		
Cornstarch	¾ cup	
Cold water	1 cup	

(continued)

Procedure

1. Press the tofu (p. 474) while preparing the other ingredients.
2. Sauté the onions in oil until they are translucent.
3. Add the carrots, peppers, dill, and marjoram and cook on medium heat until the vegetables are tender. Drain.
4. Mash the pressed tofu in a large bowl using a potato masher or your fingers. The end result should be a fine crumble.
5. Mix in the sautéed vegetables and the remaining ingredients thoroughly. Tofu has little taste without its immersion in added flavors.
6. This "meatloaf" is not baked in loaf pans. Instead, press an equal amount of the loaf into four lightly oiled shallow pans.
7. Bake, uncovered, at 350° for 30 minutes and then cut each pan into 6 squares.
8. While the tofu loaf is baking, prepare the gravy. Sauté the sliced mushrooms in oil and soy sauce until the mushrooms are tender. Add the sherry and stock or water and bring to a boil and then reduce to a low boil. Dissolve the cornstarch in cold water and add it slowly to the pot, stirring continuously until the gravy thickens. Add salt and pepper to taste.

Servings	Calories	Protein (g)	Fat (g)	Cholesterol (mg)	Carbohydrates (g)	Fiber (g)	Sodium (mg)
1	572	16.1	31.7	0	60.7	7.5	762

Vegetable Moussaka

24 14-oz. Servings

This hearty, layered casserole is chock-full of vegetables and features two flavorful sauces.

Equipment:	4 half-size insert pans, 4-in. deep
Preparation Time:	2 hours
Baking Time:	1 hour plus 15 minutes to set up

Ingredients	Volume	Weight
Tomato Sauce		
Olive oil	⅓ cup	
Onions, chopped	1½ qts.	1 lb. 8 oz.
Garlic, pressed or minced	10 cloves or 3 Tbsp.	
Tomatoes, canned, chopped, plus juice	1 #10 can (3 qts.)	6 lbs. 6 oz.
Green peppers, chopped	1 qt.	1 lb.
Dill, fresh, chopped	2 Tbsp.	
or dried	2 tsp.	
Cinnamon	½ tsp.	
Parsley, fresh, chopped	½ cup	
Salt and black pepper to taste		
Vegetables		
Eggplant, cut in ½-in. thick rounds		6 lbs.
Zucchini, cut in ½-in. thick rounds		6 lbs.
Olive oil	¼ cup	
Custard Sauce		
Butter	1⅓ cups	
White flour	1⅓ cups	
Milk, heated	2 qts.	
Eggs, lightly beaten	4 whole eggs, 4 egg whites	

(continued)

Nutmeg, ground	¼ tsp.	
Feta cheese, grated	2 qts.	2 lbs.
Couscous, raw	3 cups	
Parmesan cheese, coarsely grated, fresh	2 qts.	2 lbs.

Procedure

1. Prepare Tomato Sauce: sauté the onions and garlic in olive oil for a few moments before adding the tomatoes. Simmer for 5 minutes; then add the remaining sauce ingredients. Continue to simmer, uncovered, for 30 minutes.
2. Spread the eggplant slices on oiled pans, salt lightly, tightly cover with aluminum foil, and bake at 375° for about 30 minutes, or until tender.
3. Sauté the zucchini in a small amount of oil until just tender.
4. Prepare Custard Sauce: melt the butter and whisk in the flour. On a low flame, cook this roux for about 5 to 7 minutes, whisking frequently. Slowly pour in the heated milk whisking continuously until the sauce thickens. Remove from the heat and whisk in the eggs and nutmeg.
5. Preheat oven to 350°.
6. In four oiled pans, layer the casseroles in the following order:
   * 2 cups Tomato Sauce
   * one-fourth of the eggplant slices
   * 1 cup feta cheese
   * 3 oz. couscous
   * 2 cups Tomato Sauce
   * one-fourth of the zucchini slices
   * 1 cup feta cheese
   * 3 oz. couscous
   * one-fourth of the Custard Sauce
   * 2 cups Parmesan cheese
7. Bake, covered, at 350° for 30 minutes, and uncovered for 15 to 20 minutes, or until the custard topping is set and golden. Allow the casserole to sit for 15 minutes before serving.
8. Cut each pan into 6 servings.

Servings	Calories	Protein (g)	Fat (g)	Cholesterol (mg)	Carbohydrates (g)	Fiber (g)	Sodium (mg)
1	669	32.7	38.5	141	50.3	6.2	1466

FISH

Even though our menu is predominantly vegetarian, we offer fish or other seafood four nights of the week. Fish is an excellent source of protein that is relatively low in fat, and many types of fish are good subjects for a variety of preparations. We tend to use regionally available fish, including firm fillets of scrod, flounder, haddock, catfish, tilapia, or bluefish, as well as steaks of tuna, salmon, swordfish, or sea bass. With the exception of the stews, all our recipes are for baked fish. The number of servings we suggest for each recipe is based on dinner-sized portions. Sometimes we serve plain broiled or grilled fish topped with one of the following sauces from the Sauces and Salsas section (p. 253–270):

- Cilantro Pesto
- Citrus Salsa
- Dill Pesto
- Fennel Mustard Sauce
- Hazelnut Pesto
- Mango Salsa
- Shallot–Herb Butter
- Taratour Sauce
- Spinach Pesto
- Pesto Genovese

Caribbean-Style Fish

24 8-oz. Servings
32 6-oz. Servings

Taste the tropics with this exotically seasoned, refreshing topping. Serve on Golden Spanish Rice (p. 329) with fried okra.

Equipment:	4 half-size insert pans, 2-in. deep
Preparation Time:	30 minutes
Baking Time:	20 minutes

Ingredients	Volume	Weight
Fish fillets		12 lbs.
Lime juice, fresh	2 cups	
Annatto seeds (p. 464)	3 Tbsp.	
Vegetable oil	¾ cup	
Onions, chopped	1½ qts.	1 lb. 8 oz.
Garlic, minced or pressed	10 cloves or 3 Tbsp.	
Chili peppers, fresh, minced	6 sm.	3 oz.
or Cayenne	½ tsp., or to taste	
Tomatoes, chopped, fresh or canned, drained	2 qts.	3 lbs.
Thyme, dried	1½ tsp.	
Coconut milk (p. 470)		28 oz.
Cilantro, fresh, chopped	1 cup	

Procedure

1. Divide the fillets among four pans. Pour 1/2 cup lime juice over each pan and refrigerate while preparing the topping.
2. Make annatto oil by sautéing the seeds in vegetable oil for a few minutes. Or microwave the seeds in oil for 1 minute. The oil should turn a deep red-orange but not brown. Drain and discard the seeds.

(continued)

3. Preheat the oven to 375°.
4. Sauté the onions, garlic, and chilies or cayenne in annatto oil for 5 minutes.
5. Add the tomatoes, thyme, and coconut milk and simmer for 5 minutes.
6. Turn off the heat and add the cilantro.
7. Top the fish with about 2 cups of sauce per pan. Bake, covered, at 350° for 20 minutes or until the fish flakes easily.

Note: Nutritional analysis calculated for 24 servings.

Servings	Calories	Protein (g)	Fat (g)	Cholesterol (mg)	Carbohydrates (g)	Fiber (g)	Sodium (mg)
1	347	47.9	12.6	112	8.8	1.3	170

Chesapeake Catfish

32 6-oz. Servings
24 8-oz. Servings

It took our Baltimore boy, Dave Dietrich, to bring Old Bay into our midst, and we're forever grateful for what it does for catfish. For Moosewood Restaurant regulars, Chesapeake Catfish is synonymous with mashed sweet potatoes and greens—either collards or kale.

Equipment:	4 half-size insert pans, 2-in. deep
Preparation Time:	15 minutes
Baking Time:	25 minutes

Ingredients	Volume	Weight
Catfish fillets		12 lbs.
Garlic, pressed	⅓ cup	
Lemon juice, fresh	¾ cup	
Old Bay seasoning (p. 472)	½ cup	

Procedure

1. Rinse and drain the fillets. Place them skin side down in four pans. Preheat the oven to 350°.
2. Cover each fillet with
   - ½ tsp. pressed garlic
   - ½ tsp. Old Bay seasoning (more for spicier fish)
   - ½ Tbsp. lemon juice
3. Bake, covered, at 350° for 20–25 minutes, or until the fish flakes easily.

Note: Nutritional analysis calculated for 32 servings.

Servings	Calories	Protein (g)	Fat (g)	Cholesterol (mg)	Carbohydrates (g)	Fiber (g)	Sodium (mg)
1	156	25.8	4.5	91	1.8	0.2	68

Creamy Fish Stew

24 12-oz. Servings

This hearty, homey meal in a bowl is delicious paired with a wedge of steaming Cornbread (p. 323) and a mixed green salad. Garnish with chopped parsley and lemon wedges.

Equipment:	2½-gallon stockpot
Preparation Time:	30 minutes
Cooking Time:	45 minutes

Ingredients	Volume	Weight
Vegetable oil	¼ cup	
Onions, chopped	1 qt.	1 lb.
Garlic, minced or pressed	6 cloves or 2 Tbsp.	
Carrots, chopped	1 qt.	1 lb. 4 oz.
Celery, chopped	1 qt.	1 lb.
Zucchini, chopped	1½ qts.	2 lbs.
Peppers, green, chopped (optional)	1 qt.	1 lb.
Vegetable Stock (p. 63) or water	2 qts.	
Bay leaves	4	
Dill, fresh, chopped	2 Tbsp.	
_or_ dried	2 tsp.	
Marjoram, dried	1½ Tbsp.	
Salt and black pepper to taste		
Potatoes, cubed	2 qts.	2 lbs.
Fish fillets, cut in bite-size pieces, raw (fish can be prebaked and cubed)		4 lbs. 8 oz.
Milk or half-and-half	1 qt.	

Procedure

1. Sauté the onions and garlic in oil until the onions soften.
2. Add the carrots and celery and sauté for 10 minutes.
3. Add the zucchini, optional peppers, stock or water, and herbs and simmer until the vegetables are tender, about 15 minutes.
4. Stir in the cubed raw fish and continue to simmer until the fish is just cooked. If using prebaked fish, stir it in at the end of the recipe.
5. While the chowder simmers, boil the potatoes in a separate pot and drain, reserving a couple of cups of potato stock.
6. In a blender or food processor, purée half the potatoes with a small amount of potato stock.
7. Add the purée and the remaining potatoes to the chowder.
8. Stir in the milk or half-and-half, salt, and pepper.

Note: This is a wonderful way to use leftover baked fish.

Servings	Calories	Protein (g)	Fat (g)	Cholesterol (mg)	Carbohydrates (g)	Fiber (g)	Sodium (mg)
1	206	22.7	4.1	50	19.9	3.2	135

Fish

Fish Algiers

24 8-oz. Servings
32 6-oz. Servings

Lemon, toasted cumin, and tomatoes are a grand combination. Serve Fish Algiers on rice, couscous (p. 470), or Bulghur Pilaf (p. 318), with steamed green beans or zucchini. Garnish with lemon wedges and parsley.

Equipment:	4–6 half-size insert pans, 2-in. deep
Preparation Time:	15 minutes
Baking Time:	20 minutes

Ingredients	Volume	Weight
Fish fillets		12 lbs.
Cumin seeds, whole	½ cup	
Olive oil	1¼ cups	
Lemon juice, fresh	1¼ cups	
Garlic, minced or pressed	12 cloves or 3½ Tbsp.	
Salt	2 tsp.	
Cayenne (optional)	½–1 tsp.	
Tomatoes, sliced and each slice cut into quarters	3 qts.	4 lbs. 8 oz.

Garnishes

Lemon wedges
Parsley, fresh, chopped

Procedure

1. Preheat the oven to 375°.
2. Rinse the fish and place, skin side down, in four to six lightly oiled pans, depending on the size of the fillets.
3. Toast the cumin seeds in a dry skillet or toaster oven until aromatic. Take care not to burn. Grind the cumin to a fine powder in a spice grinder.
4. Whisk the toasted cumin with the olive oil, lemon juice, garlic, salt, and cayenne.
5. Layer the quartered tomato slices on top of the fish, pour on the marinade, cover, and bake for 20–30 minutes, or until the fish flakes easily.

Note: Nutritional analysis calculated for 24 servings.

Servings	Calories	Protein (g)	Fat (g)	Cholesterol (mg)	Carbohydrates (g)	Fiber (g)	Sodium (mg)
1	350	47.9	14.3	112	7.3	1.1	369

Fish Cantonese

24 8-oz. Servings
32 6-oz. Servings

This is a quick and delicious Chinese dish. Don't be scared off by the black beans. They are available in all Asian stores and in the ethnic section of many supermarkets. Regular dried black beans cannot be substituted for this specially treated variety of soybeans. Serve Fish Cantonese with rice and Asian Greens (p. 315) or a simple steamed broccoli.

Equipment:	4 half-size insert pans, 2-in. deep
Preparation Time:	20 minutes
Baking Time:	30 minutes

Ingredients	Volume	Weight
Chinese fermented black beans (p. 469)	¾ cup	4.5 oz.
Water	3 cups	
Garlic, pressed	8 cloves or 2¾ Tbsp.	
Soy sauce	¾ cup	
Sesame oil, dark (p. 473)	⅓ cup	
Ginger root, fresh, grated	½ cup	4 oz.
Chinese rice vinegar (p. 469)	⅓ cup	
Fish fillets		12 lbs.

Garnish

Scallions, diagonally sliced	1 cup	3.5 oz.

Procedure

1. Soak the beans in water for about 15 minutes; then drain.
2. In a bowl or food processor, mash the beans with the other ingredients except the scallions and fish.
3. Preheat the oven to 350°.
4. Place the rinsed and drained fillets, skin side down, in four lightly oiled pans.
5. Spread one-fourth of the bean mixture (about 2/3 cup) over the fillets in each pan.
6. Bake, covered, at 350° for 25–30 minutes, or until the fish flakes easily.
7. Garnish with chopped scallions.

Note: Nutritional analysis calculated for 24 servings.

Servings	Calories	Protein (g)	Fat (g)	Cholesterol (mg)	Carbohydrates (g)	Fiber (g)	Sodium (mg)
1	260	47.7	5.0	112	3.3	0.7	566

Fish

Fish Marseilles

24 8-oz. Servings
32 6-oz. Servings

We've taken the elegant and expensive bouillabaise and transposed its mysterious and complex taste into a sauce to top more affordable types of fish. Serve with rice and a steamed vegetable.

Equipment:	4 half-size insert pans, 2-in. deep; 8-qt. stockpot
Preparation Time:	40 minutes
Baking Time:	25 minutes

Ingredients	Volume	Weight
Olive oil	¼ cup	
Leeks, chopped	1¼ qts.	1 lb. 4 oz.
Peppers, red and green, chopped	1 qt.	1 lb.
Thyme, dried	1 tsp.	
Fennel seed, ground	1 Tbsp.	
Garlic, minced or pressed	5 cloves, or 1½ Tbsp.	
Tomatoes, canned with juice, crushed	1½ qts.	3 lbs.
Red wine, dry	2¼ cups	
Orange peel, grated	1 tsp.	
Tarragon, dried	2 tsp.	
or fresh, chopped	1½ Tbsp.	
Basil, dried	1 Tbsp.	
or fresh, chopped	3 Tbsp.	
Saffron	½ tsp.	
Cayenne	1–2 pinches	
Lemon juice, fresh	2 Tbsp.	
Fish fillets		12 lbs.

Procedure

1. Sauté the leeks for 5 minutes in olive oil.
2. Add the peppers, thyme, fennel seed, garlic, tomatoes, and wine and simmer 10 minutes.
3. Add the orange peel, herbs, spices, and lemon juice and simmer an additional 15 minutes.
4. Preheat the oven to 350°.
5. Place the fish, skin side down, in four lightly oiled baking pans. Cover the fillets evenly with 3 cups of sauce per pan.
6. Bake, covered, at 375° for 20–25 minutes, or until the fish flakes easily.

Note: Nutritional analysis calculated for 24 servings.

Servings	Calories	Protein (g)	Fat (g)	Cholesterol (mg)	Carbohydrates (g)	Fiber (g)	Sodium (mg)
1	280	47.7	4.4	112	6.8	0.5	238

Fish

Fish Santorini

32 6-oz. Servings
24 8-oz. Servings

Modelled after the classic Shrimp Scorpio, this easily assembled dish has proven a perennial crowd pleaser. Serve on rice or with Greek Roasted Potatoes (p. 330) and Easy Artichokes (p. 324).

Equipment:	4 half-size insert pans, 2-in. deep
Preparation Time:	20 minutes
Baking Time:	30 minutes

Ingredients	Volume	Weight
Fish fillets		12 lbs.

Topping

Ingredients	Volume	Weight
Lemon juice, fresh	1 cup	
Red onion, thinly sliced in rounds	1 qt.	1 lb. 8 oz.
Dill, fresh, chopped	⅓ cup	
or dried	3 Tbsp.	
Tomatoes, fresh, chopped	2 qts.	3 lbs.
Feta cheese, grated	1¼ qts.	1 lb. 4 oz.

Procedure

1. Preheat the oven to 350°.
2. Lay out fillets, skin side down, in four pans that have been lightly oiled with olive oil.
3. Divide the topping ingredients among the pans of fish and layer in the order listed.
4. Bake, covered, at 350° until the fish flakes easily.

Note: Nutritional analysis calculated for 32 servings.

Servings	Calories	Protein (g)	Fat (g)	Cholesterol (mg)	Carbohydrates (g)	Fiber (g)	Sodium (mg)
1	226	38.1	5.3	100	5.1	0.8	322

Fish West African Style

24 8-oz. Servings
32 6-oz. Servings

West African cuisine blends sweet potatoes, cabbage, and lemon to yield this rich and succulent topping. Serve with rice, fried plantains, and a crisp green salad.

Equipment:	4 half-size insert pans, 2-in. deep; 4½-gallon stewpot or Dutch oven
Preparation Time:	30 minutes
Baking Time:	30 minutes

Ingredients	Volume	Weight
Vegetable oil	½ cup	
Onions, chopped	1¼ qts.	1 lb. 4 oz.
Green peppers, chopped	1½ qts.	1 lb. 8 oz.
Tomato juice	1½ cups	
Tomato paste	1½ cups	
Sweet potatoes, peeled, sliced in ¼-in. rounds		2 lbs. 8 oz.
Cabbage, shredded	1½ qts.	1 lb.
Pimiento slices		10 oz.
Salt and ground black pepper to taste		
Fish fillets		12 lbs.
Lemon juice, fresh	1 cup or more to taste	

Garnish

Cilantro, fresh, chopped (optional)

Procedure

1. Brown the onions in ¼ cup of oil.
2. Add the peppers and sauté until tender.

(continued)

3. Purée the sauté in a food processor or blender with the tomato juice and paste to make a smooth, thick sauce.
4. Using a stewpot or Dutch oven, sauté the sweet potatoes in the remaining oil.
5. When they brighten, add the cabbage, cover, and cook on low heat until the vegetables are tender.
6. Mix the tomato mixture and the pimientos into the cooked vegetables and add salt and pepper.
7. Preheat the oven to 350°.
8. Rinse and drain the fish fillets.
9. Place the fillets, skin side down, in four oiled pans. Dress each pan with 4 Tbsp. lemon juice and 4 cups of topping.
10. Bake, covered, at 350° for about 30 minutes, or until the fish flakes easily.
11. Serve topped with cilantro, if desired.

Note: Nutritional analysis calculated for 24 servings.

Servings	Calories	Protein (g)	Fat (g)	Cholesterol (mg)	Carbohydrates (g)	Fiber (g)	Sodium (mg)
1	343	48.9	6.9	112	20.4	2.2	348

Fish with Lemon and Basil

32 6-oz. Servings
24 8-oz. Servings

This dish has an aromatic, crisp topping achieved through baking, not frying. To complete the meal, accompany by an Artichoke Heart–Tomato Salad (p. 313) and Rice Pilaf with Orzo (p. 339).

Equipment:	4 half-size insert pans, 2-in. deep
Preparation Time:	25 minutes
Baking Time:	25 minutes

Ingredients	Volume	Weight
Fish fillets		12 lbs.

Topping

Lemon juice, fresh	1 cup	
Olive oil	1⅓ cups	
Garlic, minced or pressed	12 cloves or 4 Tbsp.	
Basil, fresh, chopped	1⅓ cups	
or dried	⅔ cup	
Bread crumbs (whole wheat), fresh	3½ qts.	3 lbs.
Parmesan cheese, freshly grated	1 qt.	1 lb.
Salt and black pepper to taste		

Procedure

1. Rinse and drain the fish fillets. Place the fish, skin side down, in four pans. Top with ¼ cup of lemon juice per pan.
2. Preheat the oven to 350°. Heat the olive oil in a large skillet and sauté the garlic very briefly.

(continued)

3. Add the basil and bread crumbs. Continue to sauté, stirring constantly until the crumbs are toasted and lightly browned.
4. Remove from the heat and toss with grated Parmesan, black pepper, and salt if desired.
5. Cover the fish evenly with the topping and bake at 350°, covered, for 15 minutes. Uncover and bake 10–15 minutes longer, until the topping is crisp and the fish flakes easily.

Note: Nutritional analysis calculated for 32 servings.

Servings	Calories	Protein (g)	Fat (g)	Cholesterol (mg)	Carbohydrates (g)	Fiber (g)	Sodium (mg)
1	433	45.7	17.1	95	24.1	3.9	641

Fish with Artichoke Hearts and Red Peppers

24 8-oz. Servings
32 6-oz. Servings

Serve this easily prepared dish for an elegant or special occasion with Greek Roasted Potatoes (p. 330) and Tzatziki (p. 344).

Equipment:	4 half-size insert pans, 2-in. deep; 2½-gallon stockpot
Preparation Time:	30 minutes
Baking Time:	30 minutes

Ingredients	Volume	Weight
Onions, thinly sliced	1½ qts.	1 lb. 8 oz.
Olive oil	⅓ cup	
Bell peppers, red, thinly sliced	1½ qts.	1 lb. 8 oz.
Artichoke hearts, canned, drained, quartered	30 whole or 2 qts. (1 #10 can)	3 lbs. 6 oz.
Paprika	1½ Tbsp.	
Dill, fresh, chopped	3 Tbsp.	
or dried	1 Tbsp.	
Parsley, fresh, chopped	¼ cup	
White wine, dry	2 cups	
Lemon juice, fresh	½–¾ cup	
White flour	¼ cup	
Fish fillets		12 lbs.

Procedure

1. Briefly sauté the onions in olive oil, about 3–4 minutes.
2. Add the red peppers and continue to sauté until the peppers just soften.
3. Stir in the artichoke hearts and the remaining ingredients, except the flour, and bring to a simmer.

(continued)

Fish

4. Using a ladle, remove one cup of liquid from the sauce and whisk it with the flour. Add the dissolved flour mixture to the sauce and simmer briefly.
5. Preheat the oven to 350°. Rinse and drain the fish fillets. Place the fillets, skin side down, in lightly oiled pans. Spoon one-fourth of the sauce over each pan of fillets and bake, covered, at 350° for 20–30 minutes, or until the fish flakes easily.

Note: Nutritional analysis calculated for 24 servings.

Servings	Calories	Protein (g)	Fat (g)	Cholesterol (mg)	Carbohydrates (g)	Fiber (g)	Sodium (mg)
1	318	50.1	5.2	112	14.6	4.9	234

Flounder with Spinach and Almonds

24 (8 oz.) Servings
2 Rolls Per Serving

Rolled fish offers a multilayered experience—the filling serves as both complement and surprise. This dish always wins us accolades.

Equipment:	4 half-size insert pans, 2-in. deep
Preparation Time:	20 minutes
Baking Time:	20 minutes

Ingredients	Volume	Weight
Vegetable oil or butter	½ cup	
Onions, chopped	1¼ qts.	1¼ lbs.
Fresh spinach, stemmed, chopped	4 10-oz. bags	2 lbs. 8 oz.
or frozen, thawed, and drained		1 lb. 4 oz.
Dill or basil, fresh, chopped	⅓ cup	
or dried	2 Tbsp.	
Nutmeg	1 tsp.	
Almonds, toasted, finely chopped	2 cups	8 oz.
Lemon juice, fresh	½ cup	
Bread crumbs, fresh	2½ cups	5 oz.
Parsley, fresh, minced	½ cup	
Flounder fillets	48 4-oz. fillets	12 lbs.

Procedure

1. Sauté the onions, dill, and nutmeg in oil or butter until the onions are translucent.
2. Add the fresh spinach and cook, covered, until the spinach is wilted. If using frozen spinach, drain well and combine it with the seasoned onions.
3. Remove from the heat and drain.

(continued)

4. Add the remaining ingredients, except for the fish, mix well, and allow to cool.
5. Preheat the oven to 375°. Lay out the flounder fillets skinned side up. Spoon a small amount of the filling onto each fillet and then roll it up.
6. Place the rolls, seam-side down, in lightly oiled baking pans. Bake, covered, at 375° for 20 minutes, until the fish is flaky.
7. Serve on rice or orzo if desired, spooning the juices over each serving.

Servings	Calories	Protein (g)	Fat (g)	Cholesterol (mg)	Carbohydrates (g)	Fiber (g)	Sodium (mg)
1	500	54.0	24.5	147	14.7	3.0	520

Mediterranean Fish Stew

24 12-oz. Servings

This stew is a meal unto itself and a natural, uncompromising way of using prebaked fish. Play with the herbs, substitute seafood, in whole or part, and serve with bread that is fresh and aromatic.

Equipment:	2½-gallon stockpot
Preparation Time:	30 minutes
Cooking Time:	45 minutes

Ingredients	Volume	Weight
Vegetable or olive oil	¼ cup	
Onions, chopped	1 qt.	1 lb.
Garlic, minced or pressed	6 cloves or 2 Tbsp.	
Carrots, chopped	1 qt.	1 lb. 4 oz.
Potatoes, cubed	2 qts.	2 lbs.
Bay leaves	4	
Basil, fresh, chopped	3 Tbsp.	
or dried	1 Tbsp.	
Marjoram, dried	1 Tbsp.	
Summer squash, yellow, chopped	1 qt.	1 lb. 4 oz.
Peppers, red or green, chopped	1 qt.	1 lb.
Green beans, halved	1 qt.	1 lb.
Tomatoes, canned with juice, crushed	3 qts. (1 #10 can)	6 lbs. 6 oz.
Vegetable Stock (p. 63) or water	1 qt.	
Red wine, dry	¼ cup	
Salt and black pepper to taste		
Fish fillets, raw, cut in bite-sized pieces (fish can be prebaked and cubed)		4 lbs. 8 oz.

Procedure

1. Sauté the onions and garlic in oil until the onions soften.
2. Add the carrots, potatoes, bay leaves, and herbs and sauté for 10 minutes.

(continued)

3. Add the rest of the ingredients, except for the fish, bring to a boil, and then simmer for 20 minutes until all the vegetables are tender.
4. Stir in the fish and continue to simmer for 10 minutes more until the fish is just cooked and flakes easily with a fork. Adjust the seasonings. Serve, if desired, with a side of bread.

Note: Leftover Fish Santorini (p. 174), Fish with Artichoke Hearts and Red Peppers (p. 179), or Fish Marseilles (p. 172) can be easily incorporated into this stew. If using Fish Marseilles, substitute the seasonings used in that recipe for the ones listed above.

Servings	Calories	Protein (g)	Fat (g)	Cholesterol (mg)	Carbohydrates (g)	Fiber (g)	Sodium (mg)
1	194	18.8	3.5	37	22.5	3.1	240

Patrani Machi

24 8-oz. Servings
32 6-oz. Servings

Rich, hot, refreshing, and intriging, Patrani Machi is a delicious puzzle for the palate. Serve on rice with a simple cucumber–yogurt salad or with fresh tomato wedges with toasted cumin.

Equipment:	4 half-size insert pans, 2-in. deep
Preparation Time:	25 minutes
Baking Time:	30 minutes

Ingredients	Volume	Weight
Chutney		
Coconut, unsweetened, shredded	1 qt.	12 oz.
Chili peppers, fresh, coarsely chopped	8 sm.	4 oz.
Garlic, pressed	12 cloves or ¼ cup	
Ginger root, fresh, grated	¼ cup	
Cilantro, fresh, chopped	2 cups	
Lime juice, fresh	1 cup	
Cumin, ground	2 Tbsp.	
Salt	2 tsp.	
Brown sugar (optional)	1 Tbsp.	
Fish fillets		12 lbs.

Procedure

1. In a blender or the bowl of a food processor, purée all of the chutney ingredients until smooth. If using a blender, it may be necessary to add a tablespoon or two of water and to blend in batches.
2. Preheat the oven to 350°. Place the rinsed and drained fillets skin side down in four lightly oiled pans.

(continued)

3. Spread one-fourth of the chutney, about 9 oz. or 1¼ cups, over the fillets in each pan.
4. Bake, covered, at 350° for 25 to 30 minutes, or until the fish flakes easily.

Note: Nutritional analysis calculated for 24 servings.

Servings	Calories	Protein (g)	Fat (g)	Cholesterol (mg)	Carbohydrates (g)	Fiber (g)	Sodium (mg)
1	299	47.6	7.0	112	9.6	1.2	399

Pompano Tampico

24 9-oz. Servings
3 Rolls Per Serving

This gourmet Mexican tour de force is well worth the effort. Fresh white fish is a splendid vehicle for ripe tomatoes, toasted almonds, lemon, and cilantro. Serve on rice with steamed carrots or green beans.

Equipment:	4 half-size insert pans, 2-in. deep
Preparation Time:	40 minutes
Baking Time:	20 minutes

Ingredients	Volume	Weight
Sun-dried tomatoes (p. 474)	4½ cups	13 oz.
Boiling water	1½ qts.	
Almonds, toasted, chopped	3 cups	12 oz.
Tomatoes, fresh, chopped	2¼ qts.	3 lbs. 6 oz.
Cilantro, fresh, chopped	1 heaping cup	3 oz.
Salt to taste		
Flounder fillets		12 lbs. (2–3 oz. fillets)
Garlic, pressed	10 cloves or 3 Tbsp.	
Cayenne	¼ to ½ tsp.	
Butter, melted	1½ cups	12 oz.
Lemon juice, fresh	1 cup	

Procedure

1. Soak the sun-dried tomatoes in boiling water for 15 minutes. Drain and chop.
2. Combine with the almonds, fresh tomatoes, and cilantro. Salt to taste.
3. Rinse the flounder and drain. Place fillets skin side up and mound 1 oz. of filling at the end of each fillet. Roll up and place the flounder rolls, seam side down, in lightly oiled pans. Preheat the oven to 375°.

(continued)

4. Sauté the garlic and cayenne in butter for a few minutes on very low heat. Add the lemon juice and pour ½–⅔ cup of the spiced butter over each pan of rolled flounder.
5. Bake, covered, at 375° for 20 to 25 minutes, or until the fish flakes easily.

Servings	Calories	Protein (g)	Fat (g)	Cholesterol (mg)	Carbohydrates (g)	Fiber (g)	Sodium (mg)
1	575	54.9	33.0	178	16.1	4.3	843

Fish

Salmon Teriyaki

24 4–6 oz. Salmon Steaks

Here is a quick and fat-free version of Teriyaki Sauce that loses nothing in the translation. We hope it "re-orients" your average salmon experience. Serve with rice, blanched snow peas, or steamed broccoli. This marinade is also good for vegetable kabobs or other types of baked, grilled, or broiled fish.

Equipment:	4 half-size insert pans, 2-in. deep
Preparation Time:	10 minutes
Baking Time:	20 minutes

Ingredients	Volume	Weight
Marinade		
Soy sauce	1³/₄ cups	
Ginger root, fresh, grated	3 Tbsp.	
Garlic, pressed	5 cloves or 1¹/₂ Tbsp.	
Mirin (p. 472) (dry sherry or Chinese cooking wine can substitute with the addition of ¹/₄ cup sugar)	1³/₄ cups	
Lemon juice, fresh	1 cup	
Salmon steaks	24 steaks	4–6 oz. each
Garnish		
Scallions, chopped	1 cup	2.5 oz.

Procedure

1. Preheat the oven to 350°. Whisk together the marinade ingredients.
2. Lay out six steaks per pan and ladle on 8 oz. of marinade per pan.
3. Bake in a 350° oven, covered, for about 20 minutes or until flaky.
4. Garnish with chopped scallions.

Servings	Calories	Protein (g)	Fat (g)	Cholesterol (mg)	Carbohydrates (g)	Fiber (g)	Sodium (mg)
1	341	42.1	16.8	133	1.4	0.1	338

Spicy Cajun Fish

24 8-oz. Servings
32 6-oz. Servings

Serve a dish that brings the indulgent tastes of New Orleans to the table. Accompany with rice and stewed tomatoes with okra.

Equipment:	4 half-size insert pans, 2-in. deep
Preparation Time:	20 minutes
Baking Time:	20 minutes

Ingredients	Volume	Weight
Olive oil	1 cup	
Butter	1 cup	
Onions, thinly sliced	1 qt.	1 lb.
Garlic, pressed	12 cloves or 4 Tbsp. or to taste	
Thyme, dried	1 Tbsp.	
Rosemary, dried, crumbled	2 tsp.	
Ground black pepper	2 tsp.	
Cayenne	1 tsp.	
Hungarian paprika	1½ Tbsp.	
Dry white wine	2 cups	
Lemon juice, fresh	½ cup or to taste	
Fish fillets		12 lbs.

Procedure

1. Heat the oil and butter until the butter has melted. Add the onions and garlic and sauté on medium heat until the onions are softened.
2. Stir in the herbs and spices and sauté for 2 to 3 minutes.
3. Pour in the wine and lemon juice and simmer for 5 minutes more.
4. Preheat the oven to 350°. Rinse and drain the fish fillets. Place the fillets, skin side down, in four pans, 3 lbs. per pan. Pour 2 cups of the topping over each pan of fish.
5. Bake, covered, at 350° for about 20 minutes, or until the fish flakes easily.

Note: Substitute shrimp for fillets and bake until pink and firm.
Note: Nutritional analysis calculated for 32 servings.

Servings	Calories	Protein (g)	Fat (g)	Cholesterol (mg)	Carbohydrates (g)	Fiber (g)	Sodium (mg)
1	295	35.4	14.3	100	2.8	0.5	180

Fish

LEGUMES

Beans and soy products are important sources of vegetable proteins, complex carbohydrates, fiber, and B vitamins. Traditional pairing with grains such as rice, corn, or wheat enhances the nutritional and food appeal of legumes. Versatility, low fat content, and good economy are additional reasons to develop a repertoire of bean dishes that go beyond the simple side dish.

Tofu, made from soybeans, is the object of unfair ridicule, primarily because people lack the expertise to prepare tasty tofu-based dishes. Tofu's blandness can be an asset when it is used as a base for other flavors. This high-in-protein product fills a multitude of roles in this section—it is an essential part of a not-fried croquette, Tofu-Vegetable Croquettes; a highly seasoned, Jamaican-style Jerk Tofu; a vegetarian burger, and back to its Chinese roots, five-spice Seasoned Tofu.

Bean dishes are a regular menu item at Moosewood, and we most often use dried beans in their preparation. We buy bulk quantities of dried beans for economy. Our prep routine includes sorting, soaking, and cooking beans for the day's meals. Pressure cookers dramatically reduce the cooking time of beans. Canned beans can be useful when there are time constraints. However, they are usually heavily salted and contain preservatives. We usually give canned beans a quick rinse to reduce saltiness. Canned beans tend to be drier, firmer, and lighter than beans cooked in the soak-and-boil method.

For the convenience of those of you who opt to cook dried beans ahead of time, we've listed dried bean quantities in the recipes. We caution you that volume–weight equivalents are different for canned beans and cooked-from-scratch beans, with canned beans weighing less. The weights we list are based on industry charts for canned beans.

As our fresh salsa repertoire has expanded, we've found our bean dish repertoire growing also, because fresh tropical fruits make delicious toppings for a variety of beans. We often serve smoked cheese as an optional topping for beans, to satisfy our customers who miss the flavor of smoked meats.

BBQ Tempeh and Peppers

24 6-oz. Servings

This is our tribute to down-home cooking. Serve with rice, as a filling for pita sandwiches, or over split cornbread or biscuits. Or, serve as part of a combination plate with Sara's Greens (p. 342), mashed sweet potatoes, and coleslaw.

Equipment:	4½-gallon stockpot	
Preparation and Cooking Time:	40 minutes	

Ingredients	Volume	Weight
Vegetable oil	½ cup	
Onions, chopped	2¼ qts.	2 lbs. 4 oz.
Garlic, minced or pressed	10 cloves or 3 Tbsp.	
Peppers, green and/or red, chopped	2 qts.	2 lbs.
Tempeh (p. 474), thawed slightly if frozen, cubed into ½-in. pieces		3 lbs.

Sauce

Dijon mustard	2 Tbsp.	
Soy sauce	½ cup	
Tomato paste	1 cup	
Molasses or brown sugar	⅓ cup	
Water	1 qt.	
Coriander seed, ground	3 Tbsp.	
Fennel seed, ground	1½ Tbsp.	
Tabasco or other hot sauce	3–4 tsp.	
Salt to taste		

Procedure

1. Sauté the onions and garlic in oil for 3–4 minutes.
2. Add the peppers and continue to sauté until they begin to soften.

(continued)

3. Add the cubed tempeh and sauté, stirring often, for 5 minutes.
4. Combine the sauce ingredients and set aside.
5. Sprinkle the coriander and fennel over the tempeh and vegetables, add the sauce, and simmer on low heat for 5 minutes.
6. Add Tabasco or other hot sauce to taste and salt if desired.

Servings	Calories	Protein (g)	Fat (g)	Cholesterol (mg)	Carbohydrates (g)	Fiber (g)	Sodium (mg)
1	212	12.6	9.4	0	22.8	1.2	382

Caribbean Black Beans

24 9-oz. Servings

This Moosewood favorite is quick and sophisticated with an aroma redolent of the Spice Islands. Serve beans on Golden Spanish Rice (p. 329) or Coconut Rice (p. 322) topped with Mango Salsa (p. 264).

Equipment:	4-in. deep insert pan
Preparation Time:	45 minutes
Cooking Time:	3½ hours with dried beans or 1 hour with cooked beans

Ingredients	Volume	Weight
Black beans, dried	3 qts.	5 lbs.
or cooked and drained	6 to 7 qts.	9 to 10 lbs.
	(2 #10 cans)	
Olive oil	½ cup	
Onions, chopped	2 qts.	2 lbs.
Garlic, minced or pressed	6 cloves or	
	2 Tbsp.	
Ginger root, fresh, grated	⅓ cup	6 oz.
Thyme, dried	1 Tbsp.	
Allspice, ground	1 Tbsp.	
Orange juice	1 qt.	
Salt, black pepper, and Tabasco to taste		

Procedure

1. If using dried beans, pick over for stones, rinse, and soak overnight in water to cover; or bring to a boil, remove from the heat, and soak for 1–2 hours. After the beans have soaked, drain and cook until tender in 2–3 gallons of water for 30–45 minutes. Drain.
2. While the beans cook, sauté the onions and garlic in oil until the onions are translucent.

(continued)

3. Stir in the ginger, thyme, and allspice and continue sautéing until the onions are very soft. Stir frequently to prevent sticking.
4. Pour the beans into an insert pan, adding the orange juice, onions, salt, pepper, and Tabasco.
5. Tightly cover with foil and bake at 350° for 30–45 minutes or until the beans are piping hot.

Servings	Calories	Protein (g)	Fat (g)	Cholesterol (mg)	Carbohydrates (g)	Fiber (g)	Sodium (mg)
1	243	11.7	5.5	0	38.5	0.8	700

Chili Blanco

24 9-oz. Servings

We call this our white bean chili. It is creamy and tangy and has converted many of our customers to lima beans. Serve in a bowl with tortilla chips. Or serve as a tostada on a corn tortilla with shredded lettuce, hot sauce, and chopped black or Spanish olives.

Equipment:	6-in. deep half-size insert pan
Preparation Time:	15 minutes
Cooking Time:	20 minutes

Ingredients	Volume	Weight
Lima beans, dried	2 qts.	3 lbs.
or cooked, drained	5¾ qts. (2 #10 cans white beans)	9 lbs.
Neufchâtel or cream cheese, cubed, softened		2 lbs.
Vegetable oil	½ cup	
Onions, chopped	2 qts.	2 lbs.
Garlic, minced or pressed	8 cloves or 2 Tbsp.	
Cumin, ground	2 Tbsp.	
Coriander seed, ground	1 Tbsp.	
Cayenne	¼ tsp. more to taste	
Chili powder	2 Tbsp.	
Peppers, green or red, diced	2½ qts.	2 lbs. 8 oz.
Carrots, diced	2 qts.	2 lbs. 10 oz.
Salt to taste		

Procedure

1. If using dried beans, start with 2 qts. of beans, pick over for stones, rinse, and soak overnight in water to cover; or bring to a boil, remove from heat, and soak

(continued)

for 1–2 hours. After the beans have soaked, drain and cook until tender in 2–3 gallons of water for 20–30 minutes. Drain.

2. Mash the drained beans with the cream cheese.
3. Sauté the onions and garlic in oil until the onions soften.
4. Add the spices, peppers, and carrots, and cook, stirring often, until the vegetables are tender.
5. Combine the beans and vegetable sauté and salt to taste.
6. Tightly cover with foil and bake for 40 minutes at 350° or until thoroughly heated.

Servings	Calories	Protein (g)	Fat (g)	Cholesterol (mg)	Carbohydrates (g)	Fiber (g)	Sodium (mg)
1	372	16.7	14.6	29	46.2	2.7	246

Creole Beans and Rice

24 8-oz. Servings with 4 oz. of Rice

The classic version of this dish is distinguished by Andouille or other types of smoked sausage. At Moosewood, we've created a vegetarian creole dish that has its own compelling charm.

Equipment:	4-in. deep insert pan
Preparation Time:	2 hours with dried beans, 1 hour with cooked beans
Cooking Time:	45 minutes

Ingredients	Volume	Weight
Kidney beans, dried	2¼ qts.	3 lbs. 8 oz.
or cooked, drained	5–6 qts.	9 lbs.
	(2 #10 cans)	
Cayenne	¼ tsp.	
Allspice, ground	½ tsp.	

Salsa (yields 2½ qts.)

Scallions, chopped	1 cup	2 oz.
Cucumbers, peeled, seeded, diced	3 cups	1 lb.
Tomatoes, fresh, diced	1¼ qts.	2 lbs.
Parsley, fresh, chopped	1½ cups	8 oz.
Vegetable oil	¾ cup	
Vinegar	½ cup plus 2 Tbsp.	

Salt, to taste
Tabasco or other hot pepper sauce to taste

Brown rice, raw	2 qts.	3 lbs. 4 oz.

Vegetable Sauté

Vegetable oil	¼ cup	
Onions, chopped	2¼ qts.	2 lbs. 4 oz.
Garlic, minced or pressed	18 cloves or 6 Tbsp.	

(continued)

Celery, chopped	1 qt.	1 lb.
Carrots, chopped	2 qts.	2 lbs. 10 oz.
Peppers, green, chopped	2 qts.	2 lbs.

Sauce

Tomato paste	1 cup
Red wine, dry	3/4 cup
Vinegar	1 Tbsp.
Brown sugar or molasses	1½ Tbsp.
Dijon mustard	1 Tbsp.
Salt	1 Tbsp.
Oregano, dried	1½ tsp.
Cayenne to taste	
Allspice, ground	3/4 tsp.

Garnish

Sour cream (optional)	2½ cups	1 lb. 8 oz.

Procedure

1. If using dried beans, pick over for stones, rinse, and soak overnight in water to cover; or bring to a boil, remove from heat, and soak for 1–2 hours. After the beans have soaked, drain and add the cayenne and allspice and cook until tender in 2–3 gallons of water for 45 minutes to 1 hour. If using canned or precooked beans, spread them in a 4-in. deep insert pan. Mix in the cayenne and allspice; then set aside.
2. In a separate bowl, combine the salsa ingredients. Refrigerate for an hour, stirring occasionally. Add more Tabasco for a hotter salsa.
3. Cook the rice for about 50 minutes (p. 468).
4. Meanwhile, sauté the onions and garlic in oil until the onions are translucent.
5. Add the celery and carrots and sauté over medium heat for 10 minutes, stirring occasionally.
6. Stir in the green peppers and continue to sauté until all the vegetables are tender. Covering the vegetables part way through yields a juicier mixture and does not detract from the taste.
7. In a bowl, whisk together the sauce ingredients. Add the sauce and the cooked vegetables to the pan of cooked beans. Stir thoroughly.
8. Cover tightly with foil and bake at 350° for 30–45 minutes, or until steaming.
9. For each serving, spoon 8 oz. of beans on 4 oz. of rice and top with 2 oz. of salsa and a dollop of sour cream, if desired.

Servings	Calories	Protein (g)	Fat (g)	Cholesterol (mg)	Carbohydrates (g)	Fiber (g)	Sodium (mg)
1	493	21.8	9	0	84.3	3.8	463

Legumes

East-West Braised Eggplant

24 Stuffed Eggplant Halves

This dish was fashioned after a Japanese appetizer that two of our cooks swooned over. Here, an adventuresome mix of ingredients creates a rich and exotically seasoned entrée.

Equipment:	4 insert pans, 4-in. deep
Preparation Time:	1 hour 45 minutes
Baking Time:	30 minutes

Ingredients	Volume	Weight
Braising Liquid		
Dry sherry	3 cups	
Soy sauce	1 cup	
Molasses	½ cup	
Eggplants, halved lengthwise	12 med.	
Filling		
Vegetable oil	¾ cup	
Tempeh (p. 474), cubed		3 lbs.
Onions, chopped	4 qts.	4 lbs.
Fennel seed, ground	2 Tbsp.	
Cayenne	¼ tsp.	
Coriander seed, ground	1 Tbsp.	
Peppers, green and/or red, diced	1½ qts.	1 lb. 8 oz.
Mushrooms, sliced	6¼ qts.	5 lbs.
Tomato paste	1 cup	
Salt to taste		
Garnish		
Sesame seeds, toasted	½ cup	
Scallions, chopped	2 cups	5 oz.

Procedure

1. Whisk together the braising liquid ingredients and pour equal amounts into four insert pans.
2. Place the eggplant halves cut side down in the pans and cover each pan tightly with aluminum foil. Bake at 350° for 45 minutes, or until tender.
3. While the eggplants braise, brown the tempeh with 1 qt. of the onions, 1 Tbsp. fennel, ¼ tsp. cayenne, and ½ cup oil. Stir often to prevent burning.
4. In a separate pot or large skillet, sauté the remaining onions and fennel with the coriander and remaining ¼ cup oil, until the onions are translucent.
5. Add the peppers and mushrooms and continue to sauté until the peppers soften.
6. Combine the tempeh with the other sautéed vegetables. Stir in the tomato paste and ⅔ cup braising liquid from the baked eggplants.
7. Using a fork, mash the pulp of the baked eggplant, then push it to the sides, creating a hollow in each half.
8. Fill the hollow with 1 cup of filling per eggplant half.
9. Return filled eggplants to original baking pans, cover tightly, and bake at 350° for 20–30 minutes, until heated through.
10. Serve each eggplant half on a bed of rice, if desired, basting the eggplant with a little of the pan juices. Sprinkle the top with 1 tsp. sesame seeds and chopped scallions.

Servings	Calories	Protein (g)	Fat (g)	Cholesterol (mg)	Carbohydrates (g)	Fiber (g)	Sodium (mg)
1	360	16.7	14.1	0	44.5	8.5	646

Greek-Style Cannellini
and Vegetables

24 12-oz. Servings

Inspired by pasta e fagioli, we've created a Greek-style one-pot meal enlivened with artichoke hearts and red wine vinegar. This dish combines vegetables, beans, and pasta into a fine tasting, nutritious whole.

Equipment:	2½-gallon stockpot
Preparation Time:	30 minutes
Cooking Time:	45 minutes

Ingredients	Volume	Weight
Olive oil	½ cup	
Onions, chopped	2 qts.	2 lbs.
Garlic, pressed	10 cloves or 3 Tbsp.	
Mint, fresh, minced	¼ cup	
or dried	1 Tbsp.	
Dill, fresh, minced	½ cup	
or dried	2 Tbsp.	
Marjoram, fresh, chopped	2 Tbsp.	
or dried	2 tsp.	
Carrots, diced	2¼ qts.	3 lbs.
Peppers, red or green, chopped	1½ qts.	1 lb. 8 oz.
Zucchini, chopped	1½ qts.	2 lbs.
25 Artichoke hearts, quartered	2 qts. (1 #10 can)	2 lbs. 8 oz.
Tomatoes, canned with juice, crushed	3 qts. (1 #10 can)	6 lbs. 6 oz.
Cannellini, white kidney, or dried lima beans,	1¼ qts.	2 lbs.
or cooked, drained	3 qts. (1 #10 can)	4 lbs. 8 oz.
Orzo, dry (p. 472)	2 cups	
Water	1 qt.	
Red wine vinegar	½ cup	
Salt and black pepper to taste		

Procedure

1. If using dried beans, sort through for stones, rinse, and soak overnight in water to cover; or bring to a boil, remove from heat, and soak for 1–2 hours. After the beans have soaked, drain and cook in 1 gallon water for 20–30 minutes, or until tender.
2. In a 2½-gallon stockpot, sauté the onions and garlic in oil.
3. Add the dried herbs and continue to sauté until the onions are soft. If you are using fresh herbs, set aside.
4. Add the carrots and sauté for 10 minutes.
5. Add the peppers and zucchini and continue to sauté for 10 minutes more.
6. Stir in the artichoke hearts, tomatoes, and cooked beans to the sauté. Simmer, stirring occasionally, until the vegetables are tender.
7. Meanwhile, cook the orzo until it is al dente. Drain.
8. When the vegetables and beans are hot, add the fresh herbs, orzo, vinegar, salt, and pepper.

Servings	Calories	Protein (g)	Fat (g)	Cholesterol (mg)	Carbohydrates (g)	Fiber (g)	Sodium (mg)
1	319	13.3	5.9	0	57.1	10.8	260

Legumes

Honolulu Beans

24 10-oz. Servings

This dish provides the popularity of baked beans without the hours involved yet offers some surprises to the discerning palate. Serve on Coconut Rice (p. 322) or with Cornbread (p. 323) and add Asian Cabbage Slaw (p. 314).

Equipment:	6-in. deep half-size insert pan
Preparation Time:	20 minutes
Baking Time:	40 minutes

Ingredients	Volume	Weight
Onions, chopped	2 qts.	2 lbs.
Vegetable oil	1/3 cup	
Kidney beans, dried	2 1/4 qts.	3 lb. 4 oz.
or cooked, drained	6 qts. (2 #10 cans)	9 lbs.
Hoisin sauce (p. 471)	3/4 cup	
Dijon mustard	2 Tbsp.	
Tomato paste	1/2 cup	
Soy sauce	1/2 cup	
Sesame oil, dark (p. 473)	2 Tbsp.	
Cumin, ground	2 Tbsp.	
Orange peel, grated	2 Tbsp.	
Pineapple, unsweetened, canned, crushed	1 qt.	

Procedure

1. If using dried beans, sort through for stones, rinse, and soak overnight in water to cover; or bring to a boil, remove from heat, and soak for 1–2 hours. After the beans have soaked, drain and cook in 2 gallons of water for 45 minutes to 1 hour, or until tender.
2. Sauté the onions in oil until lightly browned.
3. Mash one-third of the beans and combine them with the remaining beans, onions, and the rest of the ingredients.
4. Cover with foil and bake at 350° for 30–40 minutes.

Servings	Calories	Protein (g)	Fat (g)	Cholesterol (mg)	Carbohydrates (g)	Fiber (g)	Sodium (mg)
1	313	17.6	5.4	0	51.6	0.8	421

Hoppin' John

24 7-oz. Servings with 3.5 oz. Rice

Here is our rendition of the Southern classic that welcomes in each New Year. This simple bean dish is made interesting by the contrasting colors, textures, and tastes of its toppings.

Equipment:	6-in. deep half-size insert pan
Preparation Time:	20 minutes
Cooking Time:	1 hour 15 minutes

Ingredients	Volume	Weight
Black-eyed peas, dried	2¼ qts.	4 lbs.
or cooked, canned, or frozen	6 qts. (2 #10 cans)	9 lbs.
Bay leaves	4	
Water	2 gals.	
Garlic, whole cloves, peeled	12 cloves	
Vegetable oil	¼ cup	
Onions, diced	3 qts.	3 lbs.
Allspice, ground	1 tsp.	
Cayenne	¼ tsp.	
Soy sauce	½ cup	
Black pepper and additional salt to taste		
Brown rice, cooked (p. 468)	3 qts.	

Toppings

	Volume	Weight
Tomatoes, fresh, chopped	1½ qts.	2 lbs. 4 oz.
Scallions, chopped	2 cups	5 oz.
Smoked Cheddar cheese, grated	1½ qts.	1 lb. 2 oz.

Procedure

1. If using dried black-eyed peas, sort through for stones. Cook the peas with bay leaves, whole garlic cloves, and water, until tender—about 45 minutes. For frozen or canned, drain peas, cook with bay leaves and garlic cloves in water to just cover for 20 minutes. Place the bay leaves and garlic cloves in cheesecloth for easy removal.
2. Drain the cooked beans, reserving the liquid. Remove the bay leaves. Press or mash the cooked garlic into the beans.
3. Sauté the onions in oil with the allspice and cayenne until the onions are softened and golden.
4. Add the sauté and soy sauce to the cooked peas, along with 2–3 cups of the reserved cooking liquid.
5. Using a flame tamer, gently heat the peas, stirring often to allow the flavors to blend. Alternatively, bake the peas for 30 minutes at 350°, in a tightly covered 6-in. deep half-size insert pan.
6. Serve the peas on ½ cup cooked rice, topped with ¼ cup smoked Cheddar, ¼ cup chopped tomato, and a sprinkling of scallions.

Servings	Calories	Protein (g)	Fat (g)	Cholesterol (mg)	Carbohydrates (g)	Fiber (g)	Sodium (mg)
1	374	16.8	11.4	22	52.6	6.9	925

Jerk Tofu
7 lbs. 8 oz.

Jay Solomon is an Ithaca restauranteur and cookbook author. Our adaptation of his multipurpose Jamaican marinade transforms plain tofu into an intensely seasoned and flavorful ingredient. Serve with Caribbean Vegetable Stew (p. 351) or Roasted Vegetables (p. 340).

Equipment:	2 insert pans, 2-in. deep
Preparation Time:	25 minutes
Baking Time:	1 hour

Ingredients	Volume	Weight
Tofu, pressed (p. 474)		10 lbs. (unpressed)

Jerk Sauce

Ingredients	Volume	Weight
Scallions, chopped	2 cups	5 oz.
Onions, chopped	1 qt.	1 lb.
Chili peppers, minced	4 sm.	2 oz.
Soy sauce	2 cups	
Red wine vinegar	¾ cup	
Vegetable oil	½ cup	
Brown sugar	½ cup	
Thyme, dried	1 Tbsp.	
Garlic, pressed	10 cloves or 3 Tbsp.	
Ginger root, fresh, grated	1 Tbsp.	
Black pepper	2 tsp.	
Cloves, ground	1 tsp.	
Nutmeg, ground	1 tsp.	
Allspice, ground	1 tsp.	
Cinnamon, ground	½ tsp.	

Procedure

1. While the tofu is pressing, prepare, measure, and blend the jerk sauce ingredients in the bowl of a food processor.
2. Once the tofu is pressed and drained, slice the cakes horizontally into thirds, and then once vertically on a diagonal to yield 6 triangles per cake.
3. Arrange the triangles in a single layer in shallow pans and pour an equal amount of jerk sauce over each pan of tofu.
4. Bake, uncovered, in a convection oven if possible, at 350° for 45 minutes to 1 hour, turning the tofu every 10–15 minutes.

Servings	Calories	Protein (g)	Fat (g)	Cholesterol (mg)	Carbohydrates (g)	Fiber (g)	Sodium (mg)
1	158	4.6	6.5	0	21.8	0.6	1093

Lentil Dhal

24 7-oz. Servings

Dhals are popular Indian side dishes that provide variety and enhance the protein content of many vegetarian meals. Lentils and split peas are soft beans that cook up quickly, making the preparation of a complete Indian meal even more possible. Serve with Eggplant-Spinach Curry (p. 355) or Eggplant Bombay (p. 401).

Equipment:	2-gallon stockpot
Preparation Time:	15 minutes
Cooking Time:	1 hour

Ingredients	Volume	Weight
Lentils or split peas, dried	2½ qts.	5 lbs.
Water or Vegetable Stock (p. 63)	2 gals.	
Turmeric	1 Tbsp.	
Salt	1 Tbsp.	
Vegetable oil	½ cup	
Onions, diced	2 qts.	2 lbs.
Garlic, minced or pressed	4 cloves or 1½ Tbsp.	
Cumin, ground	1 Tbsp.	
Turmeric	2 Tbsp.	
Cayenne	¼ tsp.	
Black pepper	½ tsp.	
Coconut milk, unsweetened (p. 470)	1 can	14 oz.

Procedure

1. Cook the lentils with water, salt, and turmeric until soft. Add 1–2 additional cups of water if needed to avoid scorching.
2. In a 2-gallon pot, sauté the onions, garlic, and the rest of the spices in oil. Stir often, until the onions are softened.
3. Drain the lentils, reserving the cooking liquid, if any. Stir the lentils into the sautéed onions, along with the coconut milk. Heat gently if necessary, adding some of the reserved cooking liquid if the dhal is too thick or dry.

Note: For a lighter version, substitute 2 cups of chopped tomatoes for the coconut milk.

Servings	Calories	Protein (g)	Fat (g)	Cholesterol (mg)	Carbohydrates (g)	Fiber (g)	Sodium (mg)
1	258	10.8	7.0	0	40.3	11.1	337

Legumes

Refritos

24 6-oz. Servings
Total Yield: 1 gallon

Refritos, or refried beans, can be put to many uses. In casseroles, tamale pies, on tostadas, or as a filling for burritos or peppers, Refritos are a flavorful way of producing meatless, high-protein meals.

Equipment:	6-in. deep half-size insert pan
Preparation Time:	30 minutes
Cooking Time:	2 hours with dried beans, or 30 minutes with cooked beans

Ingredients	Volume	Weight
Pinto beans, dried	2 qts.	3 lbs. 3 oz.
or cooked and drained, reserve 1–2 cups of liquid	6 qts. (2 #10 cans)	9 lbs.
Vegetable oil	½ cup	
Onions, chopped	3 qts.	3 lbs.
Garlic, minced or pressed	15 cloves or 5 Tbsp.	
Cayenne	¼ tsp.	
Cumin, ground	2 Tbsp.	
Coriander seed, ground	1 Tbsp.	
Soy sauce	½ cup	
Salt and black pepper to taste		
Tabasco, to taste		

Procedure

1. If using dried beans, sort through for stones, then soak overnight in water to cover; or bring the beans to a boil, remove from the heat, and soak for 1–2 hours. After soaking, drain and cook the beans until tender in 2 gallons of water to cover for 30–45 minutes.
2. Sauté the onions and garlic in oil until the onions are soft.
3. Stir in the cayenne, cumin, and coriander seed and sauté for 2–3 minutes, stirring continuously.
4. Mash the beans and then combine them with the sautéed onions, soy sauce, salt, and pepper in a half-size insert pan. Add a few splashes of Tabasco for a spicier dish.
5. Tightly cover with aluminum foil and bake at 350° for 30 minutes. Add some of the reserved liquid if the refritos are too dry.

Servings	Calories	Protein (g)	Fat (g)	Cholesterol (mg)	Carbohydrates (g)	Fiber (g)	Sodium (mg)
1	267	12.9	5.7	0	43.1	13.0	284

Seasoned Tempeh

24 2³/₄-oz. Servings

Tempeh, a popular source of soy protein in Indonesia, adds a "meaty" taste and texture to soups, sautés, stews, and pita sandwiches.

Preparation Time: 15 minutes
Cooking Time: 1 hour

Ingredients	Volume	Weight
Tempeh (p. 474), frozen, thawed, cubed		4 lbs. 8 oz.

Marinade

Vinegar	1¹/₂ cups	
Soy sauce	1¹/₂ cups	
Water	³/₄ cup	
Fennel seed, ground	2 Tbsp.	
Garlic, pressed	10 cloves or 3 Tbsp.	
Vegetable oil	³/₄ cup	
Salt and black pepper to taste		

Note: To adapt Seasoned Tempeh to different ethnic cuisines, add the following herbs to the marinade:
- Mexican: 1 Tbsp. cumin, ground
          1 Tbsp. oregano, dried
- Italian: 1 Tbsp. basil, dried
- Greek: 1 Tbsp. oregano, dried
          1 Tbsp. mint, dried

Procedure

1. Combine the marinade ingredients.
2. Add the tempeh to the marinade and let it sit until the marinade is absorbed.
3. In two separate batches, heat the oil and sauté the tempeh until it is crisp and golden. Stir often to prevent sticking. Add salt and pepper to taste, serve at once.
4. Refrigerated seasoned tempeh will keep for up to 5 days.

Servings	Calories	Protein (g)	Fat (g)	Cholesterol (mg)	Carbohydrates (g)	Fiber (g)	Sodium (mg)
1	235	16.4	13.6	0	15.2	0.0	215

Seasoned Tofu

Total Yield: 1½ lbs.

Tofu has a great talent for absorbing flavor. This is our version of the well-known Chinese five-spice tofu. We use sliced seasoned tofu in salads, sandwiches, and stir-fries.

Equipment:	2-in. deep half-size insert pan
Preparation Time:	40 minutes
Baking Time:	1 hour

Ingredients	Volume	Weight
Tofu (p. 474)		2 lbs.
Soy sauce	¼ cup	
Water	¼ cup	
Five-spice powder (p. 471)	¼ tsp.	
Star anise (p. 467)	3 stars	
or anise seed, ground (p. 467)	½ tsp.	
or fennel seed, ground	2 tsp.	

Procedure

1. Press the tofu by placing the cakes between two plates or baking sheets and balancing a weight (e.g., a heavy book or a stack of plates) on the top plate for at least 20 minutes. Drain. Pressing excess water from tofu allows it to absorb flavorings more intensely.
2. Cut each pressed cake in half, horizontally, to yield 2 slices per cake.
3. Arrange the tofu in a single layer in a baking pan. Whisk together the remaining ingredients and pour over the tofu.
4. Bake at 350° for 1 hour, turning the tofu once after 30 minutes.
5. Refrigerated seasoned tofu will keep for up to 5 days.

Servings	Calories	Protein (g)	Fat (g)	Cholesterol (mg)	Carbohydrates (g)	Fiber (g)	Sodium (mg)
1	23	1.0	0.5	0	3.8	0	138

Tropical Fruit Salad (p. 466)

Salat Morocain (p. 102)

Pasta e Fagioli (with cooked beans) (p. 239)

Peach Parfait with Amaretto Cream (p. 448)

Spicy Chick-Peas

25 4-oz. Servings

This is a succulent addition to any Indian meal, offering a rich and tangy accent to milder dishes. Try it beside Roti (p. 293) or Eggplant Bombay (p. 401).

Equipment:	4-qt. stainless steel saucepan
Preparation Time:	15 minutes
Cooking Time:	1 hour or 1½ hours if cooking beans

Ingredients	Volume	Weight
Chick-peas, dried	3 cups	1 lb. 5 oz.
or canned, drained	2¼ qts.	3 lbs. 8 oz.
Onions, chopped	1¼ qts.	1 lb. 4 oz.
Garlic, pressed	12 cloves or 4 Tbsp.	
Chili peppers, fresh, coarsely chopped	4 to 6 sm.	2 to 3 oz.
or Cayenne	¼ to ½ tsp.	
Vegetable oil	¼ cup	
Tamarind concentrate (p. 474)	⅓ cup	
Hot water	1 cup	
Tomatoes, fresh, chopped	1¼ qts.	2 lbs.
Ginger root, fresh, peeled, grated	5 Tbsp.	
Salt	1 Tbsp.	

Procedure

1. If using cooked beans, set aside. If cooking dried beans, pick through for stones, rinse, and soak overnight in water to cover. Or bring to a boil, remove from the heat, and soak for 1–2 hours. After soaking, drain and cook the beans until tender in 1 gallon of water, for 30–45 minutes. Drain.
2. Sauté the onions, garlic, and chilies in oil until the onions are golden, about 15–20 minutes.
3. In a small bowl, dissolve the tamarind concentrate in the hot water.

(continued)

4. Using a blender or a food processor, purée the onions with the dissolved tamarind and the remaining ingredients (except for the chick-peas) into a smooth sauce.
5. Transfer the chick-peas and sauce to a stainless steel saucepan. Simmer, uncovered, for 30–45 minutes. Stir occasionally.

Servings	Calories	Protein (g)	Fat (g)	Cholesterol (mg)	Carbohydrates (g)	Fiber (g)	Sodium (mg)
1	101	3.2	2.7	0	17.1	3.1	400

Tofu Burgers

24 8-oz. Burgers

These burgers are our McMoosewood Special. Serve open-face on toasted whole wheat bread atop a bright green leaf of curly lettuce. Cover with Russian dressing and a juicy slice of ripe tomato. Don't forget the pickle!

Equipment:	large baking trays
Preparation Time:	30 minutes
Baking Time:	30 minutes

Ingredients	Volume	Weight
Tofu, pressed (p. 474)		7½ lbs. (unpressed weight)
Vegetable oil	½ cup	
Onions, chopped	1½ qts.	1 lb. 8 oz.
Carrots, grated	3½ cups	1 lb. 4 oz.
Peppers, diced	1 qt.	1 lb.
Basil, dried	3½ Tbsp.	
Marjoram, dried	2½ Tbsp.	
Bread crumbs, fresh	3½ cups	7 oz.
Walnuts, chopped	2½ cups	10 oz.
Tahini (p. 474)		6 oz.
Dijon mustard	2½ Tbsp.	
Soy sauce	½ cup	
Lemon juice, fresh	3 Tbsp.	
Salt and black pepper to taste		

Procedure

1. Sauté the onions in oil until they are translucent.
2. Add the vegetables and herbs and continue sautéing until the vegetables are softened.

(continued)

3. Mash the pressed and drained tofu in a large bowl. Add the remaining ingredients and the cooked vegetables. Combine thoroughly.
4. Form into 24 burgers and place on lightly oiled baking sheets or in shallow insert pans.
5. Bake at 375°, uncovered, for about 30 minutes, or until browned and firm.

Servings	Calories	Protein (g)	Fat (g)	Cholesterol (mg)	Carbohydrates (g)	Fiber (g)	Sodium (mg)
1	332	9.8	18.6	0	35.0	3.0	470

Tofu-Vegetable Croquettes

24 6-oz. Servings
3 Croquettes Each

These creamy, crunchy baked croquettes are the centerpiece of a meal when smothered with Sweet and Sour Vegetables (p. 377). Or roll the batter into smaller balls and serve as an appetizer with a duck or plum dipping sauce.

Equipment:	large baking trays
Preparation Time:	45 minutes
Baking Time:	40 minutes

Ingredients	Volume	Weight
Tofu, pressed (p. 474), mashed		5 lbs. 4 oz. (unpressed weight)
Dijon mustard	2 tsp.	
Peanut butter	1 cup	9 oz.
Soy sauce	⅓ cup	
Ginger root, fresh, grated	¼ cup	
Cayenne	½ to 1 tsp.	
Scallions, chopped	2 bunches	
Mushrooms, chopped	1 qt.	10 oz.
Water chestnuts, drained, chopped	1 cup	6 oz.
Peppers, green and/or red, minced	2 cups	8 oz.

Procedure

1. Mix all the ingredients in a large bowl.
2. Form the tofu mixture into 2-in. balls and place on an oiled baking tray.
3. Bake at 375° for 30–45 minutes until browned and firm.

Servings	Calories	Protein (g)	Fat (g)	Cholesterol (mg)	Carbohydrates (g)	Fiber (g)	Sodium (mg)
1	151	6.3	7.1	0	17.2	1.2	273

PASTA

If our customers' preferences are any indication, pasta may rank as the most popular entrée of all. Beloved by young and old alike, this appealing food is uniquely satisfying.

The recipes here fall into two categories: casseroles and pasta with sauce. Although casseroles require more preparation time, once assembed, they can sit refrigerated until baking time, and are easily served when completed. Our casserole pasta dishes include Balkan Moussaka, Pasta al Cavolfiore, Spinach Lasagna Putanesca, Ziti with Chard, and Lasagna Verdure. The following pasta sauces can be prepared ahead of time and hold well in the steam table: Artichoke Sauce Allegro, Fettucine Toscana (steam cauliflower as needed), Pasta e Fagioli, Pasta Tutto Giardino, Pasta with Beans and Greens, and Pasta with Spinach and Ricotta. Pasta Therese and Very Fresh Tomato-Basil Sauce are best prepared an hour or so before serving at room temperature.

Portions here are for home-style dinner entrées. Salad and bread need be the only accompaniments.

Artichoke Sauce Allegro

24 12-oz. Servings

This fairly instant but palate-pleasing sauce is especially good with a filled pasta such as ravioli or tortellini.

Equipment:	2-gallon pot
Preparation and Cooking Time:	20 minutes

Ingredients	Volume	Weight
Olive oil	2 cups	
Butter	2 cups	1 lb.
Garlic, pressed	20 med. cloves or ⅓ cup	
Artichoke hearts, packed in brine, drained, quartered	1⅓ #10 cans	4 lbs. 8 oz.
Basil, fresh, chopped	1 cup	
or dried	2 Tbsp.	
Lemon juice, fresh	½ cup	
Black pepper to taste		
Pasta: linguine, spaghetti, ravioli		6 lbs.
Parmesan cheese, grated (optional)	1½ qts.	1 lb. 8 oz.

Procedure

1. Heat the oil and butter. When the butter has melted, add the garlic and sauté for 5–7 minutes until the garlic is golden but not browned.
2. Remove from the heat and emulsify in a blender. This will keep the sauce from separating.
3. Return the sauce to the stove. Add the quartered artichoke hearts, basil, and lemon and gently heat through.

(continued)

4. Cook the pasta and drain.
5. Serve ¼ lb. of pasta per serving in heated bowls. Ladle on 7 oz. of sauce and top with 1 oz. of Parmesan cheese.

Servings	Calories	Protein (g)	Fat (g)	Cholesterol (mg)	Carbohydrates (g)	Fiber (g)	Sodium (mg)
1	534	11	36.2	79	46.4	9.4	306

Balkan Moussaka

24 14-oz. Servings

The flavors of the eastern Mediterranean are highlighted in our variation on the classic lasagna. This tour de force needs only a simple green salad as an accompaniment.

Equipment:	4 half-size insert pans, 4-in. deep
Preparation Time:	2 hours
Baking Time:	50 minutes

Ingredients	Volume	Weight
Sauce		
Vegetable oil	¹/₂ cup	
Onions, chopped	2 qts.	2 lbs.
Mushrooms, sliced	5¹/₂ qts.	4 lbs. 8 oz.
Soy sauce	¹/₃ cup	
White wine, dry	1 cup	
Tomatoes, canned, with juice, crushed	1 #10 can (3 qts.)	6 lb. 6 oz.
Basil, fresh	¹/₃ cup	
or dried	2 Tbsp.	
Dill, fresh	¹/₃ cup	
or dried	2 Tbsp.	
Salt and black pepper to taste		
Vegetable oil	¹/₄ cup	
Zucchini or yellow summer squash, sliced in ¹/₄-in. rounds		9 lbs.
Garlic, minced or pressed	6 cloves or 2 Tbsp.	
Hungarian paprika, sweet	1 Tbsp.	
Feta cheese, grated	3 qts.	3 lbs.
Eggs, lightly beaten	18 lg., 4¹/₂ cups	2 lb. 4 oz.
Cottage cheese	1¹/₂ qts.	3 lbs.
Dill, fresh	1 Tbsp.	
or dried	1 tsp.	
Lasagna noodles, raw (noodles do not need to be precooked)		6 lbs.

(continued)

Procedure

1. Prepare the sauce. Sauté the onions in vegetable oil until the onions are translucent. Add the mushrooms, soy sauce, and wine. Simmer for a few minutes before adding the tomatoes, herbs, salt, and black pepper. Continue to simmer for an additional 15 minutes.
2. Sauté the zucchini or yellow squash in oil with garlic, paprika, and a sprinkle of salt until barely tender.
3. Combine 2 qts. of the feta cheese with the beaten eggs, cottage cheese, and dill. Reserve 1qt. of feta.
4. Preheat oven to 350°.
5. In four oiled pans, layer each pan in the following order:
   - 2 cups tomato–mushroom sauce
   - lasagna noodles
   - one-eighth of the squash or zucchini
   - lasagna noodles
   - 4½ cups feta–cottage cheese mixture
   - lasagna noodles
   - one-eighth of the squash or zucchini
   - lasagna noodles
   - 2 cups tomato sauce
   - 1 cup reserved feta
6. Bake at 350°, covered, for 40 minutes, and uncovered for 10 minutes until topping is golden and bubbly.
7. Cut each pan into 6 servings.

Servings	Calories	Protein (g)	Fat (g)	Cholesterol (mg)	Carbohydrates (g)	Fiber (g)	Sodium (mg)
1	587	30.7	29.1	295	51.5	5.4	1279

Fettucine Toscana

24 12-oz. Servings

Pasta topped with a creamy spinach sauce and cauliflower is both attractive and satisfying.

Equipment:	2½-gallon stockpot
Preparation and Cooking Time:	90 minutes

Ingredients	Volume	Weight
Bechamel Sauce (2 qts.)		
Butter	1 cup	½ lb.
White flour	1 cup	
Milk, warmed	1½ qts.	
Nutmeg, ground	½ tsp.	
Salt	1½ tsp.	
Black pepper	½ tsp.	
Dijon mustard	2 tsp.	
Vegetable or olive oil	¼ cup	
Onions, chopped	1¼ qts.	1 lb. 4 oz.
Thyme, dried	2 tsp.	
Bay leaves	4	
Spinach, stemmed, rinsed	2 10-oz. bags	1 lb. 4 oz.
Lemon juice, fresh	¼ cup	
Cauliflower, cut in florets	1 gal.	7 lbs. 4 oz.
Parmesan cheese, grated (optional)	2 qts.	2 lbs.
Fettucine		6 lbs.

Procedure

1. Prepare the bechamel sauce by first melting the butter in a heavy-bottomed pot. Whisk in the flour and simmer the roux at a low heat for 5–7 minutes, whisking

(continued)

frequently. Gradually add the warm milk, whisking as you pour. Turn up the heat to medium and continue to whisk until the roux and milk thicken into a white sauce. Stir in the salt, pepper, nutmeg, and mustard, insert a heat diffuser between the pot and the flame, and cook at a low heat for 20 minutes, stirring occasionally.

2. In a separate pot, sauté the onions, thyme, and bay leaves in oil until the onions are softened.
3. Add the spinach and cook, covered, on a low heat until the spinach wilts. Remove the bay leaves.
4. In a food processor or blender, purée the spinach and onions with the lemon juice.
5. Add to the bechamel sauce. Stir thoroughly.
6. Steam the cauliflower.
7. Serve each ¼-lb. portion of fettucine, topped with 3 oz. cauliflower, 4 oz. sauce, and 1 oz. Parmesan cheese, if desired.

Servings	Calories	Protein (g)	Fat (g)	Cholesterol (mg)	Carbohydrates (g)	Fiber (g)	Sodium (mg)
1	330	11.1	13.6	62	43.1	5.8	301

Lasagna Verdure

24 16-oz. Servings
48 8-oz. Servings

This lasagna is full of surprises: two sauces—one lusty, one creamy—layered with a medley of vegetables.

Equipment:	3 half-size insert pans, 4-in. deep
Preparation Time:	1½ hours
Baking Time:	50 minutes

Ingredients	Volume	Weight
Tomato Sauce (see Ziti with Chard's Simple Tomato Sauce, p. 251), double the recipe	2 gals.	
Bechamel Sauce (see Fettucine Toscana, p. 233)	2 qts.	
Carrots, sliced in ¼-in. rounds	1¾ qts.	2 lbs. 4 oz.
Zucchini (and/or yellow squash), sliced in ¼-in. rounds	1¾ qts.	2 lbs. 4 oz.
Broccoli, cut into florets, stems sliced into ¼-in. rounds		2 lbs. 8 oz.
Mushrooms, thickly sliced (if small, can be left whole)		2 lbs.
Parmesan cheese, grated	4½ qts.	4 lbs. 8 oz.
Mozzarella cheese, grated	1½ qts.	1 lb. 2 oz.
Lasagna noodles, raw (noodles do not need to be precooked)		4 lbs. 8 oz.

Procedure

1. If making the sauces from scratch, prepare them first. Let the tomato sauce simmer while preparing the other ingredients.
2. Steam or blanch each vegetable until just tender. Cool in four separate pans.
3. Combine the grated cheeses.

(continued)

4. Preheat the oven to 350°.
5. Lightly oil three pans and layer the lasagna in each pan in the following order:
    - 1 cup of tomato sauce
    - layer of uncooked noodles
    - 2 cups tomato sauce
    - 2²/₃ cups cheese
    - noodles
    - 1–1¹/₄ cups bechamel sauce
    - one-third of the carrots and zucchini
    - 2 cups tomato sauce
    - 2²/₃ cups cheese
    - noodles
    - 1–1¹/₄ cups bechamel sauce
    - one-third of the broccoli and mushrooms
    - noodles
    - 3 cups tomato sauce
    - 2²/₃ cups cheese
6. Bake, covered, at 350° for 50 minutes, and then uncovered for 10 minutes.
7. Cut each pan into 8 or 16 servings.

Note: Nutritional analysis calculated for 48 servings.

Servings	Calories	Protein (g)	Fat (g)	Cholesterol (mg)	Carbohydrates (g)	Fiber (g)	Sodium (mg)
1	475	29.7	19.2	80	47.2	3.4	1106

Pasta al Cavolfiore

24 12-oz. Servings

Creamy and comforting, this dish is elegant enough for any occasion.

Equipment:	3 half-size insert pans, 4-in. deep
Preparation Time:	1½ hours
Baking Time:	35 minutes

Ingredients	Volume	Weight
Cheese Sauce		
Butter	1½ cups	12 oz.
White flour	1½ cups	
Milk, heated	2 qts.	
Parmesan cheese, grated	2 cups	8 oz.
Nutmeg	2 tsp.	
Dijon mustard	4½ tsp.	
Salt and black pepper to taste		
Olive oil	¼ cup	
Garlic	4 cloves or 1 Tbsp.	1 oz.
Onions, chopped	2¼ qts.	2 lbs. 4 oz.
Basil, dried	3 Tbsp.	
Cauliflower	5 qts.	3 lbs. 12 oz.
Tomatoes, fresh or canned (drained), chopped or crushed	1½ qts.	2 lbs. 4 oz.
Pasta: medium shells, ziti, penne		3 lbs.
Mozzarella cheese, grated	2 qts.	1 lb. 8 oz.

Procedure

1. In 1-gallon saucepan melt the butter. Whisk in the flour and simmer, whisking continuously, for about 10 minutes. Gradually add the heated milk and continue whisking until the sauce thickens.

(continued)

2. Stir in the Parmesan until well melted.
3. Add the nutmeg, mustard, and salt and pepper to taste. Remove from heat.
4. Sauté the garlic, onions, and basil in oil until the onions are translucent.
5. Add the cauliflower and sauté until it is just tender.
6. Stir in the tomatoes and shut off the heat.
7. Bring a large pot of water to a boil for the pasta. Add the pasta. When the water returns to a boil, remove the pot from the heat and drain the pasta.
8. Preheat oven to 350°.
9. In a large mixing bowl combine the pasta, vegetables, cheese sauce, and mozzarella.
10. Oil three baking pans and distribute the casserole equally among the pans. Bake, covered, at 350° for 20 minutes. Uncover and bake an additional 10–15 minutes until heated through and golden.
11. Cut each pan into 8 servings.

Servings	Calories	Protein (g)	Fat (g)	Cholesterol (mg)	Carbohydrates (g)	Fiber (g)	Sodium (mg)
1	521	23.7	19.8	45	62.5	5.1	439

Pasta e Fagioli
(with Cooked Beans)

24 11½-oz. Servings

This traditional home-style dish is enhanced by herbs and nutritious greens.

Equipment:	2½-gallon stockpot
Preparation Time:	20 minutes
Cooking Time:	40 minutes

Ingredients	Volume	Weight
White beans (cannellini, navy, pea, great northern), cooked, drained	1 qt.	1 lb. 8 oz.
or dried, uncooked beans	1⅔ cups	10¼ oz.
Olive oil	½ cup	
Onions, chopped	2 qts.	2 lbs.
Carrots, sliced in half-moons	1½ qts.	2 lbs.
Celery, chopped	2 qts.	2 lbs.
Garlic, minced or pressed	10 cloves or 3 Tbsp.	
Plum tomatoes, canned, with juice, crushed	1 #10 can (3 qts.)	6 lbs. 6 oz.
Fennel seed, ground	2 tsp.	
Parsley, fresh, chopped	1 cup	1.3 oz.
Basil, fresh, chopped	½ cup	
or dried	2 Tbsp.	
Oregano (optional)	1 Tbsp.	
Zucchini, sliced in half-moons	1½ qts.	2 lbs.
Swiss chard, coarsely chopped, stems removed		1 lb.
or spinach		1 lb.
Salt and black pepper to taste		
Pasta, a chunky variety: ziti, spirals, or shells		4 lbs.
Parmesan cheese, grated (optional)		1 lb. 8 oz.

(continued)

Procedure

1. If using dried beans, soak 1⅔ cups of beans overnight in water to cover; or bring them to a boil, remove from heat, and let soak for 1–2 hours. After soaking, drain and cook the beans until tender in 2 qts. of water for 30–45 minutes. Avoid overcooking. Drain and set aside the cooked beans.
2. Sauté the onions in oil until the onions are translucent.
3. Add the carrots, celery, and garlic and sauté briskly, stirring often, for 5–10 minutes.
4. Add the tomatoes, cooked white beans, fennel seed, and herbs. Cover and bring to a simmer.
5. Add the zucchini and simmer for 20 minutes more, stirring frequently. Test the carrots for tenderness.
6. Mix in the chard or spinach, cook until the greens just wilt. Adjust salt and pepper.
7. Cook the pasta until it is al dente and drain.
8. Serve each 2½-oz. portion of pasta topped with 9 oz. bean stew and 1 oz. Parmesan cheese, if desired.

Servings	Calories	Protein (g)	Fat (g)	Cholesterol (mg)	Carbohydrates (g)	Fiber (g)	Sodium (mg)
1	270	9.7	6.2	0	46.2	4.2	229

Pasta Therese

24 12-oz. Servings

Well suited for hot weather menus, this straightforward, uncooked sauce highlights the fresh flavors of a few simple ingredients.

Equipment: 2½-gallon stockpot, 8-oz. ladle
Preparation Time: 45 minutes

Ingredients	Volume	Weight
Tomatoes, ripe, chopped	5½ qts.	8 lbs.
Garlic, minced or pressed	12 cloves or 3½ Tbsp.	
Mushrooms, sliced		3 lbs.
Basil, fresh, chopped	2 cups	
Olive oil	1½ cups	
Mozzarella cheese (fresh, if possible), cut in small cubes or grated	3 qts.	2 lbs. 4 oz.
Salt and black pepper to taste		
Pasta: linguine, spaghetti, or fettucine		6 lbs.
Parmesan cheese, grated (optional)	1½ qts.	1 lb. 8 oz.

Procedure

1. Combine all ingredients except the pasta and Parmesan cheese and allow to sit at room temperature for 1 hour before serving.
2. Cook pasta and drain.
3. Serve pasta immediately in warmed bowls and top with sauce and Parmesan cheese.

Servings	Calories	Protein (g)	Fat (g)	Cholesterol (mg)	Carbohydrates (g)	Fiber (g)	Sodium (mg)
1	425	15.4	25.5	71	35.2	3.0	182

Pasta Tutto Giardino

24 10-oz. Servings
Total Yield: 2 gals.

In this offering, vegetables from "the whole garden" are simmered with wine and herbs and combined with a cream sauce.

Equipment:	2½-gallon stainless steel stockpot
Preparation Time:	1 hour
Cooking Time:	1 hour

Ingredients	Volume	Weight
Onions, chopped	1 qt.	1 lb.
Garlic, pressed	8 cloves or 2 Tbsp.	
Carrots, diced	1 qt.	1 lb. 6 oz.
Olive oil	¼ cup	
Peppers, red or green, diced	1 qt.	1 lb.
Mushrooms, sliced	1¼ qts.	1 lb.
Zucchini or yellow squash, diced	1½ qts.	2 lbs.
White wine, dry	2 cups	
Marjoram, fresh, chopped	2 Tbsp.	
or dried	1 Tbsp.	
Basil, fresh, chopped	¼ cup	
or dried	2 Tbsp.	
Oregano, dried	1 tsp.	
Salt and black pepper to taste		

White Sauce

Butter	¾ cup	
White flour	1 cup	
Milk, heated	1½ qts.	
Peas, frozen or fresh		2 lbs. 8 oz.
Tomatoes, fresh, chopped	1 qt.	1 lb. 8 oz.
Lemon juice, fresh	2 Tbsp.	
Linguine or spaghetti		6 lbs.
Parmesan cheese, grated (optional)	1½ qts.	1 lb. 8 oz.

Procedure

1. Sauté the onions, garlic, and carrots in the stockpot with the olive oil until the onions are translucent.
2. Stir in the peppers, mushrooms, zucchini, wine, herbs, salt, and pepper and simmer, covered, until the vegetables are just tender.
3. Meanwhile, in the saucepan, prepare a thick white sauce with the butter, flour, and milk. Melt the butter and whisk in the flour, gradually adding milk and stirring continuously until the sauce thickens.
4. When the white sauce is cooked, add the peas to the other vegetables, increase the heat to medium, and cook for 5 minutes until the peas are bright green.
5. Add the white sauce and tomatoes to the cooked vegetables and simmer for about 2 minutes. Add the lemon juice and more salt and pepper, to taste.
6. Cook the pasta al dente and drain.
7. Ladle 1¼ cups of the sauce over ¼ lb. of pasta per serving and top with ¼ cup Parmesan cheese, if desired.

Servings	Calories	Protein (g)	Fat (g)	Cholesterol (mg)	Carbohydrates (g)	Fiber (g)	Sodium (mg)
1	366	11.6	11.3	57	50.3	6.1	161

Pasta

Pasta with Beans and Greens

24 12-oz. Servings

This pasta dish is hearty, rustic, and healthful.

Equipment:	2½-gallon stockpot
Preparation and Cooking Time:	45 minutes with cooked beans; 1 hour and 45 minutes with dried, uncooked beans

Ingredients	Volume	Weight
White beans (cannellini, Great Northern), dried, uncooked	1¼ qts.	2 lbs.
or canned, drained	3 qts. (1 #10 can)	4 lbs. 6 oz.
Pasta, a chunky variety: fusilli, penne, or orecchietti		6 lbs.
Olive oil	½ cup	
Onions, chopped	2¼ qts.	2 lbs. 4 oz.
Garlic, minced or pressed	10 med. cloves or 3 Tbsp.	
Swiss chard, escarole, or leafy endive, shredded		3 lbs.
Salt and black pepper to taste		
Italian plum tomatoes, canned, with juice	2¼ qts.	4 lbs. 8 oz.
Lemon juice, fresh	¼–½ cup	
Pecorino Romano, or Parmesan cheese, grated	1½ qts.	1 lb. 8 oz.

Procedure

1. If cooking dried beans, soak the beans overnight in water to cover; or bring the beans and water to a boil, remove from the heat, and let the beans soak for 1–2 hours. After soaking, drain and cook the beans until tender in 1–2 gallons of water to cover for 30–45 minutes. Avoid overcooking. Drain. If using precooked beans, set aside.
2. Bring a large pot of water to a boil for cooking the pasta.
3. While the pasta water heats, in another stockpot, sauté the onions and garlic in oil, until the onions are translucent.
4. Add the shredded greens and salt and pepper and cook for about 5 minutes or until the vegetable is bright green and reduced by half.
5. Begin cooking the pasta.
6. Crush the tomatoes. Add the tomatoes, their juice, and the cooked beans to the onion–greens mixture.
7. Simmer the sauce for 10 minutes, adding the lemon juice to the sauce right before draining the pasta.
8. Serve 9 oz. of the sauce over 1/4 lb. of pasta topped with 1 oz. pecorino Romano or Parmesan cheese.

Variation

Canned tuna can be added.

Servings	Calories	Protein (g)	Fat (g)	Cholesterol (mg)	Carbohydrates (g)	Fiber (g)	Sodium (mg)
1	492	27.3	14.8	22	63.9	10.4	681

Pasta

Pasta with Spinach and Ricotta

24 10-oz. Servings

Heat this delicately seasoned sauce carefully to retain its smooth, creamy texture.

Equipment:	2-gallon pot
Preparation Time:	45 minutes
Cooking Time:	45 minutes

Ingredients	Volume	Weight
Sauce		
Olive oil	¼ cup	
Onions, chopped	1½ qts.	1 lb. 8 oz.
Garlic, pressed	9 cloves or 3 Tbsp.	
Spinach, raw, large stems removed, rinsed	3 10-oz. bags	1 lb. 14 oz.
or frozen, thawed		1 lb.
Ricotta cheese	2 qts. plus 1 cup	4 lbs. 8 oz.
Lemon juice, fresh	2 Tbsp.	
Basil, fresh	3 Tbsp.	
or dried	1 Tbsp.	
Parsley, fresh, chopped	1 qt.	5 oz.
Nutmeg, ground	2 tsp.	
Black pepper	2 tsp.	
Salt	1 Tbsp.	
Pasta: linguine, spaghetti, or fettucine		6 lbs.
Toppings		
Parmesan cheese, grated (optional)	2 qts.	2 lbs.
Tomatoes, fresh, chopped (optional)	2 qts.	3 lbs.

Procedure

1. Sauté the onions and garlic in oil until the onions are translucent.
2. Rinse the spinach and add it while still damp to the onions, or add slightly thawed frozen spinach to onions. Cover the pot and heat until the fresh spinach is wilted but still bright green; heat frozen spinach to soften.
3. Purée the onion–spinach mixture with the other sauce ingredients in a food processor.
4. Return sauce to a pot and keep warm in a double boiler or by using a heat diffuser on low heat.
5. Cook and drain pasta.
6. Serve ¼ lb. of pasta in a warm bowl, topped with 6 oz. sauce, 1 oz. Parmesan cheese, and 1½ oz. chopped tomatoes, if desired.

Servings	Calories	Protein (g)	Fat (g)	Cholesterol (mg)	Carbohydrates (g)	Fiber (g)	Sodium (mg)
1	313	16.5	11.1	64	37.4	2.7	440

Pasta

Spinach Lasagna Putanesca

24 16-oz. Servings
48 8-oz. Servings
Sauce Yield: 6½ qts.

A zesty, spicy sauce enlivens this lush lasagna.

Equipment:	4 half-size insert pans, 4-in. deep
Preparation Time:	2 hours
Baking Time:	1 hour

Ingredients	Volume	Weight
Sauce		
Olive oil	¼ cup	
Onions, chopped	2 qts.	2 lbs.
Garlic, minced or pressed	7 med. cloves or 2 Tbsp.	
Peppers, green and/or red, chopped	1 qt.	1 lb.
Red pepper flakes	2 tsp.	
Tomatoes, canned, with juice, chopped	4¾ qts.	9 lbs. 8 oz.
Tomato paste (optional)	1 cup	
Capers		2 oz.
Calamata olives (p. 469), pitted, chopped	½ cup	3 oz.
Black pepper to taste		
Filling		
Spinach, stemmed, rinsed	4 10-oz. bags	2 lbs. 8 oz.
Cottage cheese	1¼ qts.	2 lbs. 8 oz.
Ricotta cheese	3 qts.	6 lbs.
Eggs, beaten	6 lg. or 1½ cups	12 oz.
Bread crumbs	1 qt.	1 lb.
Fennel seed, ground	2 Tbsp.	
Mozzarella cheese, grated	1 gal.	3 lbs.
Parmesan cheese, grated	2½ qts.	2 lbs. 8 oz.
Lasagna noodles, raw (noodles do not need to be precooked)		6 lbs.

Procedure

1. Sauté the onions and garlic in olive oil until the onions are translucent.
2. Add the peppers and the pepper flakes and continue to sauté until the peppers begin to soften.
3. Add the tomatoes, tomato paste, capers, olives, and black pepper. Simmer the sauce, uncovered, for at least 1 hour.
4. Cook the spinach in a small amount of water until it wilts but is still bright green. Drain and chop.
5. In a large bowl, combine the chopped spinach with the cottage and ricotta cheeses, eggs, bread crumbs, and fennel.
6. Preheat oven to 350°.
7. Assemble the lasagna per pan in the following order:
   - thin layer of sauce
   - layer of uncooked noodles
   - 3 cups filling
   - 2 cups sauce
   - 2 cups grated mozzarella
   - layer of uncooked noodles
   - 3 cups filling
   - 2 cups sauce
   - 2 cups grated mozzarella
   - final layer of noodles
   - 2 cups sauce
   - 2½ cups Parmesan cheese
8. Bake, covered, at 350° for 45 minutes. Uncover and bake for 15 minutes, until golden. Remove from the oven and allow an additional 15 minutes for the lasagna to set up.
9. Cut each pan into 6 or 12 servings.

Note: Nutritional analysis calculated for 48 servings.

Servings	Calories	Protein (g)	Fat (g)	Cholesterol (mg)	Carbohydrates (g)	Fiber (g)	Sodium (mg)
1	496	34.3	21.9	116	40.6	2	1081

Pasta

Very Fresh Tomato-Basil Sauce

24 8-oz. Servings

This fragrant sauce is quickly and easily prepared with summer ingredients.

Equipment: 2½-gallon stockpot
Preparation Time: 30 minutes

Ingredients	Volume	Weight
Spanish or red onions, coarsely chopped	2 cups	8 oz.
Garlic cloves, coarsely chopped	½ cup	4 oz.
Tomatoes, ripe, quartered	2 gals.	12 lbs.
Olive oil	1 cup	
Basil leaves, fresh, lightly packed	1 qt.	
Salt and black pepper to taste		
Pasta		6 lbs.
Parmesan cheese, grated	3 cups	12 oz.

Procedure

1. In a blender or food processor, purée in batches the onions, garlic, tomatoes, and olive oil.
2. Chop the basil and add it to the sauce. Add salt and pepper.
3. Cook and drain the pasta.
4. Serve hot pasta in warmed bowls immediately. Top with the uncooked sauce and Parmesan cheese.

Servings	Calories	Protein (g)	Fat (g)	Cholesterol (mg)	Carbohydrates (g)	Fiber (g)	Sodium (mg)
1	369	13.9	15.3	11	46.0	4.2	294

Ziti with Chard

24 1-lb. Servings

The addition of garlic-sautéed greens makes this a nutritious and appealing pasta casserole.

Equipment:	4 half-size insert pans, 4-in. deep
Preparation Time:	2 hrs.
Baking Time:	50 minutes

Ingredients	Volume	Weight
Prepared tomato sauce	1 gal.	
or		

Simple Tomato Sauce

Olive oil	¼ cup	
Onions, chopped	1¼ qts.	1 lb. 4 oz.
Garlic, pressed	4 cloves or 1 Tbsp.	
Bay leaves	4	
Basil, dried	2½ Tbsp.	
Thyme, dried	1½ tsp.	
Tomatoes, canned, with juice, crushed	4¾ qts.	9 lbs. 9 oz.
Ziti or penne noodles		2 lbs.
Chard, kale, or spinach, rinsed, stemmed, chopped		5 lbs. 5 oz.
Olive oil	⅓ cup	
Garlic, pressed	7 cloves or 2 Tbsp.	
Eggs, lightly beaten	8 lg. or 2 cups	1 lb.
Ricotta cheese	2 qts.	4 lbs.
Mozzarella cheese, grated	2 qts.	1 lb. 8 oz.
Parmesan cheese, grated	2 qts.	2 lbs.

(continued)

Procedure

1. If making tomato sauce from scratch, prepare as follows: sauté the onions and garlic in olive oil until the onions are translucent. Add the herbs and tomatoes, and simmer for 1 hour, stirring occasionally.
2. Cook the pasta until barely al dente. Drain.
3. Mix pasta with a little sauce or oil to prevent clumping.
4. Sauté the greens with the olive oil and garlic until tender.
5. Transfer to a bowl and mix with the eggs and ricotta.
6. In a separate container, combine the mozzarella and Parmesan cheeses.
7. Preheat oven to 350°.
8. Lightly oil four pans, dividing the ingredients between the pans in the following order:
   - Sauce
   - Pasta
   - Greens and ricotta
   - Mozzarella and Parmesan cheeses
   - Repeat the layers
9. Bake at 350° for 40 minutes, covered, and for 10 minutes, uncovered. The top will be crusty and golden.
10. Cut each pan into 6 servings.

Servings	Calories	Protein (g)	Fat (g)	Cholesterol (mg)	Carbohydrates (g)	Fiber (g)	Sodium (mg)
1	650	43.4	31.0	158	50.5	4.3	1254

SAUCES AND SALSAS

Sauces and salsas enhance and enliven foods to create a sum that transcends each of its parts. Caribbean Black Beans, tasty in its own right, is given a decided lift by a topping of Mango Salsa. Salsas or sauces can also dress up a presentation; grilled fish looks and tastes better with a dollop of Cilantro Pesto. We offer four pestos in addition to the more familiar Pesto Genovese. These concentrated seasonings are useful in adding rich, fresh herb flavors to an array of simply prepared foods.

This section also includes four highly flavored sauces that are especially low in fat: Asian Marinade, Citrus Salsa, Hot Sauce, and Mango Salsa.

Use these recipes to top a wide range of dishes: steamed or raw vegetables, grains, beans, fish, pasta, and filled tortillas or crepes. We hope the menu suggestions we've included will warm up your imagination and that you'll find many creative uses for these salsas and sauces.

Aioli

Yields: 1 qt.

This almost instant topping is delicious on steamed vegetables, especially potatoes, carrots, broccoli, and cauliflower. Enhance simple baked fish with a dollop per serving or use as a dipping sauce for whole cooked artichokes.

Preparation Time: 1 minute

Ingredients	Volume	Weight
Mayonnaise, commercial	1 qt.	
Olive oil	1/4 cup	
Garlic, pressed	10 cloves or 3 Tbsp.	
Black pepper to taste		

Procedure

1. In a small skillet, gently sauté the garlic in olive oil on low heat for 1 minute.
2. In a mixing bowl, combine all the ingredients.
3. Refrigerate until ready to serve.

Note: Aioli will keep about 1 week when tightly covered and refrigerated.

Servings	Calories	Protein (g)	Fat (g)	Cholesterol (mg)	Carbohydrates (g)	Fiber (g)	Sodium (mg)
1	128	0.3	11.2	7	7.3	0	202

Asian Marinade

Yields: 3½ cups

After years of creating many different versions, we think this is the best marinade for tofu or tempeh and a flavorful sauce for steamed or sautéed vegetables and grilled or baked fish.

Equipment:	small nonreactive saucepan
Preparation Time:	5 minutes
Cooking Time:	10 minutes

Ingredients	Volume	Weight
Ginger root, fresh, 3-in.-long piece, cut into thin slices		2.5 oz.
Soy sauce	1½ cups	
Dry sherry	1½ cups	
Brown sugar or honey	6 Tbsp.	
Chinese rice vinegar (p. 469)	¾ cup	

Procedure

1. Combine everything in a small saucepan and bring to a boil. Reduce heat to a simmer and cook for 1 minute.
2. Cool for 10 minutes; then strain and discard the ginger slices.

Note: Kept covered and refrigerated, this marinade will keep indefinitely.
Note: Four ounces of marinade will season six 6-oz. fish steaks.

Servings	Calories	Protein (g)	Fat (g)	Cholesterol (mg)	Carbohydrates (g)	Fiber (g)	Sodium (mg)
1	28	0.7	0	0	4.3	0	697

Avocado Salsa

Yields: 2 qts.

This array of flavorful ingredients adds color and zest to Mexican, Caribbean, or African-style bean dishes, burritos, and enchiladas.

Preparation Time: 30 minutes

Ingredients	Volume	Weight
Avocados, peeled, chopped	4 sm.	1 lb. 4 oz.
Lime juice, fresh	1 cup	
Tomatoes, fresh, diced	1 qt.	1 lb. 8 oz.
Cucumbers, peeled, seeded, diced	3 cups	¾ lb.
Mint, fresh, chopped (optional)	3 Tbsp.	
or dried	1 tsp.	
Cilantro, fresh, chopped	½ cup	
Chili peppers, minced	2 sm.,	1 oz.
	1½ Tbsp.	
Honey (optional)	1 Tbsp.	
Salt to taste		

Procedure

1. In a blender or food processor, purée the avocados with the lime juice.
2. Pour it over the remaining ingredients and combine. Serve at room temperature or chilled.

Note: Avocado Salsa will keep for about 2 days when tightly covered and refrigerated.

Servings	Calories	Protein (g)	Fat (g)	Cholesterol (mg)	Carbohydrates (g)	Fiber (g)	Sodium (mg)
1	18	0.3	1.4	0	1.7	0.7	5

Cilantro Pesto

Yields: 3 cups

Here a lively blend of flavors creates an interesting pita filling combined with sliced seitan (p. 472), avocado, and tomato. Toss this pesto with pasta or vegetables to create exotic side dishes for Mexican, Indian, or Caribbean menus.

Preparation Time: 20 minutes

Ingredients	Volume	Weight
Almonds, whole	1½ cups	7 oz.
Cilantro, fresh, loosely packed leaves	1 qt.	2 oz.
Parsley, fresh, loosely packed leaves	1 qt.	1.5 oz.
Chili peppers, fresh, coarsely chopped (seeded if very hot)	3–4 sm.	2 oz.
Garlic, coarsely chopped	8 cloves or 2½ Tbsp.	
Lime juice, fresh	½ cup	
Vegetable oil	1 cup	

Salt and black pepper, to taste

Procedure

1. Spread the almonds on a baking sheet and toast lightly in a 350° oven for 5–10 minutes. In a food processor, coarsely chop the almonds.
2. Process the almonds with the rest of the ingredients until fairly smooth in a food processor.
3. Add salt and pepper.
4. Serve at room temperature.

Note: Cilantro Pesto will keep about 4 days when tightly covered and refrigerated.

Servings	Calories	Protein (g)	Fat (g)	Cholesterol (mg)	Carbohydrates (g)	Fiber (g)	Sodium (mg)
1	138	1.9	13.8	0	3.0	1.2	11

Citrus Salsa

Yields: 3 qts.

These refreshing fruit flavors combine especially well with spicy red or black beans. Try substituting orange sections for the pineapple to create a more dominant citrus taste.

Preparation Time: 20 minutes
Sitting Time: 30 minutes

Ingredients	Volume	Weight
Tomatoes, fresh, chopped	1½ qts.	2 lbs. 4 oz.
Peppers, red, chopped	1 qt.	1 lb.
Chili peppers, minced	3–4 sm.	2 oz.
or Tabasco sauce to taste		
Garlic, pressed	4 cloves or 1 Tbsp.	
Salt	½ tsp.	
Lime or lemon juice, fresh	½–1 cup	
Cilantro, fresh, chopped	½ cup	
Pineapple chunks, canned, unsweetened, with juice	1 qt.	2 lbs. 8 oz.

Procedure

1. Combine all the ingredients. Refrigerate and allow the flavors to mingle and intensify for at least 30 minutes.

Note: Citrus Salsa will keep for about 2 days when tightly covered and refrigerated.

Servings	Calories	Protein (g)	Fat (g)	Cholesterol (mg)	Carbohydrates (g)	Fiber (g)	Sodium (mg)
1	12	0.2	0.1	0	2.9	0.3	14

Dill Pesto

Yields: 1 qt.

Try tossing this delightful pesto with steamed or Roasted Vegetables (p. 340) and serve with crackers and Brie or Havarti cheese. Dill Pesto is also an excellent topping for spinach pasta and grilled or baked fish.

Preparation Time: 15 minutes

Ingredients	Volume	Weight
Dill, fresh, leaves loosely packed	1 qt.	3 oz.
Scallions, green and white, coarsely chopped	2 cups	2 oz.
Cheddar cheese, sharp, grated	2 cups	6 oz.
Walnuts, coarsely chopped	2 cups	8 oz.
Vegetable oil	1 cup	
Salt and black pepper to taste		

Procedure

1. Purée the ingredients, in batches, in a food processor. Whisk in 1/2 cup of water if the purée is too thick.

Note: Dill Pesto will keep for about 4 days when tightly covered and refrigerated.

Servings	Calories	Protein (g)	Fat (g)	Cholesterol (mg)	Carbohydrates (g)	Fiber (g)	Sodium (mg)
1	137	2.9	13.4	6	3.0	0.4	45

Fennel Mustard Sauce

Yields: 1 qt.

Simply pour this tempting Mediterranean-style sauce over fish fillets or seafood, cover the pan, and bake. Use it to dress up steamed asparagus or other vegetables.

Preparation Time: 8 minutes

Ingredients	Volume	Weight
Dijon mustard	1¾ cups	
Lemon juice, fresh	¾ cup	
Fennel seed, ground	2 Tbsp.	
Tarragon, dried	1 Tbsp.	
Honey	⅓ cup	
Olive oil	1¾ cups	
Salt and black pepper to taste		

Procedure

1. Whisk together all the ingredients except the olive oil, salt, and pepper.
2. Slowly drizzle in the oil, whisking all the while to form a thick sauce. Add salt and pepper to taste.

Note: Kept covered and refrigerated, this sauce will keep indefinitely.

Servings	Calories	Protein (g)	Fat (g)	Cholesterol (mg)	Carbohydrates (g)	Fiber (g)	Sodium (mg)
1	132	0.7	13.0	0	4.4	0	161

Hazelnut Pesto

Yields: 3 cups or 1 lb. 8 oz.

For an elegant side dish, toss with a small-shaped pasta or with steamed vegetables. Use as a spread for biscuits or French bread. To fill 12 lbs. of flounder fillets, triple the yield and use 1 oz. of pesto per flounder roll.

Preparation Time: 30 minutes

Ingredients	Volume	Weight
Hazelnuts, whole, toasted, skinned	2 cups	10 oz.
Parsley leaves, loosely packed	1¼ qts.	6 oz.
Thyme, fresh or dried	2 Tbsp.	
Lemon juice, fresh	¼ cup	
Lemon peel, grated	2 tsp.	
Vegetable oil	1 cup	
Salt and black pepper to taste		

Procedure

1. Bake the hazelnuts at 325° for 10 minutes. Cool.
2. With a small towel rub off as much of the skins as possible. In a food processor, coarsely chop the hazelnuts.
3. In batches, process all the ingredients in a food processor.
4. Serve at room temperature.

Note: Hazelnut Pesto will keep for about 2 days when tightly covered and refrigerated.

Servings	Calories	Protein (g)	Fat (g)	Cholesterol (mg)	Carbohydrates (g)	Fiber (g)	Sodium (mg)
1	163	1.8	16.9	0	2.8	1.0	12

Hot Sauce

Yields: 1 gallon

Our favorite, easy Hot Sauce is a vivid topping for Pepper Cheese Enchiladas (p. 288), Chilaquile Casserole (p. 133), Creole Beans and Rice (p. 201), Caribbean Black Beans (p. 197), or Refritos (p. 216).

Preparation Time: 10 minutes
Cooking Time: 30 minutes

Ingredients	Volume	Weight
Olive oil	¼ cup	
Onions, chopped	1 qt.	1 lb.
Peppers, green, chopped	1 qt.	1 lb.
Chili peppers, minced (more to taste)	4 sm.	2 oz.
Coriander seeds, ground	2 Tbsp.	
Cumin, ground	2 Tbsp.	
Tomatoes, canned, undrained	3 qts. (1# 10 can)	6 lbs. 6 oz.
Salt to taste		

Procedure

1. Sauté the onions, peppers, and chilies in oil for 15 minutes, stirring frequently.
2. Add the spices and sauté for a few minutes more.
3. In a blender, purée the tomatoes with the onion–spice mixture.
4. Reheat. Salt to taste.

Note: Hot Sauce will keep for about 2 days when tightly covered and refrigerated.

Servings	Calories	Protein (g)	Fat (g)	Cholesterol (mg)	Carbohydrates (g)	Fiber (g)	Sodium (mg)
1	24	0.7	1.1	0	3.3	0.2	63

Mango Salsa

Yield: 2 qts.

The lush flavor of mangos harmonizes with lime, cilantro, and peppers. Used as a topping, Mango Salsa adds exquisite color to Caribbean Black Beans (p. 197) and an interesting twist to Groundnut Stew (p. 363).

Preparation Time: 30 minutes

Ingredients	Volume	Weight
Mangoes, ripe, peeled, chopped	5 lg.	
Cucumber, peeled, seeded, diced	2 cups	10 oz.
Tomatoes, fresh, diced	1 qt.	1 lb. 8 oz.
Garlic, pressed	3 cloves or 1 Tbsp.	
Lime juice, fresh	1/3 cup	3 oz.
Chili peppers, fresh, minced *or* Tabasco, to taste	1–2 sm.	1 oz.
Cilantro, fresh, chopped	1/4 cup	.5 oz.
Salt (optional)	dash	

Procedure

1. Combine all the ingredients and allow flavors to mingle for at least 20 minutes.
2. Serve at room temperature or chilled.

Note: Mango Salsa will keep for about 2 days when tightly covered and refrigerated.

Servings	Calories	Protein (g)	Fat (g)	Cholesterol (mg)	Carbohydrates (g)	Fiber (g)	Sodium (mg)
1	29	0.5	0.2	0	7.3	0.9	4

Peanut Sauce

Yields: 6 cups
24 2-oz. Servings

One very popular Moosewood entrée is simply steamed broccoli, cabbage, and carrots, served over rice, topped with this tasty peanut sauce and garnished with hard-boiled eggs. We also stuff pita bread with Seasoned Tofu (p. 220), grated carrots, fresh spinach, and Peanut Sauce for a marvelous Indonesian-style sandwich. Use leftovers as the base for Groundnut Stew (p. 363) or West African Peanut Soup (p. 65).

Equipment:	saucepan
Preparation and Cooking Time:	25 minutes

Ingredients	Volume	Weight
Oil, preferably peanut or vegetable	¼ cup	
Onions, chopped	3 cups	¾ lb.
Cayenne	¼ tsp. (more to taste)	
Ginger, ground	½ tsp.	
Tomato juice	1½ cups	
Apple or apricot juice	¾ cup	
Lemon juice, fresh, or white vinegar	2 Tbsp.	
Peanut butter	2 cups	
Salt to taste		
Honey or brown sugar (optional)	2 Tbsp.	
or banana, ripe, mashed (optional)	1	

Procedure

1. Sauté the onions in oil until the onions are translucent.
2. Mix in the cayenne and ginger and sauté for 5 minutes more.
3. Add the juices and simmer for 10 minutes.

(continued)

4. Stir in the peanut butter and salt and simmer on a heat diffuser until ready to serve.
5. For a sweeter flavor add the honey or banana and stir thoroughly. If the sauce becomes too thick, add more juices while it simmers.

Note: Peanut Sauce will keep for about 1 week when tightly covered and refrigerated.

Servings	Calories	Protein (g)	Fat (g)	Cholesterol (mg)	Carbohydrates (g)	Fiber (g)	Sodium (mg)
1	144	4.9	11.9	0	6.7	1.4	142

Pesto Genovese

Yields: 3 cups

The preparation of this brilliant classic becomes effortless when using a food processor or blender. Its haunting flavor is best served as a dollop ladled over hot pasta topped with chopped tomatoes and extra Parmesan cheese. Use it as a delicious spread on toasted Italian garlic bread or add a spoonful to a serving of traditional minestrone soup. We prepare summery salad plates by tossing Pesto Genovese with potatoes, fresh green beans, sun-dried tomatoes, and mozzarella cheese.

Preparation Time: 10 minutes

Ingredients	Volume	Weight
Basil, fresh leaves, loosely packed	1½ qts.	9 oz.
Almonds or pine nuts, toasted	⅔ cup	3 oz.
Parmesan cheese, grated	1 cup	4 oz.
Garlic, pressed	6 cloves or 2 Tbsp.	
Olive oil	1 cup	

Salt and black pepper to taste

Procedure

1. In the bowl of a food processor or in a blender, process all the ingredients except the oil until well chopped.
2. Add the oil in a thin stream to form a smooth paste. Add salt and pepper to taste.

Note: This sauce may be kept for several weeks refrigerated in an airtight jar. Cover the sauce with a thin layer of olive oil or lay a sheet of plastic wrap over the top surface to prevent it from discoloring.

To freeze, prepare without the cheese, freeze in ice cube trays, and store the frozen squares in plastic bags in the freezer. Thaw and reblend with the cheese.

Servings	Calories	Protein (g)	Fat (g)	Cholesterol (mg)	Carbohydrates (g)	Fiber (g)	Sodium (mg)
1	130	3.0	12.8	4	1.7	0.4	96

Shallot–Herb Butter

24 1-oz. Servings

This creamy, tangy sauce is especially good on baked salmon or other fish. Create a variety of toppings for steamed vegetables by substituting tarragon, dill, thyme, or marjoram for the basil.

Preparation Time: 20 minutes
   Cooking Time: 20 minutes

Ingredients	Volume	Weight
Shallots or leeks (white part of leeks), minced	1 cup	5 oz.
Vinegar: cider, wine, or herb	1/3 cup	
Water	3/4 cup	
Butter, cut in 1/2-in. pieces, softened		3 lbs.
Basil, fresh, chopped	1/3 cup	
or dried	2 Tbsp.	
Parsley, fresh, chopped	2/3 cup	
Scallion greens or chives, finely chopped	1/4 cup	
Lemon juice, fresh	1/2 cup	
Salt and black pepper to taste		

Procedure

1. Simmer the shallots or leeks, vinegar, and water in a stainless steel saucepan, until the volume is reduced by half, or most of the liquid has evaporated, about 10–15 minutes. Remove from heat.
2. Whisk the butter into the shallots or leeks, a few pieces at a time. The butter should be soft and creamy, with a consistency like mayonnaise, but not melted.
3. When the sauce is smooth, stir in the herbs, lemon juice, salt, and pepper.

Note: Shallot–Herb Butter will keep for about 1 week when tightly covered and refrigerated.

Servings	Calories	Protein (g)	Fat (g)	Cholesterol (mg)	Carbohydrates (g)	Fiber (g)	Sodium (mg)
1	413	0.7	46.0	124	1.8	0.2	478

Spinach Pesto

Yields: 1 qt.

When fresh basil is unavailable, Spinach Pesto is more than a substitute; our customers enjoy it year round. Olive oil infused with garlic and dried basil is the key to this topping. In addition to serving this pesto with pasta, try it with steamed green beans and potatoes, or in a pita sandwich with chopped tomatoes, greens, and fresh mozzerella cheese.

Equipment: food processor
Preparation Time: 20–30 minutes

Ingredients	Volume	Weight
Basil, dried	²/₃ cup	
Olive oil	½ cup	
Spinach, fresh, stemmed, rinsed	2 10-oz. bags	1 lb. 4 oz.
Vegetable oil	½ cup	
Lemon juice, fresh	½ cup	
Almonds, whole	1 cup	
Parmesan cheese, grated	1½ cups	6 oz.
Garlic, minced or pressed	6 cloves or 2 Tbsp.	
Parsley, fresh, chopped	½ cup	
Salt, to taste		

Procedure

1. If possible, soak the basil in the olive oil for ½ hour before processing.
2. Coarsely chop the almonds.
3. In the bowl of a food processor, purée all the ingredients in batches until smooth. Add salt to taste.

Note: Spinach Pesto will keep for about 2 days when tightly covered and refrigerated.

Servings	Calories	Protein (g)	Fat (g)	Cholesterol (mg)	Carbohydrates (g)	Fiber (g)	Sodium (mg)
1	122	4.1	11.2	5	2.5	1.1	134

Taratour Sauce

Yields: 1¹/₂ qts.
24 ¹/₄-cup servings

This quickly prepared sauce transforms baked or grilled fish into a Middle Eastern specialty. It can be used as an exciting topping for roasted potatoes or as a dip for artichokes and crudités. Serve at room temperature or chilled.

Preparation Time: 10 minutes

Ingredients	Volume	Weight
Almonds, whole, slightly toasted	2 cups	10 oz.
Bread crumbs	3 cups	6 oz.
Lemon juice, fresh	¹/₄ cup	
Dijon mustard	1¹/₂ tsp.	
Garlic, minced or pressed	6 cloves or 1¹/₂ Tbsp.	
Olive oil	1¹/₂ cups	
Water	2 cups	
Parsley, fresh, chopped	¹/₂ cup	
Chives, dill, or marjoram, fresh, chopped (use one or combination)	¹/₂ cup	
Salt and black pepper to taste		

Procedure

1. In the bowl of a food processor or blender, combine the almonds, bread crumbs, lemon juice, mustard, garlic, olive oil, and 1 cup of the water. If using a blender, chop the almonds before blending. Process or blend until smooth.
2. Add the parsley and remaining 1 cup of water and process or blend until smooth.
3. Stir in the herbs and salt and pepper to taste.

Note: Covered and refrigerated, this sauce will keep for up to 1 week.

Servings	Calories	Protein (g)	Fat (g)	Cholesterol (mg)	Carbohydrates (g)	Fiber (g)	Sodium (mg)
1	227	3.5	20.8	0	8.5	1.6	75

SAVORY PASTRIES

Savory pastries have an undeniable appeal, whether composed of humble tortillas or elegant, flaky filo pastry. Hearty and satisfying, pastries are a good introduction for less adventurous diners unfamiliar with vegetarian cuisine.

Portion sizes in this section are for ample dinner entrées. Smaller servings could be used for lunch, brunch, or starter courses. Labor-saving products such as frozen pie shells or puff pastry shells can be used in place of homemade pastry. Whole wheat and wheat-free pie shells, as well as whole wheat tortillas, are available through natural food suppliers.

Savory pastries are well paired with simple, lighter fare such as a green or other vegetable salad, a steamed vegetable, or appropriate side dishes. Note the suggestions listed on the recipes.

Filo Pastry Assembly

Procedure

For each 14 x 18 x 1-in. baking pan:

1. Butter the pan with a large pastry or paint brush.
2. Unfold a 1-lb. box of filo leaves and cover them with a damp cloth to prevent drying; 1 lb. of filo is needed per pan.
3. Lay 3 filo leaves, overlapped, across the width of a buttered baking pan, letting the edges drape over the sides of the pan. Brush the tops of the leaves with butter out to their edges.
4. Repeat with 3 more leaves finishing the bottom layer. Butter, and spoon half the filling onto the filo. Smooth and even out the filling with a rubber spatula. Fold any overhanging filo leaves over the filling.
5. For the top layers, lay down 6 layers, 3 leaves at a time, overlapping and buttering each layer from edge to edge, until the filo is used up. Tuck the overhanging filo leaves under the filo pastry. The bottom layers will use 6 leaves, and the top layers will use 18 leaves, for a total of 24 leaves.
6. Repeat this process for your second strudel, using the remaining filling and a second box of filo.

Note: If any excess leaves remain in the box, layer on top and butter.

Black Bean–Sweet Potato Burritos

24 (1 large each) 8-oz. Servings

This savory nondairy filling is brimming with vivid colors and tastes. For complete protein, serve on a bed of rice. Top with Mango Salsa (p. 264), Citrus Salsa (p. 259), or Hot Sauce (p. 263).

Equipment:	4 half-size insert pans, 4-in. deep
Preparation Time:	1 hour, after beans have cooked
Baking Time:	20 minutes

Ingredients	Volume	Weight
Black beans, dried	5¼ cups	2 lbs. 4 oz.
or cooked, drained	3 qts. (1 #10 can)	4 lbs. 8 oz.
Vegetable oil	½ cup	
Ginger root, fresh, grated	3 Tbsp.	
Garlic, minced	10 cloves or 3 Tbsp.	
Cayenne	¼–½ tsp.	
Onions, chopped	1½ qts.	1 lb. 8 oz.
Cumin, ground	2 Tbsp.	
Celery, chopped	2 cups	8 oz.
Green peppers, chopped	2 cups	8 oz.
Thyme, dried	2 tsp.	
Sweet potatoes, peeled, diced	3 qts.	6 lbs.
Orange juice concentrate	1 cup	
Orange peel, grated fine	2 tsp.	
Salt to taste		
Wheat tortillas, 8-in.	24	

Procedure

1. If using dried beans, soak in water to cover overnight; or bring to a boil, remove from heat, and let soak 1–2 hours. After soaking, drain the beans and cook until tender in 2–3 gallons of water for 30–45 minutes. Drain.

(continued)

2. Sauté the ginger and garlic in oil for 1 minute.
3. Add the cayenne, onions, and cumin and sauté until the onions are softened.
4. Stir in the celery, peppers, and thyme and sauté until tender.
5. In a separate pot, cook the diced sweet potatoes at a rapid boil, until they are tender but not overcooked.
6. Combine the well-drained beans and the cooked sweet potatoes with the vegetable mixture, the orange juice concentrate, and peel.
7. Salt to taste.
8. Preheat the oven to 350°.
9. Fill each tortilla with ¾ cup of the bean filling. Roll up and place, seam side down, in lightly oiled pans. Approximately 4–5 burritos fill each pan.
10. Bake, tightly covered, at 350° for 15–20 minutes.

Servings	Calories	Protein (g)	Fat (g)	Cholesterol (mg)	Carbohydrates (g)	Fiber (g)	Sodium (mg)
1	365	12.4	7.9	0	62.9	9.6	86

Cauliflower Tart

25 12-oz. Servings, 1/5 of a 10-in. pie

Here is an Italian pie lush with cheeses and cauliflower and seasoned with garlic, basil, and sun-dried tomatoes. Serve with steamed asparagus, green beans, or Easy Artichokes (p. 324).

Equipment:	10-in. pie plates
Preparation Time:	90 minutes if preparing pie crust; 45 minutes if using premade crusts
Baking Time:	60 minutes

Ingredients	Volume	Weight
Pie Crust, unbaked, (p. 290), 10-in.	5	
Olive oil	1/3 cup	
Onions, chopped	1 1/4 qts.	1 lb. 4 oz.
Garlic, pressed or minced	10 cloves or 3 Tbsp.	
Basil, dried	2 Tbsp.	
Cauliflower, cut into small florets		4 lbs.
Sun-dried tomatoes	1 1/2 cups	

Custard

Milk	2 qts.	
Eggs	36 lg. or 2 1/4 qts.	4 lbs. 8 oz.
White flour	5 Tbsp.	
Dijon mustard	1 1/2 Tbsp.	
Salt	1 Tbsp.	
Black pepper to taste		
Mozzarella cheese, grated	1 1/4 qts.	1 lb.
Parmesan cheese, grated, fresh	3 3/4 cups	1 lb.

Procedure

1. If making the pie crust from scratch, roll out and chill (p. 290).
2. Sauté the onions, garlic, and basil in oil until the onions are translucent.

(continued)

3. Add the cauliflower and continue to sauté until it is tender.
4. While the cauliflower cooks, soak the sun-dried tomatoes in an equal amount of boiling water for 10–15 minutes. Drain, chop, and add to the cauliflower.
5. Whisk together the custard ingredients.
6. Preheat the oven to 350°.
7. Assemble the pie in each crust in layers in the following order:
   - ½ cup custard
   - ½ cup mozzarella cheese
   - 4 cups cauliflower mixture
   - ½ cup mozzarella cheese
   - 3 cups custard
   - ¾ cup Parmesan cheese
8. Bake at 350° for about 1 hour, until the custard is set and nicely browned.

Servings	Calories	Protein (g)	Fat (g)	Cholesterol (mg)	Carbohydrates (g)	Fiber (g)	Sodium (mg)
1	678	32.9	41.8	461	44.2	5.0	1351

Cheese Borekas

24 6-oz. Servings

Here filo pastry is stuffed with an extravagant cheese filling and presented in an easy-to-serve triangle. Offset the richness of this entrée with a simple Artichoke Heart–Tomato Salad (p. 313) or tangy Marinated Vegetables (p. 333).

Equipment:	2 baking pans, 18 x 14 x 1 in.
Preparation Time:	75 minutes
Baking Time:	20 minutes

Ingredients	Volume	Weight
Filling		
Mozzarella cheese, grated	2¼ qts.	1 lb. 12 oz.
Feta cheese, grated	2½ qts.	10 oz.
Sharp Cheddar cheese, grated	2 qts.	1 lb. 8 oz.
Eggs, beaten	6 lg., 1½ cups	12 oz.
Parsley, fresh, chopped	3 cups	4 oz.
Scallions, chopped	2 cups	5 oz.
Black pepper to taste		
Filo pastry		2 lbs.
Butter, melted	1½ cups	12 oz.
Sesame seeds (optional)		

Procedure

1. Combine the filling ingredients.
2. Lay out three stacked sheets of filo with one of the short sides nearest to you. Fold the stack lengthwise so that the edges meet.
3. Butter the top surface of the filo and spread ½–¾ cup of filling down the middle, leaving 1-in. margins on the sides.
4. Preheat the oven to 350°.

(continued)

Savory Pastries

5. Fold the lower left corner of the filo up and over diagonally so that the bottom edge is aligned with the right side. Fold straight up and then to the left. Continue folding in this manner, as you would a flag, to make a triangular pastry.

6. Lightly butter or oil the baking pans. Lay the triangles in pans. Brush the top of the triangle with butter, sprinkle with sesame seeds, and bake at 350° for 20 minutes until puffy and golden.

Servings	Calories	Protein (g)	Fat (g)	Cholesterol (mg)	Carbohydrates (g)	Fiber (g)	Sodium (mg)
1	455	20.1	37.7	152	9.6	0.3	633

Feta–Spinach Pizza
24 10-oz. Servings

Here's a pizza that Zeus would have loved. Our flaky filo crust adds a new dimension to an Italian-American classic. Serve with a green salad and a cup of Tomato–Garlic Soup (p. 58) or Lebanese Vegetable Soup (p. 39); or in combination with other Mediterranean specialties such as Artichoke Heart–Tomato Salad (p. 313) and Tzatziki (p. 344).

Equipment:	2 baking pans, 15 x 21 x 1 in.
Preparation Time:	40 minutes
Baking Time:	30 minutes

Ingredients	Volume	Weight
Spinach, fresh, stemmed	5 10-oz. bags	3 lbs. 2 oz.
or frozen, thawed, drained		1 lb. 8 oz.
Scallions, chopped	2 cups	
Dill, fresh, chopped	¼ cup	
or dried	1½ Tbsp.	
Feta cheese, grated	1¾ qts.	1 lb. 12 oz.
Ricotta cheese	2 qts.	4 lbs.
Black pepper to taste		
Filo pastry		1 lb. box
Butter, melted	1½ cups	12 oz.
Tomatoes, fresh, thinly sliced		3 lbs. 8 oz.

Procedure

1. Cook the fresh spinach. Drain thoroughly and chop. If using frozen spinach, drain well.
2. Add the scallions, dill, feta, ricotta, and black pepper.
3. To assemble a filo pastry crust, lay six filo leaves on a buttered baking pan: three on the right side overlapped with three on the left side. Brush with butter. Repeat with two more layers of six leaves each. Brush butter between the layers and on

(continued)

the top layer. Fold any overhanging leaves into the pan to create a slightly raised crust around the perimeter of the pan.

4. Preheat the oven to 400°.
5. Divide the filling between the two pizzas, placing the sliced tomatoes as a top layer.
6. Bake in a 400° oven for 20 minutes until the filling is heated through and the crust is golden.
7. Cut each pan into 12 servings.

Servings	Calories	Protein (g)	Fat (g)	Cholesterol (mg)	Carbohydrates (g)	Fiber (g)	Sodium (mg)
1	272	16.0	17.5	53	14.5	2.3	535

Italian-Style Tofu Pizza

24 11-oz. Servings

Serve our delicious vegetarian version of an Italian sausage pizza with Roasted Egg-plant–Pepper Salad (p. 83) or Easy Artichokes (p. 324).

Equipment:	2 baking pans, 16 x 24 x 1 in.
Preparation Time:	30 minutes
Baking Time:	20 minutes

Ingredients	Volume	Weight
Tofu, pressed (p. 474), and crumbled or frozen, thawed, shredded		4 lbs. 8 oz. (unpressed and unfrozen)
Olive oil	½ cup	
Fennel seed, ground	¼ cup	
Garlic, minced or pressed	10 cloves or 3 Tbsp.	
Cayenne	¼ tsp.	
Soy sauce	⅓ cup	
Tomato paste	⅓ cup	
Oregano, dried	2 Tsp.	
Tomato sauce, prepared (or see Ziti with Chard, p. 251)	3¼ qts.	
Mozzarella cheese, grated	2 qts.	1 lb. 8 oz.
Parmesan cheese, grated	1 qt.	1 lb.
Pizza shells, prebaked (if frozen, thawed)	2 23 x 15 in.	

Procedure

1. Set aside the prepared tofu.
2. Sauté the garlic and fennel in olive oil for a couple of minutes.
3. Add the tofu and cook on a fairly high heat for 3–4 minutes.
4. Add the cayenne, soy sauce, tomato paste, and oregano. Stir well.
5. Add the tomato sauce. Remove from the heat and adjust the seasonings.

(continued)

6. Preheat the oven to 450°.
7. Divide the topping between the two pizzas; sprinkle with cheeses.
8. Bake at 450° for 15–20 minutes until heated through and bubbly.
9. Cut each pizza into 12 servings.

Note: Frozen tofu (p. 475) will yield a firmer, chewier product than the softer fresh tofu.

Servings	Calories	Protein (g)	Fat (g)	Cholesterol (mg)	Carbohydrates (g)	Fiber (g)	Sodium (mg)
1	382	22.3	17.4	31	36.3	1.8	1595

Mexican Seitan

24 10-oz. Servings

Seitan is a high-protein, low-fat alternative to meat and is especially well suited for soaking up the flavors of sauces, seasonings, and marinades. Mexican Seitan is a wonderful topping for split Cornbread (p. 333), rice, or tortillas and is a tasty filling in burritos or pita bread.

Equipment:	large skillet
Preparation and Cooking Time:	1 hour

Ingredients	Volume	Weight
Chili peppers, seeded, chopped	¼ cup	1 oz.
Onions, chopped	3 qts.	3 lbs.
Garlic, minced or pressed	10 med. cloves or 3 Tbsp.	
Olive oil	½ cup	
Bell peppers, red or green, chopped	3 qts.	3 lbs.
Cumin, ground	3 Tbsp.	
Coriander seed, ground	2 Tbsp.	
Seitan (p. 472), diced or grated		7 lbs. 8 oz.
Oregano, dried	2 Tbsp.	
Basil, dried	2 Tbsp.	
Soy sauce	¼ cup	
Tomatoes, canned, with juice	1½ qts. (½ of a #10 can)	3 lbs. 3 oz.
Corn, frozen		2 lbs. 8 oz.

Tabasco, soy sauce, or salt to taste

Procedure

1. Sauté the chilies, onions, and garlic in oil until the onions are translucent.
2. Add the peppers, cumin, and coriander seed and sauté briefly.

(continued)

3. Add the seitan, herbs, soy sauce, and tomatoes and simmer for 15 minutes.
4. Stir in the corn and adjust seasonings with more salt or soy sauce plus Tabasco, if needed.
5. Simmer for a final 10 minutes.

Servings	Calories	Protein (g)	Fat (g)	Cholesterol (mg)	Carbohydrates (g)	Fiber (g)	Sodium (mg)
1	260	8.4	8.4	0	42.3	2.9	240

Mu Shu Vegetables

24 Servings of 2 6-oz.
Filled "Pancakes"

This Chinese delicacy pairs crunchy sautéed vegetables and gingery tofu in a delicate wrapper. When we want to serve a stellar nondairy entrée, this is frequently our choice.

Equipment:	2 insert pans, 2-in. deep
Preparation Time:	30 minutes
Cooking Time:	stir-fry 30 minutes; baking, 20 minutes

Ingredients	Volume	Weight
Shiitake mushrooms, dried (p. 473)	3 cups	2.5 oz.
Vegetable oil	as needed	
Cabbage, shredded	2³/₄ qts.	2 lbs.
Peppers, green and/or red, thinly sliced	2 qts.	2 lbs.
Carrots, grated	2 qts.	2 lbs. 8 oz.
Onions, thinly sliced	2 qts.	2 lbs.
Ginger root, fresh, grated	¹/₃ cup	
Garlic, pressed	12 cloves or 3¹/₂ Tbsp.	
Mung bean sprouts	3 qts.	2 lbs.
Seasoned tofu, baked (p. 220), or commercial five-spice tofu, julienned		1 lb. 8 oz.
Soy sauce	¹/₂ cup	
Hoisin sauce (p. 471)	¹/₂ cup	
Chili paste with garlic (p. 469) (optional)	1 tsp.	
Wheat tortillas	48 8-in.	
Hoisin sauce	2 to 3 14-oz. jars	

Procedure

1. Cover the shiitake mushrooms with boiling water and set aside to soften; then drain and coarsely chop, removing stems if necessary.

(continued)

2. In a wok or large skillet, stir-fry the cabbage, peppers, and carrots separately in approximately 2 Tbsp. oil. They should be crisp and barely tender. Stir-fry the onions with the garlic and ginger. Briefly stir-fry the mung bean sprouts.
3. As each batch is completed, put into a large pot.
4. Mix together the hoisin sauce, soy sauce, and chili paste. Add to the vegetables with the tofu and shiitake mushrooms.
5. Empty the pot into a large colander placed over a large pot to collect the excess juices and keep the vegetables from becoming soggy. Reserve these juices. Season the vegetable mixture with additional salt or chili paste as desired.
6. Preheat the oven to 350°.
7. Place ¾ cup of the vegetable mixture in a horizontal line across the center of each tortilla. Roll up and place seam side down in a lightly oiled pan. Approximately 8–10 rolled pancakes fill a pan. Bake, tightly covered with foil, at 350° for 20 minutes.
8. Serve the "pancakes" on rice topped with a drizzle of hoisin sauce. We like to thin two 14-oz. jars of hoisin sauce with 1 cup of the reserved vegetable juices.

Note: Alternatively, serve the stir-fried vegetables Chinese-style—fresh from the wok with warmed pancakes (which can be steamed briefly in a vegetable steamer) and hoisin sauce. Diners spread a drizzle of sauce on each pancake, add vegetables and tofu, roll up the pancakes, and eat it like an egg roll.

Servings	Calories	Protein (g)	Fat (g)	Cholesterol (mg)	Carbohydrates (g)	Fiber (g)	Sodium (mg)
1	473	13.8	9.1	0	87.9	3.9	1297

Mushroom and Smoked Cheese Pizza

24 8-oz. Servings

This gourmet pizza features the unusual flavors of rosemary and sage. The smoked cheese provides depth and interest.

Equipment:	2 baking pans, 16 x 24 x 1 in.
Preparation Time:	40 minutes
Baking Time:	15 minutes

Ingredients	Volume	Weight
Onions, finely diced	2½ qts.	2 lbs. 8 oz.
Vegetable oil	½ cup	
Sage, dried, crumbled	2 tsp.	
Rosemary, dried, ground	2 tsp.	
Mushrooms, fresh, sliced		8 lbs.
Salt and black pepper to taste		
Dijon mustard	3 Tbsp.	
Smoked cheese (Cheddar or Swiss), grated	1¼ qts.	1 lb. 4 oz.
Mild cheese (muenster, mozzarella, or Monterey Jack), grated	1¼ qts.	1 lb. 4 oz.
Pizza shells, prebaked (if frozen, thawed)	2 (23 x 15 in.)	

Procedure

1. Sauté the onions and herbs in oil until the onions are softened.
2. Add the mushrooms and sauté on high heat until they release their juices.
3. Add salt, pepper, and mustard and cook 1–2 minutes longer. Drain if very juicy.
4. Preheat the oven to 450°.
5. Divide the onion–mushroom mixture between the two pizzas; sprinkle with cheeses. Bake at 450° for 10 to 15 minutes until the cheeses are melted and golden.
6. Cut each pizza into 12 servings.

Servings	Calories	Protein (g)	Fat (g)	Cholesterol (mg)	Carbohydrates (g)	Fiber (g)	Sodium (mg)
1	341	17.1	21.0	46	23.2	2.9	446

Pepper–Cheese Enchiladas

24 Servings of 2 3-oz. Enchiladas

Confetti-colored sweet peppers are combined with the bite of hot pepper, creamy cheeses, and aromatic cumin. This richly flavored dish is complete served on a bed of rice topped with Hot Sauce (p. 263).

Equipment:	4 half-size insert pans, 4-in. deep
Preparation Time:	1½ hours
Baking Time:	30 minutes

Ingredients	Volume	Weight
Onions, chopped	2½ qts.	2 lbs. 8 oz.
Garlic, minced or pressed	12 cloves or 3½ Tbsp.	
Chili peppers, minced (seeded only if very hot)	⅓ cup	
Cumin, ground	¼ cup	
Vegetable oil	½ cup	
Peppers, green, red, and yellow if possible, chopped	1 gal.	4 lbs.
Neufchâtel or cream cheese, cubed, softened		2 lbs.
Cheddar cheese, sharp, grated	2 qts.	1 lb. 8 oz.
Cottage cheese	3 cups	1 lb. 8 oz.
Corn tortillas	48 5-in.	
Vegetable oil for frying		

Procedure

1. Sauté the onions, garlic, chilies, and cumin in vegetable oil until the onions begin to soften.
2. Add the peppers, cover the pot, and cook on low heat, stirring often until the peppers are tender.
3. Remove from the heat and stir in the cheeses. Adjust seasonings.
4. To soften the tortillas either
    - Brush each tortilla lightly with oil and place on a baking sheet. Bake very briefly in a 400° oven for no longer than 2 minutes. Remove and allow to cool. Keep covered if not immediately proceeding with recipe.
    - Fry the tortillas in at least ½ in. of hot oil for a couple of seconds on each side. Do not allow the tortillas to become crisp.
5. Preheat the oven to 350°.
6. Fill each tortilla with ⅓ cup of the filling on the half of the tortilla closest to you. Roll and place seam side down in an oiled pan. Approximately six enchiladas fill a pan. Bake, tightly covered, at 350° for 20 minutes.

Servings	Calories	Protein (g)	Fat (g)	Cholesterol (mg)	Carbohydrates (g)	Fiber (g)	Sodium (mg)
1	463	20.0	27.4	63	37.0	1.7	547

Pie Crust

5 10-in. Pie Crusts

Equipment: food processor
Preparation Time: 10 minutes

Ingredients	Volume	Weight
Unbleached white flour (up to half whole wheat pastry flour can be used)	1¾ qts.	
Butter, chilled, cut in small pieces	2½ cups	1 lb. 4 oz.
Ice water	1–1½ cups	

Procedure

1. Add the butter pieces to the flour in the bowl of a food processor.
2. Pulse on and off until the butter pieces are pea-sized. Continue to pulse while adding the water. Use the larger amount of water if the dough seems dry.
3. Form into five balls and roll out on a lightly floured board.

Servings	Calories	Protein (g)	Fat (g)	Cholesterol (mg)	Carbohydrates (g)	Fiber (g)	Sodium (mg)
1	278	3.5	18.7	50	24.2	1.0	188

Pissaladiere

25 12-oz. Servings

Our version of a French-style pizza is presented as a golden pie beautifully topped with tomato slices and olives. Serve with a simple steamed vegetable or Easy Artichokes (p. 324).

Equipment:	5 10-in. pie plates
Preparation Time:	90 minutes if making pie crusts; 45 minutes if using premade crusts
Baking Time:	50–60 minutes

Ingredients	Volume	Weight
Pie Crusts (p. 290), unbaked	5 10-in.	
Olive oil	¼ cup	
Onions, chopped	2 qts.	2 lbs.
Garlic, pressed	15 med. cloves or 5 Tbsp.	
Basil, fresh, chopped	¾ cup	
or dried	2 Tbsp.	

Custard

Milk	1¼ qts.	
Eggs	25 lg., 1½ qts.	3 lbs. 2 oz.
White flour	5 Tbsp.	
Dijon mustard	5 tsp.	
Salt	5 tsp.	
Parmesan cheese, grated	1¼ qts.	1 lb. 4 oz.
Mozzarella cheese, grated	1¼ qts.	1 lb. 2 oz.
Black olives [California, calamata (p. 469), or niçoise], chopped	5 Tbsp.	
Tomatoes, fresh, sliced in rounds		3 lbs. 12 oz.

Procedure

1. If making the pie crusts from scratch, roll out and chill.
2. Sauté the onions and garlic in oil until the onions are translucent. If using dried

(continued)

basil, sauté it with the onions and garlic. If using fresh basil, stir it into the onion–garlic mixture when the onions are done.

3. In a mixing bowl, whisk together the custard ingredients.
4. Preheat the oven to 350°.
5. To assemble each pie, layer the ingredients in each crust in the following order:
   - ½ cup custard
   - ½ cup mozzarella cheese
   - ⅕ of the onion–basil sauté
   - ½ cup of mozzarella cheese
   - 1 Tbsp. chopped olives
   - tomato slices to cover
   - 1⅓–1½ cups custard
   - 1 cup Parmesan cheese
6. Bake at 350° for 50–60 minutes, or until the custard has set and the topping is golden.
7. Cut each pie into five pieces.

Servings	Calories	Protein (g)	Fat (g)	Cholesterol (mg)	Carbohydrates (g)	Fiber (g)	Sodium (mg)
1	621	28.7	39.9	347	37.3	2.4	1394

Roti

Yields: 24 11-oz. Rotis

A squash filling lavishly seasoned with lime, coconut milk, and rum. Create a Caribbean feast by serving on Coconut Rice (p. 322) with Sara's Greens (p. 342).

Equipment:	4 insert pans, 2-in. deep
Preparation Time:	30 minutes with cooked squash
Baking Time:	25 minutes

Ingredients	Volume	Weight
Winter squash (acorn, butternut, buttercup), whole		12 lbs.
or frozen, thawed	1 gal.	

Seasonings

Ingredients	Volume	Weight
Cayenne	¼ tsp.	
Coriander seeds, ground	½ cup	
Mustard, dry	4 Tbsp.	
Garlic, pressed	30 cloves or ½ cup	
Turmeric	2 tsp.	
Vegetable oil	¼ cup	
Onions, chopped	2½ qts.	2 lbs. 8 oz.
Peppers, red and green, chopped	2½ qts.	2 lbs. 8 oz.
Corn, frozen or cut	3 cups	1 lb. 8 oz.
Seitan (p. 472) (optional)	1¾ qts.	1 lb. 2 oz.
White flour	4 Tbsp.	
Coconut milk, unsweetened (p. 470)	2 cups	14 oz.
Lime or lemon juice, fresh	½ cup	
Dark rum	¾ cup	
Scallions, chopped	1 cup	2.5 oz.
Salt	3 Tbsp.	
Black pepper, to taste		
Wheat tortillas, 10-in.	24	

(continued)

Procedure

1. If using whole squash, halve and seed them. Place the squash, cut side down, on oiled trays, or in insert pans with a small amount of water covering the bottom of the pan. Tightly cover the pans and bake at 375° for 45–60 minutes until the squash is tender. Cool.
2. Meanwhile, combine the seasonings and set aside.
3. Sauté the onions in oil until the onions are translucent.
4. Add the peppers, corn, and seitan, if using, and continue to sauté until the peppers soften.
5. Stir in the seasonings and flour, and continue sautéing, stirring continuously, for a few minutes more.
6. Add the coconut milk, lime juice, rum, and scallions, and simmer for 10 minutes.
7. When the squash cools, scoop out the pulp and coarsely chop it.
8. In a large bowl, combine the chopped or frozen squash with the onion–vegetable mixture. Adjust for salt and pepper.
9. Spoon 1 cup of filling along one edge of each tortilla and roll it up. Place the roti seam side down in four lightly oiled insert pans. Approximately nine Roti fill each pan. Cover tightly with aluminum foil and bake at 350° for 20–30 minutes until the filling is heated through.
10. Cut each Roti in half, serve topped with Mango Salsa (p. 264) or Citrus Salsa (p. 259), alone, or on a bed of rice.

Servings	Calories	Protein (g)	Fat (g)	Cholesterol (mg)	Carbohydrates (g)	Fiber (g)	Sodium (mg)
1	317	10.0	8.6	0	50.5	7.0	90

Spanakopita

24 11-oz. Servings

Serve this ever-popular Greek specialty with Marinated Vegetables (p. 333) or halve each of our serving sizes into a triangle to present a combination platter with Carrot Salad (p. 321) and stuffed grape leaves.

Equipment:	2 baking pans, 18 x 14 x 1 in.
Preparation Time:	1 hour
Baking Time:	50–60 minutes

Ingredients	Volume	Weight
Olive oil	1/3 cup	
Onions, chopped	1 qt.	1 lb.
Garlic, pressed or minced	8 cloves or 2 1/2 Tbsp.	
Dill, fresh, chopped	1 Tbsp.	
or dried	1 tsp.	
Oregano, dried	1 Tbsp.	
Spinach, fresh, stemmed	4 10-oz. bags	2 lbs. 8 oz.
or frozen, thawed, drained		1 lb. 4 oz.
Eggs	12 lg. or 3 cups	1 lb. 8 oz.
White flour	1/2 cup	
Cottage cheese	3 1/2 qts.	7 lbs.
Cream cheese or Neufchâtel, softened, cubed		1 lb. 8 oz.
Feta cheese, grated	3 qts.	3 lbs.
Filo pastry		2 lbs.
Butter, melted	1 1/2 cups	12 oz.
Fennel seeds (optional)		

Procedure

1. Sauté the onions, garlic, and herbs in oil until the onions are softened and golden.

(continued)

2. In a separate pot, steam or blanch the raw spinach until it is wilted but still bright green. Drain and press out as much water as possible and coarsely chop. If using frozen spinach, drain well.
3. In a large bowl, blend the eggs with flour and then combine with the cheeses, spinach, and sautéed onions.
4. Preheat the oven to 350°.
5. Assemble the filo pastry (p. 272), sprinkling the top filo layer with fennel seeds, if desired.
6. Bake at 350° for 50 minutes to 1 hour, or until the filling has set and the top is crisp and golden.
7. Cut each pan into 12 pieces.

Variation of Spanakopita

Artichoke Heart–Red Pepper Strudel

1. Replace spinach with

Ingredients	Volume	Weight
Artichoke hearts, canned, drained, quartered	1¼ qts.	2 lbs.
Roasted red peppers, canned, drained, thinly sliced	2 cups	1 lb. 4 oz.

2. Reduce the following cheeses to

Cottage cheese	2½ qts.	5 lbs.
Feta cheese	2 qts.	2 lbs.

3. Replace dill with

Basil, dried	1 Tbsp.	

Servings	Calories	Protein (g)	Fat (g)	Cholesterol (mg)	Carbohydrates (g)	Fiber (g)	Sodium (mg)
1	746	34.1	58.3	265	22.8	1.3	1520

Spinach Tofu Borekas

24 6¹/₂-oz. Servings

Our dairy-free filo turnover has the Turkish influence of cinnamon, lemon, and currants. The filling is wrapped in flaky pastry and folded into an easy-to-serve triangle. Accompany with the Middle Eastern version of Carrot Salad (p. 321).

Equipment:	2 baking pans, 18 x 14 x 1 in.
Preparation Time:	1 hour (excluding freezing and thawing tofu)
Baking Time:	20 minutes

Ingredients	Volume	Weight
Olive oil	¹/₂ cup	
Onions, chopped	2 qts.	2 lbs.
Garlic, minced or pressed	5 cloves or 1¹/₂ Tbsp.	
Cinnamon	1 tsp.	
Dill, fresh, chopped	¹/₄ cup	
or dried	2 Tbsp.	
Carrots, diced	1 qt.	1 lb. 5 oz.
Tofu (p. 474), frozen, then thawed	7 cakes	6 lbs. (unfrozen)
Soy sauce	3 Tbsp.	
Tomato paste	¹/₄ cup	
Spinach, fresh, stemmed	4 10-oz. bags	2 lbs. 8 oz.
or frozen, thawed, drained		1 lb. 4 oz.
Currants, dried	1 cup	
Lemon juice, fresh	1 Tbsp.	
Salt and black pepper to taste		
Filo pastry		2 lbs.
Margarine, melted	1¹/₂ cups	12 oz.
Sesame seeds (optional)	¹/₄ cup	

(continued)

Savory Pastries

Procedure

1. Sauté the onions and garlic in olive oil for 2–3 minutes.
2. Add the cinnamon, dill, and carrots and continue to sauté until the vegetables are tender.
3. Squeeze the liquid from the thawed, sponge-like tofu. Finely chop or put through the grating blade of a food processor.
4. Add the tofu to the vegetables and stir in the soy sauce and tomato paste.
5. If using raw spinach, cook it separately, drain well, and chop. If using frozen spinach, drain well.
6. Add spinach to the tofu–vegetable mixture, along with the currants, lemon juice, salt, and pepper.
7. Preheat the oven to 350°.
8. Lay out three stacked sheets of filo with one of the short sides nearest to you. Fold the stack lengthwise and brush the top surface of the filo with margarine. Spread 1 cup of filling down the middle, leaving 1-in. margins on each side.
9. Fold the bottom left corner of the filo up and over diagonally so that the bottom edge is aligned with the right side. Fold straight up, and then to the left. Continue folding in this manner, as you would a flag, to make a triangular pastry.
10. Brush the top of the triangle with margarine, sprinkle with sesame seeds, and bake at 350° for 20 minutes until puffy and golden.

Note: Olive oil can be substituted for margarine with the addition of salt and a tablespoon of crushed garlic.

Servings	Calories	Protein (g)	Fat (g)	Cholesterol (mg)	Carbohydrates (g)	Fiber (g)	Sodium (mg)
1	370	6.3	26.0	0	30.6	2.7	370

Spinach–Feta Pie

25 12-oz. Servings

Easy to prepare and serve, this rich and flavorful vegetarian quiche makes an excellent lunch or brunch entrée served with fresh fruit or a green salad.

Equipment:	5 10-in. pie plates
Preparation Time:	90 minutes if preparing pie crusts, 45 minutes if using premade crusts
Baking Time:	1 hour

Ingredients	Volume	Weight
Pie crusts, unbaked (p. 290)	5 10-in.	
Olive oil	½ cup	
Garlic, pressed	10 med. cloves or 3 Tbsp.	
Onions, chopped	2½ qts.	2 lbs. 8 oz.
Spinach, fresh, stemmed	3 10-oz. bags	1 lb. 14 oz.
or frozen, thawed, drained		1 lb. 8 oz.
Eggs	25 lg. or 1½ qts.	3 lbs. 2 oz.
Ricotta cheese	1¼ qts.	2 lbs. 8 oz.
Feta cheese, grated	1 gal.	4 lbs.
Dill, fresh, chopped		2 oz.
Oregano, dried	1 Tbsp.	
Ground black pepper	1¼ tsp.	

Procedure

1. If making the pie crusts from scratch, roll out and chill.
2. Sauté the garlic and onions in olive oil until the onions are translucent . Set aside.
3. Cook the spinach in a small amount of water until just wilted. Drain, press out excess water, and chop. If using frozen spinach, drain well.
4. Preheat the oven to 350°.

(continued)

Savory Pastries

5. Beat the eggs in a large mixing bowl. Add the onions, spinach, and remaining ingredients, combining thoroughly.
6. Divide the filling among five pie crusts. Bake at 350° for approximately 1 hour, or until the eggs have set and the pie is golden.
7. Cut each pie into 5 pieces.

Servings	Calories	Protein (g)	Fat (g)	Cholesterol (mg)	Carbohydrates (g)	Fiber (g)	Sodium (mg)
1	731	30.1	51.1	401	38.9	2.6	1261

Savory Pastries

Tarte Lyonnaise

25 12-oz. Servings

The traditional tastes of quiche lorraine are recreated in our vegetarian version with smoked cheese and golden onions flavored with thyme. Serve with a colorful steamed vegetable.

Equipment:	5 10-in. pie plates
Preparation Time:	90 minutes if preparing pie crusts; 45 minutes if using premade crusts
Baking Time:	45–60 minutes

Ingredients	Volume	Weight
Pie crusts, unbaked (p. 290)	5 10-in.	
Onions, chopped	5 qts.	5 lbs.
Vegetable oil	¼ cup	
Thyme, dried	2 Tbsp.	
Swiss cheese, grated	1½ qts.	1 lb. 8 oz.
Gruyere cheese, grated	2 cups	8 oz.
Smoked cheese, grated	2 cups	8 oz.
Eggs	30 lg., 1¾ qts.	3 lbs. 12 oz.
Milk	1¼ qts.	
White flour	6 Tbsp.	
Dijon mustard	5 tsp.	
Salt	5 tsp.	
Black pepper to taste		

Procedure

1. If making the pie crusts from scratch, roll out and chill.
2. Slowly sauté the onions and thyme in oil (preferably in a cast iron skillet) until the onions are golden.
3. Combine the grated cheeses.

(continued)

4. Preheat the oven to 350°.

5. Whisk together the remaining ingredients.

6. Assemble the pies in the following order:
   - Spread 1 cup grated cheese on bottom of pastry crust.
   - Spoon 1½ cups onions on top of cheese.
   - Add 1 cup grated cheese.
   - Pour 1½–2 cups custard on top.

6. Bake for 45–60 minutes at 350°, or until the custard has set and the pie is golden.

7. Cut each pie in 5 pieces.

Servings	Calories	Protein (g)	Fat (g)	Cholesterol (mg)	Carbohydrates (g)	Fiber (g)	Sodium (mg)
1	655	28.4	43.4	415	37.8	2.3	952

Tofu Burritos

24 Servings of 10 burritos

Low-fat and deliciously Tex-Mex, these burritos can also be served with side dishes such as Spanish rice, Refritos (p. 216), or guacamole. Top with a tomato salsa or Hot Sauce (p. 263).

Equipment:	5 insert pans, 2- or 4-in. deep
Preparation Time:	90 minutes
BakingTime:	20 minutes

Ingredients	Volume	Weight
Onions, chopped	2 qts.	2 lbs.
Vegetable oil	½ cup	
Garlic, minced or pressed	10 cloves or 3 Tbsp.	
Chili peppers, fresh, seeded, minced	4 sm.	
or Cayenne	¼–½ tsp.	
Peppers, red or green, chopped	2½ qts.	2 lbs. 8 oz.
Paprika	2 Tbsp.	
Cumin, ground	4 Tbsp.	
Coriander seed, ground	2 Tbsp.	
Oregano, dried	1 Tbsp.	
Corn, frozen or cut	1¼ qts.	2 lbs.
Tofu, pressed (p. 474), then crumbled or mashed		7 lbs. (unpressed)
Tomato paste	1½ cups	
Soy sauce	½ cup	
Green olives, chopped (optional)	1 cup	
Salt and black pepper to taste		
Wheat tortillas, 10-in.	24	

Procedure

1. Sauté the onions, garlic, and chilies or cayenne, in oil for a couple of minutes.
2. Stir in the peppers and sauté on medium heat until the onions soften.

(continued)

3. Add the paprika, cumin, coriander seed, oregano, corn, and crumbled tofu and continue to sauté.
4. When the vegetables are tender, stir in tomato paste, soy sauce, olives, salt, and pepper.
5. Preheat oven to 350°.
6. Lightly oil a baking pan. Place 1 cup of the filling in the center of each tortilla and roll up to form a cylinder. Place each burrito seam side down in the pan. Usually 9–10 burritos fill each pan.
7. Bake at 350°, in pans tightly covered with foil, for 20 minutes, or until heated thoroughly.

Servings	Calories	Protein (g)	Fat (g)	Cholesterol (mg)	Carbohydrates (g)	Fiber (g)	Sodium (mg)
1	353	17.1	14.4	0	44.6	4.0	465

Savory Pastries

Torta Fiorentina

24 11-oz. Servings

Our elegant Italian strudel is layered with mushrooms, garlicky spinach, and mellow cheeses. Accompany this lavish pastry with a crisp green salad.

Equipment:	2 baking pans, 18 x 14 x 1 in.
Preparation Time:	90 minutes
Baking Time:	45 minutes

Ingredients	Volume	Weight
Olive oil	¼ cup	
Onions, chopped	2 qts.	2 lbs.
Garlic, minced or pressed	12 cloves or 3 Tbsp.	
Mushrooms, sliced	3¾ qts.	3 lbs.
Spinach, fresh, stemmed, chopped	4 10-oz. bags	2 lbs. 8 oz.
or frozen, thawed, drained		1 lb. 4 oz.
Ricotta cheese	1½ qts.	3 lbs.
Parmesan cheese, freshly grated	1½ qts.	1 lb. 8 oz.
Sour cream	1 qt.	2 lbs.
Eggs, beaten	12 lg. or 3 cups	1 lb. 8 oz.
Bread crumbs, fresh	2 cups	4 oz.
Parsley, chopped	1 cup	1.33 oz.
Filo pastry		2 lbs.
Butter, melted	1½ cups	12 oz.
Sesame seeds (optional)	1 Tbsp.	

Procedure

1. Sauté the onions and garlic in oil until the onions are translucent.
2. Add the mushrooms and spinach and continue to sauté on high heat until the mushrooms soften and the spinach wilts. Drain vegetable juices if any.

(continued)

3. Combine the cheeses, sour cream, eggs, bread crumbs, and parsley in a large mixing bowl.
4. Add the drained vegetables.
5. Preheat the oven to 350°.
6. Assemble the filo pastry with the melted butter (see p. 272). Top the final layer of pastry with a sprinkling of sesame seeds, if desired.
7. Bake at 350° for 45 minutes until golden and set.
8. Allow the strudel to sit for 10 minutes before cutting.
9. Cut each pan in 12 pieces.

Servings	Calories	Protein (g)	Fat (g)	Cholesterol (mg)	Carbohydrates (g)	Fiber (g)	Sodium (mg)
1	619	27.7	46.9	220	23.7	2.6	901

Ukrainian Vegetable Strudel

24 11-oz. Servings

This elegant, sumptuous fall or winter strudel is complemented by applesauce or a baked apple and pickled beets.

Equipment:	2 baking pans, 18 x 14 x 1-in.
Preparation Time:	45–60 minutes
Baking Time:	45–60 minutes

Ingredients	Volume	Weight
Vegetable oil	½ cup	
Onions, chopped	1½ qts.	1 lb. 8 oz.
Cabbage, thinly shredded	3 qts.	2 lbs.
Carrots, sliced in half-moons	1¼ qts.	1 lb. 11 oz.
Salt	1 Tbsp.	
Dill, dried	1½ Tbsp.	
Tarragon, dried	2 tsp.	
Basil, dried	1 Tbsp.	
Thyme, dried	2 tsp.	
Mushrooms, sliced	3 qts.	2 lbs. 6 oz.
Black pepper	1½ tsp.	
Cottage cheese	1½ qts.	3 lbs.
Neufchâtel or cream cheese, softened, cubed	3 cups	1 lb. 8 oz.
Sharp Cheddar, grated	1¼ qts.	1 lb.
Eggs, beaten	1 doz. lg. or 3 cups	1 lb. 8 oz.
White flour	1 cup	
Butter, melted	1½ cups	12 oz.
Filo pastry		2 lbs.

Procedure

1. Sauté the onions in oil until they are translucent.
2. Add the cabbage, carrots, and salt and sauté until the cabbage is wilted.

(continued)

3. Add the herbs, mushrooms, and black pepper. Cook until the mushrooms are juicy and reduced in size.
4. Drain the vegetables, reserve the stock for other uses if desired.
5. Add the cheeses to the drained vegetables.
6. Blend the eggs with the flour and combine with the vegetable–cheese mixture.
7. Preheat the oven to 350°.
8. Assemble the filo pastry with the melted butter (p. 272).
9. Bake for 45–60 minutes at 350° until the filo pastry is golden and set. Allow to sit for 10 minutes before cutting.
10. Cut each pan in 12 pieces.

Servings	Calories	Protein (g)	Fat (g)	Cholesterol (mg)	Carbohydrates (g)	Fiber (g)	Sodium (mg)
1	556	21.7	43.5	213	21.2	2.3	991

Vegetable Piroshki
24 6-oz. Servings

These savory Eastern European-style pastries are wonderful served with applesauce and Sweet and Sour Red Cabbage (p. 343).

Equipment:	2 baking pans, 18 x 14 x 1 in.
Preparation Time:	75 minutes
Baking Time:	35 minutes

Ingredients	Volume	Weight
Pastry		
White flour	1¹/₂ qts.	1 lb. 8 oz.
Salt	1 tsp.	
Butter	2 cups	1 lb.
Ice water	³/₄ to 1¹/₄ cups	
Potatoes, sliced	2 qts.	2 lbs.
Vegetable oil	¹/₄ cup	
Cabbage, thinly sliced	2 qts.	1 lb. 8 oz.
Onions, chopped	1¹/₄ qts.	1 lb. 4 oz.
Cottage cheese	1 qt.	2 lbs.
Sharp Cheddar cheese, grated	1¹/₄ qts.	1 lb.
Eggs, lightly beaten	4 lg. or 1 cup	8 oz.
Dill weed, fresh, chopped	¹/₄ cup	
or dried	2 Tbsp.	
Scallions, chopped	¹/₂ cup	1 oz.
Black pepper	1 tsp.	
Egg Wash		
Eggs, beaten with	2 lg. or ¹/₂ cup	4 oz.
water	¹/₄ cup	
Poppy seeds	3 Tbsp.	

(continued)

Procedure

1. Prepare the pastry by thoroughly mixing the flour and salt. Cut in the butter until the mixture resembles coarse cornmeal. Using a fork and a minimum number of strokes, mix in the ice water until the mixture can be formed into a ball. Chill the dough for 15 minutes. Form into six balls and refrigerate for up to 1 hour.
2. Boil the sliced potatoes in salted water until tender. Drain.
3. Sauté the cabbage and onions in oil until they are softened and golden.
4. Mash the potatoes and combine with the sautéed vegetables, cheeses, the beaten cup of eggs, dill, scallions, and black pepper.
5. Divide each ball of dough into four equal pieces. Roll each piece into a 6-in. diameter circle.
6. Preheat the oven to 350°.
7. Place ½ cup of filling in the center of each circle. Brush the edges with the egg wash and fold over to form a turnover, pressing the edges together with a fork.
8. Lift the piroshki with a spatula onto an oiled baking sheet or pan. Brush the tops with the egg wash and sprinkle with poppy seeds.
9. Bake for 25–35 minutes, at 350°, until lightly browned.

Servings	Calories	Protein (g)	Fat (g)	Cholesterol (mg)	Carbohydrates (g)	Fiber (g)	Sodium (mg)
1	452	16.0	28.3	133	34.1	2.8	553

SIDE DISHES

The recipes in this section can be used to harmonize or contrast with, or in some other way augment, other foods in a given meal. Some, like Cornbread, are clearly meant to play a supporting role. Others, like Roasted Vegetables, are destined to be in a more starring position but need back-up players to create a satisfying meal. Following are some examples of how to use recipes from this section in combination with other dishes:

- Autumn Squash Gratin with Cornbread and Sara's Greens
- Bulghur Pilaf with Lebanese Vegetable Soup (p. 39) and Tzatziki
- Golden Orzo with Easy Artichokes and Fresh Mozzarella and Sun-dried Tomatoes
- Marinated Vegetables with Italian-Style Tofu Pizza (p. 281)
- Pasta with Peas and Onions with Roasted Eggplant–Pepper Salad (p. 83)
- Roasted Vegetables with Seasoned Tempeh (p. 218) and Golden Orzo
- Cantonese Roasted Vegetables with Vegetable Tofu Almondine (p. 110) and rice
- Rice Pilaf with Orzo with Turkish Spinach-Lentil Soup (p. 59) and Artichoke Heart–Tomato Salad
- Golden Spanish Rice with BBQ Tempeh and Peppers (p. 195)

Artichoke Heart–
Tomato Salad

24 5-oz. Servings

The tangy flavor of this easily prepared marinated dish suggests its use as an accompaniment to rich strudels or savory pies.

Preparation Time: 20 minutes

Ingredients	Volume	Weight
Artichoke hearts, canned (packed in brine), drained	2 qts. (1 #10 can)	3 lbs. 8 oz.
Tomatoes, fresh	12 med.	3 lbs. 6 oz.

Marinade

Olive or vegetable oil	¾ cup
Red wine vinegar	½ cup
Garlic, pressed	5 cloves or 1½ Tbsp.
Basil, dill, oregano (choose one or two), fresh, chopped	3 Tbsp.
or dried	1 Tbsp.

Procedure

1. Halve the artichoke hearts and cut the tomatoes into wedges.
2. Blend the marinade.
3. Combine marinade with the vegetables.

Servings	Calories	Protein (g)	Fat (g)	Cholesterol (mg)	Carbohydrates (g)	Fiber (g)	Sodium (mg)
1	112	2.9	7.4	0	11.0	4.3	69

Asian Cabbage Slaw

24 4-oz. Servings

Hold the mayo! Here's a unique cabbage slaw that is as beautiful to look at as it is delectable to taste. Serve with Udon Noodles and Vegetables (p. 108), Honolulu Beans (p. 208), or Salmon Teriyaki (p. 189).

Preparation Time: 30 minutes

Ingredients	Volume	Weight
Cabbage, finely shredded	1 gal.	3 lbs.
Carrots, grated	1½ qts.	1 lb. 4 oz.
Peppers, red and/or green, julienned	3 cups	12 oz.

Dressing

Vegetable oil	¾ cup	
Chinese rice vinegar (p. 469)	¾ cup	
Soy sauce	6 Tbsp.	
Brown sugar	¼ cup	
Ginger root, fresh, grated	1 Tbsp.	
Chili oil or Tabasco sauce	1 tsp. or to taste	

Garnishes

Peanuts, roasted, chopped	2 cups	8 oz.
or Sesame seeds, toasted	6 Tbsp.	

Procedure

1. Combine the vegetables and set aside.
2. Whisk together the dressing ingredients.
3. Pour the dressing over the vegetables and toss well.
4. Marinate for 10 to 15 minutes.
5. Garnish with chopped peanuts or sesame seeds if desired.

Servings	Calories	Protein (g)	Fat (g)	Cholesterol (mg)	Carbohydrates (g)	Fiber (g)	Sodium (mg)
1	158	3.6	12.0	0	11.2	3.1	226

Asian Greens

24 4-oz. Servings

This side dish is a very tasty and authentic way of preparing healthful greens. Serve with Cantonese Roasted Vegetables (p. 319) or Salmon Teriyaki (p. 189).

Equipment:	wok or 2½-gallon stockpot
Preparation Time:	15 minutes
Cooking Time:	15 minutes

Ingredients	Volume	Weight
Vegetable oil	½ cup	
Garlic, pressed	10 cloves or 3 Tbsp.	
Ginger root, fresh, grated	3 Tbsp.	
Greens (kale, collards, chard, mustard, bok choy, rapini), fresh, chopped		6 lbs.
Sherry, Chinese rice wine (p. 469), or mirin (p. 472)	1½ cups	
White vinegar or lemon juice, fresh (optional)	4–6 Tbsp.	
Sugar or honey	1–2 Tbsp.	
Water	¾ cup	
Soy sauce or fish sauce (p. 470)	½ cup	

Procedure

This dish will probably need to be done in at least three batches, depending on the size of your wok or pot. Divide the ingredients proportionally for each batch.

1. Sauté the garlic and ginger in oil on medium heat for 1 or 2 minutes.
2. Add the greens and stir-fry for 1 minute.
3. Add the remaining ingredients, except the soy or fish sauce. Continue to stir-fry until the greens are tender.
4. Toss the soy or fish sauce with the greens right before serving.

Servings	Calories	Protein (g)	Fat (g)	Cholesterol (mg)	Carbohydrates (g)	Fiber (g)	Sodium (mg)
1	87	1.8	5.0	0	7.5	1.8	288

Autumn Squash Gratin

24 10 oz. Servings

The sweetness of squash nicely combines with sharp cheddar cheese in this New England home-style dish. Use a tart apple for further contrast. Serve with Portuguese Kale and White Bean Soup (p. 49) or baked beans.

Equipment:	4 half-size insert pans, 4-in. deep
Preparation Time:	45–60 minutes
Baking Time:	45 minutes

Ingredients	Volume	Weight
Winter squash, raw, peeled and cubed		4 lbs. 8 oz.
or cooked and mashed	1 gal.	7 lbs. 8 oz.
Onions, chopped	2½ qts.	2 lbs. 8 oz.
Thyme, dried	2 tsp.	
Vegetable oil	¼ cup	
Apples, peeled, cored, thinly sliced	2½ qts.	2 lbs. 12 oz.
White flour	¼ cup	
Cheddar cheese, sharp, grated	2 qts.	1 lb. 8 oz.
Bread crumbs	1 cup	4 oz.
Salt and black pepper to taste		

Procedure

1. Bake or boil the cubed squash if using the raw vegetable. Drain and mash.
2. Gently sauté the thyme and onions in oil until the onions are soft and golden, for about 20 minutes.
3. In one mixing bowl, toss the apple slices with flour. In another bowl, mix the Cheddar cheese with the bread crumbs.
4. Combine the squash and sautéed onions. Add salt and pepper.
5. Oil the baking pans and layer in the following order:
   - squash and onions
   - apple slices
   - Cheddar and bread crumbs
6. Bake at 350° for 30 minutes covered, and 15 minutes, uncovered, or until golden and bubbly.

Servings	Calories	Protein (g)	Fat (g)	Cholesterol (mg)	Carbohydrates (g)	Fiber (g)	Sodium (mg)
1	239	10.2	12.7	30	24.0	5.8	212

Bulghur Pilaf

24 3.5-oz. Servings

Bulghur has a mild, nutty flavor and is easy to prepare. This versatile wheat product deserves more attention than it currently enjoys. Here is an herbed pilaf that is a good companion for steamed or sautéed vegetables or for baked fish prepared with herb butters or sour cream sauces.

Equipment:	2-gallon pot
Preparation Time:	20 minutes
Cooking Time:	30 minutes

Ingredients	Volume	Weight
Onions, finely chopped	1 qt.	1 lb.
Olive oil	¼ cup	
Salt	2 Tbsp.	
Black pepper	¼ tsp.	
Basil, dried	1½ Tbsp.	
Rosemary or marjoram, dried	1 tsp.	
Bulghur, raw (p. 468)	1½ qts.	2 lbs. 4 oz.
Hot water	2¼ qts.	

Procedure

1. Sauté the onions in oil until they are translucent.
2. Add the herbs and seasonings, cover the pot, and cook until the onions begin to brown.
3. Stir in the bulghur and continue sautéeing until the grain begins to darken.
4. Add the water, cover tightly, and bring to a boil. Reduce the heat to low, insert a heat diffuser, and let the pilaf steam for 20 minutes, until the bulghur grains are separate and tender. If the bulghur is underdone, add more hot water sparingly. This dish should not be mushy.

Servings	Calories	Protein (g)	Fat (g)	Cholesterol (mg)	Carbohydrates (g)	Fiber (g)	Sodium (mg)
1	174	5.5	3.0	0	34.0	8.0	603

Cantonese Roasted Vegetables

24 9-oz. Servings

East meets West in this dish, which combines a traditional Chinese savory and sweet sauce with a Mediterranean way of cooking vegetables. Serve on a bed of steamed greens with baked tofu (see Vegetable–Tofu Almondine, p. 110) or wedges of hard-boiled egg. Garnish with mung bean sprouts or chopped scallions, if desired.

Equipment:	3 insert pans, 2-in. deep
Preparation Time:	1 hour
Baking Time:	45 minutes to 1 hour

Ingredients	Volume	Weight
Sweet potatoes, cut in 1-in. cubes	2½ qts.	3 lbs.
White potatoes, cut in 1-in. cubes	2½ qts.	3 lbs. 6 oz.
Onions, thickly sliced	2½ qts.	2 lbs. 8 oz.
Eggplant, cut in 1 × 2-in. strips	3 qts.	3 lbs.
Zucchini and/or yellow squash, cut in 1 × 2-in. strips	1 gal.	4 lbs.
Mushrooms, halved or whole if small		2 lbs.

Braising Sauce

	Volume	Weight
Hoisin sauce (p. 471)	2 14-oz. jars or 2 cups	28 oz.
Sherry	1¼ cups	
Soy sauce	1¼ cups	
Vegetable oil	¾ cup	
Honey	¾ cup	
Garlic, pressed	6 cloves or 2 Tbsp.	

Procedure

1. Parboil the sweet and white potatoes for 5 minutes. Drain.
2. Preheat the oven to 400°.

(continued)

3. Divide the vegetables among three insert pans, with a good mix of vegetables in each pan.
4. Whisk together the braising ingredients and toss with vegetables, using 2 cups per insert pan.
5. Bake uncovered at 400° for about 1 hour, turning the vegetables every 15 minutes.

Servings	Calories	Protein (g)	Fat (g)	Cholesterol (mg)	Carbohydrates (g)	Fiber (g)	Sodium (mg)
1	333	5.7	9.4	0	59.3	5.6	951

Carrot Salad

24 2-oz. Servings

A nutritious carrot salad with a garden-fresh flavor, this easily prepared dish can be paired with most savory entrées or used in a salad bar.

Preparation Time: 20 minutes

Ingredients	Volume	Weight
Carrots, grated	12 cups	3 lbs.
Lemon juice, fresh	½ cup	
Vegetable oil	¾ cup	
Parsley, fresh, finely chopped	3 cups	4 oz.
Salt and black pepper to taste		
Garlic, pressed	3 cloves or 1 Tbsp.	

Variations

Add one or two of the following seasonings:

Coriander seed, ground	1½ Tbsp.
Mint, fresh, chopped	¼ cup
or dried	1 Tbsp.
Chives or scallions, fresh, chopped	¼ cup

For an Asian salad, substitute rice vinegar for the lemon juice and dark sesame oil (p. 473) for the vegetable oil, and add

Ginger root, fresh, grated	1 Tbsp.

Procedure

1. Combine and chill.

Carrot Salad

Servings	Calories	Protein (g)	Fat (g)	Cholesterol (mg)	Carbohydrates (g)	Fiber (g)	Sodium (mg)
1	91	0.8	7.2	0	6.7	1.9	30

Coconut Rice

24 4-oz. Servings

Lightly golden and sweetly fragrant, this rice is a delicious base for curried dishes and Caribbean or African-style stews or beans.

Equipment:	2-gallon pot
Preparation Time:	10 minutes
Cooking Time:	45 minutes

Ingredients	Volume	Weight
Vegetable oil	¼ cup	
Brown rice, raw	2 qts.	3 lbs. 4 oz.
Turmeric	1 Tbsp.	
Shredded coconut, unsweetened	2 cups	
Water	3 qts.	
Cinnamon stick	1 (1–1½-in. long)	
Salt	2 tsp.	

Procedure

1. Sauté the rice, turmeric, and coconut in oil for a few minutes.
2. Add the water, cinnamon stick, and salt.
3. Cover the pot and increase the heat to bring the water to a boil. Reduce the heat and simmer for about 40 minutes.
4. Remove from the heat. Allow the rice to sit for 10 minutes and then gently fluff.

Servings	Calories	Protein (g)	Fat (g)	Cholesterol (mg)	Carbohydrates (g)	Fiber (g)	Sodium (mg)
1	191	3.1	5.6	0	32.1	0.3	216

Cornbread

24 3-oz. Servings

Our standard cornbread recipe always draws rave reviews. At its best served warm from the oven, cornbread is particularly good with Southern or Southwestern-style stews and bean dishes. Try it with Creole Beans and Rice (p. 201), Hoppin' John (p. 210), Brunswick Stew (p. 347), or Santa Fe Chowder (p. 53).

Equipment:	2 half-size insert pans, 2-in. deep
Preparation Time:	15 minutes
Baking Time:	20 minutes

Ingredients	Volume	Weight
Cornmeal	3 cups	
Flour (half white and half whole wheat pastry or all white)	4 cups	
Baking powder	2½ Tbsp.	
Baking soda	2 tsp.	
Salt	2 tsp.	
Buttermilk	1 qt.	
Milk	1 cup	
Eggs, beaten	4 lg. or 1 cup	8 oz.
Brown sugar	⅓ cup	
Butter, melted	½ cup	8 oz.

Procedure

1. Preheat the oven to 400°.
2. Sift together the dry ingredients in a large bowl.
3. Combine the wet ingredients.
4. Add the wet ingredients to the dry ingredients, mixing only until the dry ingredients are moistened.
5. Pour into two oiled pans and bake at 400° for 20–25 minutes. The cornbread is done when a knife inserted at the center is dry and the edges begin to pull away from the pan.

Servings	Calories	Protein (g)	Fat (g)	Cholesterol (mg)	Carbohydrates (g)	Fiber (g)	Sodium (mg)
1	251	6.8	9.9	67	34.3	2.8	474

Easy Artichokes

24 Whole Artichokes
48 Artichoke Halves

Cooking the artichokes with some basic seasonings amplifies the flavor of this prized seasonal vegetable. Serve with Fish Santorini (p. 174) or White Bean and Tomato Salad (p. 112).

Equipment:	2 stockpots, 4½ gallons each
Preparation Time:	30 minutes
Cooking Time:	45 minutes

Ingredients	Volume	Weight
Artichokes, fresh, whole	24	
Bay leaves, whole	6	
Peppercorns, whole	2 Tbsp.	
Vinegar or lemon juice, fresh	⅓ cup	
Garlic, whole cloves, peeled	12	
Olive oil	⅓ cup	
Salt	1–2 Tbsp.	

Procedure

1. Place the artichoke on its side and slice off the stem end evenly so that the artichoke will sit flatly on its base. Cut off ½ to ¾ in. from the top of the artichoke to produce a flat top. If desired, with kitchen scissors, trim the barbed tops from the rest of the leaves (the barbs, if left on, will soften during cooking).
2. Place the artichokes in two deep pots, standing upright. Add water to half the height of the artichokes, and half of the remaining ingredients to each pot.
3. Cover, bring to a boil, reduce to a simmer, and cook for 30–45 minutes, or until the bases are tender when tested with a fork and the leaves pull off easily.
4. Drain the artichokes upside down.

Servings	Calories	Protein (g)	Fat (g)	Cholesterol (mg)	Carbohydrates (g)	Fiber (g)	Sodium (mg)
1	102	5.0	3.4	0	16.9	7.8	578

Fassoulia (Sephardic Green Beans)

24 3-oz. Servings

This stewed green bean dish is slow-cooked to allow all the flavors to gently marry. If you prefer your beans crisp-tender, reduce the simmering time by half. Serve as a side dish with Chesapeake Catfish (p. 165); or, to create a main dish, serve with the optional almonds and Bulghur Pilaf (p. 318).

Equipment:	4½-gallon stockpot
Preparation Time:	15 minutes
Cooking Time:	20–30 minutes

Ingredients	Volume	Weight
Vegetable oil	¼ cup	
Onions, thinly sliced	1½ qts.	1 lb. 8 oz.
Garlic, pressed or minced	10 cloves or 3 Tbsp.	
Tomatoes, fresh, chopped	3 cups	1 lb.
Green beans, fresh or frozen, trimmed, halved	1¼ gals.	6 lbs.
Allspice, ground	1 tsp.	
Black pepper	1 tsp.	
Salt	1 Tbsp.	
Water	1 qt.	
Brown sugar (optional)	1 tsp.	

Garnish

Almonds, chopped (optional)	½ cup	2 oz.

Procedure

1. Sauté the onions and garlic in oil until the onions are golden.
2. Mix in the tomatoes and green beans, add the spices, and continue to sauté for 5 minutes.

(continued)

3. Stir in the water and the optional sugar, bring to a boil, and reduce to a simmer for 20–30 minutes until the beans are very tender.
4. Garnish with chopped almonds.

Servings	Calories	Protein (g)	Fat (g)	Cholesterol (mg)	Carbohydrates (g)	Fiber (g)	Sodium (mg)
1	55	1.5	2.6	0	8.0	2.7	309

Side Dishes

Fresh Mozzarella and Sun-dried Tomatoes

24 3-oz. Servings

The distinctive flavor of chewy sun-dried tomatoes and the creamy texture of fresh mozzarella are featured in this elegant salad. For an appetizer or starter course, toast slices of French or Italian bread that have been rubbed with a cut clove of garlic and lightly brushed with olive oil. Then top with the mozzarella mixture. Other serving suggestions include: as an accompaniment to pasta and vegetable salads; as a pita bread filling with lettuce and fresh tomatoes; as a salad, with alternating slices of fresh tomatoes and the mozzarella arranged on a platter and topped with the sun-dried tomatoes, olive oil, and basil.

Preparation Time: 20 minutes

Ingredients	Volume	Weight
Sun-dried tomatoes	3 cups	9 oz.
Mozzarella cheese, fresh, in ¼-in. thick slices		4 lbs.
Olive oil, extra-virgin if desired	¼ cup	
Basil, fresh, chopped	¼ cup	

Procedure

1. Cover the sun-dried tomatoes with boiling water and set aside to soak for 15 minutes.
2. Drain and slice the tomatoes.
3. Gently combine with other ingredients.

Note: We prefer the more economically priced dry-packed tomatoes to the oil-packed ones.

Servings	Calories	Protein (g)	Fat (g)	Cholesterol (mg)	Carbohydrates (g)	Fiber (g)	Sodium (mg)
1	244	20.0	14.8	44	8.7	1.5	600

Golden Orzo

24 6-oz. Servings

Orzo is a small, rice-shaped pasta that we use to add variety to our repertoire of grain dishes. It readily absorbs seasonings and is naturally paired with other Mediterranean dishes such as Fish with Artichoke Hearts and Red Peppers (p. 179), Roasted Vegetables (p. 340), and Eggplant Mykonos (p. 353).

Equipment:	6-in. deep half-size insert pan
Preparation Time:	5 minutes
Cooking Time:	10 minutes

Ingredients	Volume	Weight
Orzo or rosamarina (p. 472).		3 lbs.
Olive oil	¼ cup	
Turmeric	1 Tbsp.	
Coriander seed, ground	2 tsp.	
Paprika, Hungarian sweet	2 tsp.	
Salt and black pepper to taste		

Procedure

1. Bring at least 3 gallons of water to a boil. Cook orzo until it is al dente. Drain.
2. Meanwhile, heat the olive oil in a small skillet and add the spices. Cook gently on a very low heat for 2–3 minutes while stirring.
3. Remove from the heat and toss with cooked orzo.

Variations
- Replace the coriander and paprika with 1 tsp. cinnamon and 2 tsp. ground cumin.
- Toss with annatto oil (p. 467).
- Replace the coriander and paprika wih 1 tsp. dried thyme and 2 tsp. dried oregano.

Servings	Calories	Protein (g)	Fat (g)	Cholesterol (mg)	Carbohydrates (g)	Fiber (g)	Sodium (mg)
1	260	8.1	3.5	0	47.9	2.3	9

Golden Spanish Rice

24 4.5-oz. Servings

Festively colored and seasoned, this rice dish is well paired with Pompano Tampico (p. 187), Refritos (p. 216), or Caribbean Black Beans (p. 197).

Equipment:	6-in. deep half-size insert pan
Preparation Time:	20 minutes
Cooking Time:	15 minutes with cooked rice; 50 minutes with raw rice or cold cooked rice

Ingredients	Volume	Weight
Brown rice, cooked	4½ qts.	7 lbs. 12 oz.
or raw (p. 468)	1½ qts.	2 lbs. 6 oz.
Vegetable oil	⅓ cup	
Annatto seeds (p. 467)	1½ Tbsp.	
Corn, frozen	3 cups	1 lb. 8 oz.
Tomato, fresh, cubed	1 qt.	1 lb. 8 oz.
Scallions, green and white parts, chopped	2 cups	5 oz.
Spanish olives, chopped	1 cup	6 oz.
Cilantro, fresh, chopped	½–¾ cup	
Salt and black pepper to taste		

Procedure

1. If not using precooked rice, cook the 1½ qts. of raw rice first.
2. In a small skillet, heat the oil and the annatto seeds on medium heat for 4–5 minutes, until the oil turns a deep yellow-orange.
3. Strain the oil into a large skillet and discard the seeds.
4. Add the remaining ingredients, except for the rice, salt, and pepper and cook for about 5–10 minutes, until hot.
4. Combine the sauté with the rice. Season with salt and pepper. If the rice is hot, serve immediately. If cold cooked rice is used, transfer the rice and the sauté to a lightly oiled baking pan, cover tightly with foil, and bake at 350° for 45 minutes, or until heated through.

Servings	Calories	Protein (g)	Fat (g)	Cholesterol (mg)	Carbohydrates (g)	Fiber (g)	Sodium (mg)
1	240	4.9	6.0	0	43.2	1.5	187

Greek Roasted Potatoes

24 5-oz. Servings

Crisp and lemony, these slow-cooked potatoes are a good accompaniment to Flounder with Spinach and Almonds (p. 181) and Fish with Lemon and Basil (p. 177).

Equipment:	2 insert pans, 4-in. deep
Preparation Time:	30 minutes
Cooking Time:	1–1½ hours

Ingredients	Volume	Weight
Potatoes, raw, cubed	2½ gals.	10 lbs.
Lemon juice, fresh	2 cups	
Vegetable oil	1 cup	
Olive oil	½ cup	
Salt	3 Tbsp.	
Black pepper	2 tsp.	
Oregano, dried	2 tsp.	
Garlic, minced or pressed	8 cloves or 2½ Tbsp.	
Hot water	8 cups	

Procedure

1. Preheat the oven to 475°.
2. Divide the potatoes between two insert pans.
3. Toss them with the lemon juice, oils, and seasonings.
4. Add 4 cups of hot water to each pan.
5. Bake uncovered at 475° for 1–1½ hours, in a convection oven if possible, stirring every 20 minutes. Add more water if necessary to prevent sticking; however, try to let the potatoes brown and the liquid to evaporate in the final 15 minutes.

Servings	Calories	Protein (g)	Fat (g)	Cholesterol (mg)	Carbohydrates (g)	Fiber (g)	Sodium (mg)
1	265	2.8	14.3	0	33.0	2.9	901

Kasha with Mushrooms

24 6-oz. Servings

Kasha is a hearty, staple grain used in much of Eastern Europe. Dill and mushrooms are delicious in combination with kasha, as well as being authentic compatriots. Serve with Sweet and Sour Red Cabbage (p. 343) and Apple Soup (p. 17).

Equipment:	4½-gallon stockpot	
Preparation Time:	20 minutes	
Cooking Time:	20 minutes	

Ingredients	Volume	Weight
Vegetable oil	¼ cup	
Onions, chopped	1½ qts.	1 lb. 8 oz.
Vegetable Stock (p. 63) or water	2¼ qts.	
Eggs (or egg white), lightly beaten	4 or 1 cup	8 oz.
Kasha (roasted buckwheat groats)*	4½ cups	
Mushrooms, fresh, sliced	3¾ qts.	3 lbs.
Vegetable oil	¼ cup	
Soy sauce	⅓ cup	
Dill, fresh, chopped	¼ cup	
or dried	2 Tbsp.	
Black pepper	1 tsp.	
Salt to taste		

Procedure

1. Sauté the onions in oil until they are golden.
2. In a separate pot, heat the water or stock to boiling.
3. In a bowl, combine the eggs and kasha, mixing thoroughly.
4. Add the kasha mixture to the softened, cooked onions and heat gently, stirring until the kasha kernels are dry and separate.

*Kasha is the Russian name for buckwheat. Although not related to the wheat family, the seed is roasted and treated as a grain. It is a food high in protein and vitamins, with a rich, nutty flavor.

(continued)

5. Add the boiling water or stock to the kasha mixture, cover, and gently simmer on low heat until all the liquid is absorbed and the kasha is cooked.
6. While the kasha cooks, sauté the mushrooms with the remaining 1/4-cup vegetable oil on high heat until the mushrooms soften. Drain and reserve the cooking liquid.
7. Add the mushrooms to the kasha with 1 cup of the reserved liquid. Stir in the soy sauce, dill, and black pepper. Season to taste with salt.

Servings	Calories	Protein (g)	Fat (g)	Cholesterol (mg)	Carbohydrates (g)	Fiber (g)	Sodium (mg)
1	140	4.6	6.4	44	18.2	2.1	212

Marinated Vegetables

24 6-oz. Servings

This classic Moosewood dish is employed to add a balance of flavor, color, and texture to rich dishes such as strudels or savory pastries. Marinated Vegetables can be served as a main dish salad when paired with whole grain bread and either Seasoned Tofu (p. 220), hard-boiled egg, or sliced cheese.

Equipment:	4-in. deep insert pan
Preparation Time:	40 minutes
Cooking Time:	25 minutes

Ingredients	Volume	Weight
Carrots, cut into thick matchsticks	1½ qts.	2 lbs.
Cauliflower, cut into bite-sized florets	1½ qts.	2 lbs. 4 oz.
Peppers, red and/or green, cut in strips or coarsely chopped	2 qts.	2 lbs.
Asparagus, sliced on diagonal	1 qt.	1 lb. 3 oz.
Zucchini and/or yellow squash, cut in rounds	1 qt.	1 lb. 6 oz.
Tomatoes, fresh, cut in wedges and halved	1 qt.	1 lb.

Vinaigrette

Ingredients	Volume
Vegetable oil	¾ cup
Olive oil	¾ cup
Cider or red wine vinegar	½ cup
Lemon juice, fresh	¼ cup
Garlic, minced or pressed	4 lg. cloves or 2 Tbsp.
Basil, marjoram, dill, tarragon, dried (in any combination)	1½–2 Tbsp.
Dijon mustard	1 Tbsp.
Salt and black pepper to taste	

(continued)

Procedure

1. Steam the vegetables sequentially until just tender. Allow to cool in long insert pans.
2. Whisk together the vinaigrette ingredients and toss with the steamed vegetables.
3. Serve at room temperature or chilled.

Servings	Calories	Protein (g)	Fat (g)	Cholesterol (mg)	Carbohydrates (g)	Fiber (g)	Sodium (mg)
·1	176	2.4	14.7	0	11.1	3.7	49

Oasis Chutney with Coconut and Dates

25 2-oz. Servings

This quickly prepared, sweet, and refreshing chutney complements any curry. Create an unusual canapé by spreading a layer of cream cheese or Neufchâtel on a toast round or sesame cracker topped with a thin layer of chutney.

Preparation Time: 20 minutes

Ingredients	Volume	Weight
Pitted dates, chopped	2 qts.	2 lbs. 4 oz.
Coconut, unsweetened	¾ cup	3 oz.
Lemon juice, fresh	1 cup	
Ginger root, fresh, grated	½ cup	
Fennel seeds, ground	1 Tbsp.	
Coriander seeds, ground	2 tsp.	
Salt	1½ tsp.	
Parsley, fresh, chopped	1 cup	

Procedure

1. Process all the ingredients, except the parsley, in the bowl of a food processor. If the dates are dry, add small amounts of hot water.
2. Stir in the parsley.

Servings	Calories	Protein (g)	Fat (g)	Cholesterol (mg)	Carbohydrates (g)	Fiber (g)	Sodium (mg)
1	135	1.1	1.1	0	34.0	3.5	158

Pasta with Peas and Onions

24 5-oz. Servings

A remarkably simple dish with a lightly sweet, appealing flavor. Serve with grilled or broiled fish or Roasted Vegetables (p. 340).

Equipment:	4-qt. stockpot
Preparation Time:	20 minutes
Cooking Time:	20 minutes

Ingredients	Volume	Weight
Onions, finely diced	3 qts.	3 lbs.
Olive oil	¼ cup	
Pasta, small shaped: shells, bowties, orecchietti		3 lbs.
Green peas, frozen, slightly thawed		3 lbs.
Spearmint, dried (the contents of 1 herbal mint tea bag)	1½ tsp.	
Salt	1 Tbsp.	

Topping

Parmesan or Romano cheese, grated (optional)	3 cups	12 oz.

Procedure

1. Sauté the onions in olive oil until they are soft and golden.
2. Cook the pasta.
3. Meanwhile, add the peas, spearmint, and salt to the sautéed onions, and heat to warm the peas.
4. Drain the pasta.
5. Top each serving with a cup of peas and onions or toss the mixture with the hot pasta. Sprinkle on 2 Tbsp. of cheese per serving, if desired.

Once heated, the onion–pea mixture should be held at room temperature in order to preserve the bright green color of the peas for as long as possible. This dish is recommended when fresh batches of hot pasta can be made throughout a meal. Peas and onions also taste good with brown or white rice.

Servings	Calories	Protein (g)	Fat (g)	Cholesterol (mg)	Carbohydrates (g)	Fiber (g)	Sodium (mg)
1	161	5.9	3.0	0	28.1	4.2	343

Peach Chutney
24 3.5-oz. Servings

Our Peach Chutney is a colorful sweet and savory accompaniment to Indian dishes, Caribbean Black Beans (p. 197), or Roti (p. 293).

Equipment:	2-gallon pot
Preparation Time:	20 minutes
Cooking Time:	20 minutes

Ingredients	Volume	Weight
Vegetable oil	¼ cup	
Onions, chopped	1 qt.	1 lb.
Ginger root, fresh, grated	1½ Tbsp.	
Cinnamon	1 tsp.	
Nutmeg	½ tsp.	
Cardamom	½ tsp.	
Cayenne	¼ tsp. or less to taste	
Cider vinegar	½ cup	
Brown sugar	¾ cup	
Peaches, drained, sliced	2 qts. (1 #10 can)	4 lbs. 4 oz.

Procedure

1. Sauté the onions and seasonings in vegetable oil until the onions are translucent.
2. Add the cider vinegar, brown sugar, and peaches and simmer for 15 minutes.

Note: Apricots can be used in place of peaches.

Servings	Calories	Protein (g)	Fat (g)	Cholesterol (mg)	Carbohydrates (g)	Fiber (g)	Sodium (mg)
1	92	0.8	2.5	0	18.4	1.1	7

Rice Pilaf with Orzo

24 5-oz. Servings

This colorful herbed side dish can accompany Mediterranean fish dishes such as Fish Santorini (p. 174), Fish Marseilles (p. 172), or Fish Algiers (p. 168).

Equipment:	2½-gallon stockpot
Preparation Time:	10 minutes
Cooking Time:	1½ hours (if cooking rice)

Ingredients	Volume	Weight
Olive oil	½ cup	
Onions, chopped	1 qt.	1 lb.
Marjoram, dried	1 Tbsp.	
Rosemary, dried	½ tsp.	
Turmeric, ground	½ tsp.	
Salt	1 tsp.	
Black pepper	½ tsp.	
Orzo, uncooked	2 cups	12 oz.
Water	3 cups	
Brown rice, cooked	3 qts.	5 lbs. 4 oz.
or raw (p. 468)	1 qt.	1 lb. 10 oz.
Parsley, fresh, chopped	½ cup	

Procedure

1. Sauté the onions, herbs, and turmeric in olive oil until the onions are softened and lightly browned.
2. Add the salt, pepper, and orzo and sauté for 2 minutes.
3. Add the water, bring to a boil, cover, and then simmer on low heat (using a heat diffuser if necessary) for 10–12 minutes until the orzo is tender.
4. Stir the cooked rice into the orzo and toss with the fresh parsley.

Note: If cooking rice, begin 1 hour before proceeding with recipe.

Servings	Calories	Protein (g)	Fat (g)	Cholesterol (mg)	Carbohydrates (g)	Fiber (g)	Sodium (mg)
1	220	4.6	5.9	0	37.1	0.9	101

Roasted Vegetables

48 4-oz. Side Dish Servings
24 8-oz. Main Dish Servings

Roasting creates vegetables that are crisp on the outside and tender and sweet inside. The process of roasting caramelizes the natural vegetable sugars. Roasted Vegetables become a complete entrée served on couscous, Golden Orzo (p. 328), or Sara's Greens (p. 342). Top with grated feta or Parmesan cheese. Asparagus, carrots, eggplant, and root vegetables such as parsnips or turnips can also be roasted with good results.

Equipment:	3 insert pans, 4-in. deep
Preparation Time:	1 hour
Baking Time:	1 hour

Ingredients	Volume	Weight
Potatoes, cut into bite-sized chunks	3 qts.	3 lbs.
Sweet potatoes, cut into bite-sized chunks	3 qts.	3 lbs.
Peppers, green and/or red, sliced	3 qts.	3 lbs.
Onions, ½-in. thick slices	3 qts.	3 lbs.
Yellow and green summer squash, cut into bite-sized chunks	3½ qts.	3 lbs.
Mushrooms, halved		2 lbs.

Marinade

Olive oil	2 cups	
Garlic, pressed	6 lg. cloves or 3 Tbsp.	
Rosemary, dried, crumbled	4 Tbsp.	
or fresh, chopped	4 Tbsp.	
Thyme, fresh or dried	4 tsp.	
Salt and black pepper to taste		
Lemon juice, fresh	2 cups	

Procedure

1. Bring to a boil enough water to cover 3 lbs. of potatoes. Boil, sequentially, the white and sweet potatoes for 5 minutes. Drain and set aside.
2. Preheat the oven to 375°.
3. Combine the potatoes with the other vegetables divided among three insert pans. Pour one-third of the marinade over each pan of vegetables.
4. Bake, uncovered, at 375° (in a convection oven if possible), stirring every 15 minutes. Bake until the vegetables are tender and nicely browned at the edges.

Servings	Calories	Protein (g)	Fat (g)	Cholesterol (mg)	Carbohydrates (g)	Fiber (g)	Sodium (mg)
1	166	2.1	9.8	0	19.2	2.5	11

Sara's Greens

24 2-oz. Servings

Sara Robbins is a Moosewood chef whose Southern heritage is reflected in the preparation of this nutritious and tasty dish. Serve with Scarlett's Frittata (p. 153), Black Bean– Sweet Potato Burritos (p. 273), or Spicy Cajun Fish (p. 190).

Equipment:	4½-gallon stockpot
Preparation Time:	30 minutes
Cooking Time:	20 minutes

Ingredients	Volume	Weight
Greens, fresh (unprepped): kale, collard, Swiss chard, mustard		6 lbs.
Salt and black pepper to taste		
Apple cider vinegar to taste		
Tabasco to taste		

Procedure

1. Carefully clean the greens by soaking and rinsing well. Remove any yellow leaves and tough stems. Coarsely chop the greens.
2. Place the greens in a large pot. Cover with cool water. Simmer for 20 minutes or until tender. Drain.
3. Place the greens in a serving container and toss with the seasonings.

Servings	Calories	Protein (g)	Fat (g)	Cholesterol (mg)	Carbohydrates (g)	Fiber (g)	Sodium (mg)
1	28	1.6	0.3	0	4.9	1.7	27

Sweet and Sour Red Cabbage

25 4-oz. Servings

This side dish is an unassuming yet excellent companion for savory dishes such as Vegetable Piroshki (p. 309) or Potato Kugel (p. 149).

Equipment:	2½-gallon stockpot
Preparation Time:	25 minutes
Cooking Time:	40 minutes

Ingredients	Volume	Weight
Vegetable oil	¼ cup	
Onions, chopped	1 qt.	1 lb.
Red cabbage, thinly sliced	1½ gals.	4 lbs.
Apple juice or cider	3 cups	
Salt	1 Tbsp.	
Black pepper to taste		
Dill, fresh, chopped	3 Tbsp.	
or dried	1 Tbsp.	
Caraway seeds	1 Tbsp.	
Cider vinegar	¾ cup	
Brown sugar or honey	¼ cup	

Procedure

1. Sauté the onions in oil until they are lightly browned.
2. Add the cabbage and sauté for 5 minutes.
3. Add the remaining ingredients, except for the sugar or honey. Cook on low heat, covered, for about 30 minutes. Stir occasionally.
4. Add the sugar or honey to taste.

Servings	Calories	Protein (g)	Fat (g)	Cholesterol (mg)	Carbohydrates (g)	Fiber (g)	Sodium (mg)
1	66	1.0	2.6	0	10.9	1.6	305

Tzatziki

Yield: 3 qts.

Here is a Greek version of a salad that is common throughout the Middle East, North Africa, and Eastern Europe. While appropriate as a side dish with foods of those regions, Tzatziki is also a refreshing counterpoint for a spicy Eggplant–Spinach Curry (p. 355) or Golden Curry (p. 359).

Preparation Time: 20 minutes

Ingredients	Volume	Weight
Cucumbers, peeled, grated	1½ qts.	2 lbs. 4 oz.
Garlic, pressed or minced	10 cloves or 3 Tbsp.	
Yogurt, plain, low-fat or nonfat	2 qts.	
Mint, fresh, minced	¼ cup	
or dried	1 Tbsp.	
Salt and black pepper to taste		

Procedure

1. Lightly salt the grated cucumbers, place in a colander or strainer, and allow to drain for 15 minutes.
2. Combine the drained cucumbers with the rest of the ingredients.
3. Chill for 30 minutes.

Servings	Calories	Protein (g)	Fat (g)	Cholesterol (mg)	Carbohydrates (g)	Fiber (g)	Sodium (mg)
1	56	4.4	1.2	5	7.2	0.4	62

STEWS AND SAUTÉS

Vegetarian stews and sautés are flavorful, appetizing meals and draw from a wide array of vegetables, legumes, grains, herbs, and spices. Stews such as Thai Curry, Caribbean Vegetable Stew, or Vegetable Tajine feature the exotic, aromatic seasonings of specific ethnic cuisines. Others are comforting and more familiar dishes, like Brunswick Stew, Vegetable Pot Pie, or Winter Vegetable Stew. For balanced taste and nutrition, most of our stews are best served with a grain or grain product such as bread or couscous. Menu suggestions on each recipe indicate our favorite accompanying grain for the dish, as well as a garnish or topping that may enhance it. Some of the toppings do double duty for flavor and additional protein. We'll admit to showing some of our idiosyncratic tastes; feta cheese, for example, shows up in many recipes here simply because we like it. Because all the stews and sautés are nondairy or vegan, we list dairy toppings and garnishes as options. This choice helps us better serve a more extensive range of customers.

Portions for all the recipes here are given in the weight measurement for our generous lunch servings. Our dinner portions average one third larger than lunch servings. We decided to list the slightly smaller portion size here because it's closer to the industry standard we noted in our research.

Even though many stews generally benefit from the slow melding of flavors during cooking, the color, texture, and individual flavor of each vegetable can suffer when held too long in a steam table. One method to retain vegetable integrity for stews is to partially cook the dish ahead of time and then finish when needed. When a meal service is to extend over a period of several hours, we don't try to hold sautés and stir-fries in the steam table. We have all the ingredients prepped ahead and then cook the sauté in several batches during the course of the meal. This is particularly crucial for Asian stir-fries such as Sweet and Sour Vegetables, Mapo Tofu, and Tofu with Vegetable Sauté. For all stews and stir-fries, the most delicate ingredients are added late in the cooking process, or even after a dish is cooked, as for the spinach in Eggplant Mykonos or the green peas in Vegetable Pot Pie.

Brunswick Stew

24 16-oz. Servings

Our vegetarian version of this Southern classic is so rich and flavorful, you won't miss the 'possum or squirrel. Try not to overlook the smoked cheese; it's a must. Serve steaming hot in bowls with a wedge of Cornbread (p. 323). Top with grated cheese and chopped scallions.

Equipment:	4½-gallon stockpot
Preparation Time:	25 minutes
Cooking Time:	1 hour

Ingredients	Volume	Weight
Onions, chopped	3 qts.	3 lbs.
Garlic, minced or pressed	10 cloves or 3 Tbsp.	
Vegetable oil	½ cup	
Carrots, sliced in half-moons	1½ qts.	2 lbs.
Potatoes, cut in small chunks	1½ qts.	1 lb. 8 oz.
Tomatoes, fresh, chopped or canned with juice	3 qts. (1# 10 can)	6 lbs. 6 oz.
Vegetable Stock (p. 63) or water	1 qt.	
Okra, frozen or fresh, sliced	2 qts.	2 lbs. 8 oz.
Corn, frozen or fresh cut	2 qts.	2 lbs. 14 oz.
Lima beans, frozen or fresh	3 qts.	3 lbs. 8 oz.
Worcestershire sauce	¾ cup	
Tabasco sauce	2 tsp.	
Molasses	1 cup	
Vinegar	½ cup	
Salt and black pepper to taste		
Ketchup or barbecue sauce (optional)	1 cup	
Zucchini, cut in 1-in. chunks	1½ qts.	2 lbs.
Cornstarch, dissolved in	6 Tbsp.	
Cool water	¾ cup	

Garnishes

Smoked Cheddar or smoked Swiss cheese, grated	2 qts.	1 lb. 8 oz.
Scallions, chopped	1 qt.	10 oz.

Procedure

1. In a 4½-gallon stockpot, sauté the onions and garlic in oil until the onions are golden.
2. Add the carrots, potatoes, tomatoes, and stock or water and heat to a simmer.
3. Stir in the okra, corn, lima beans, and seasonings and continue to simmer for about 30 minutes, until the vegetables are tender. Use a heat diffuser to avoid scorching.
4. Stir in the zucchini and cook until just tender.
5. Thicken with the cornstarch mixture. Adjust for Tabasco.
6. Top each serving with 1 oz. of cheese and a sprinkling of chopped scallions.

Servings	Calories	Protein (g)	Fat (g)	Cholesterol (mg)	Carbohydrates (g)	Fiber (g)	Sodium (mg)
1	411	15.4	15.3	30	56.9	5.7	399

Bulgarian Stew

24 12-oz. Servings

This is a mixed bean stew that is warming and substantial. The savory and tangy broth keeps it interesting and light. Serve with pumpernickel or rye bread.

Equipment:	2¹/₂-gallon stockpot
Preparation Time:	15 minutes plus soaking time for beans
Cooking Time:	1¹/₂ hours

Ingredients	Volume	Weight
Lentils, dried	2 cups	1 lb.
White beans, dried (navy, pea, or Great Northern)	2 cups	1 lb.
Olive oil	¹/₂ cup	
Onions, chopped	3 qts.	3 lbs.
Garlic, minced or pressed	10 cloves or 3 Tbsp.	
Peppers, mixed colors, diced	1 gal.	4 lbs.
Basil, dried	2 Tbsp.	
Marjoram, dried	1 Tbsp.	
Thyme, dried	1 Tbsp.	
Cayenne	¹/₄ tsp.	
Salt	1 Tbsp.	
Tomatoes, canned, with juice, crushed	1¹/₂ qts.	
Dry red wine	1 cup	
Vegetable Stock (p. 63) or water	2 cups	

Topping

Yogurt, plain, low-fat, or nonfat	2 cups

Procedure

1. Combine the lentils and white beans and soak in water to cover for 4 hours or overnight. Drain and set aside.

(continued)

2. Sauté the onions and garlic in oil until the onions are translucent.
3. Add the peppers, herbs, cayenne, and salt and continue to sauté until the peppers soften.
4. Stir in the lentils, beans, tomatoes, wine, and stock or water.
5. Bring to a boil and then reduce to a low simmer. Cook, covered, for about 1 to 1½ hours, until the beans are tender. Stir occasionally to prevent sticking.
6. Top with a dollop of yogurt.

Servings	Calories	Protein (g)	Fat (g)	Cholesterol (mg)	Carbohydrates (g)	Fiber (g)	Sodium (mg)
1	247	11.9	5.9	1	37.8	5.8	391

Caribbean Vegetable Stew
24 9-oz. Servings

The combination of these easily found and prepared ingredients results in a stew that is at once familiar yet exotic. Serve on rice or with Cornbread (p. 323); top with Jerk Tofu (p. 212), Seasoned Tempeh (p. 218), or wedges of hard-boiled eggs.

Equipment:	2½-gallon stock pot
Preparation Time:	30 minutes
Cooking Time:	40 minutes

Ingredients	Volume	Weight
Onions, chopped	2 qts.	2 lbs.
Vegetable oil	¼ cup	
Cabbage, chopped	2 qts.	1 lb. 8 oz.
Chili peppers, fresh, seeded, minced	4 sm.	2 oz.
or cayenne	¼–½ tsp.	
Ginger root, fresh, grated	¼ cup	
Vegetable Stock (p. 63) or water	1 qt.	
Salt, to taste		
Sweet potatoes, peeled, cubed	3 qts.	3 lbs.
Peppers, red and green, chopped	1½ qts.	1 lb. 8 oz.
Tomatoes, canned, with juice, crushed	2 qts.	4 lbs.
Zucchini, chopped	1½ qts.	2 lbs.
Okra, frozen, sliced	1½ qts.	2 lbs.
Lime juice, fresh	½–¾ cup	
Cilantro, fresh, chopped	½ cup	

Garnish

	Volume	Weight
Roasted peanuts	3 cups	15 oz.

Procedure

1. Sauté the onions in vegetable oil for 3–4 minutes.
2. Add the cabbage and chilies or cayenne and continue to sauté until the onions are translucent.

(continued)

3. Add the ginger, water or stock, and sweet potatoes with a sprinkle of salt. Bring to a boil and simmer for 3 minutes.
4. Add the peppers and tomatoes and simmer for 3 more minutes.
5. Add the zucchini and okra and simmer until all the vegetables are tender.
6. Stir in the lime juice, additional salt to taste, and cilantro.
7. Garnish with roasted peanuts and cilantro sprigs if desired.

Servings	Calories	Protein (g)	Fat (g)	Cholesterol (mg)	Carbohydrates (g)	Fiber (g)	Sodium (mg)
1	254	8.6	11.6	0	33.4	4.6	140

Eggplant Mykonos

24 11-oz. Servings

This tangy, tasty stew requires little preparation. Serve on rice, couscous, orzo, or bulghur and top with grated feta cheese.

Equipment:	2½-gallon stockpot
Preparation Time:	30 minutes
Cooking Time:	1 hour

Ingredients	Volume	Weight
Onions, chopped	3 qts.	3 lbs.
Garlic, pressed or minced	10 cloves or 3 Tbsp.	
Olive oil	¼ cup	
Eggplant, cubed	4½ qts.	4 lbs. 8 oz.
Salt	1 Tbsp.	
Peppers, green and red, chopped	2½ qts.	2 lbs. 8 oz.
Tomatoes, canned, with juice, crushed	3½ qts. (1 #10 can)	7 lbs.
Apple juice, unsweetened, or water	2½ cups	
Fennel seed, ground	1½ Tbsp.	
Dill weed, fresh, chopped	¾ cup	
or dried	¼ cup	
Lemon juice, fresh	½ cup	
Lemon peel, grated (optional)	1 lemon or 1 Tbsp.	
Spinach, fresh, stemmed, chopped, rinsed	2 10-oz. bags	1 lb. 4 oz.

Topping

Feta cheese, grated	1 qt.	1 lb.

Procedure

1. In a 2½-gallon stockpot, sauté the onions and garlic in oil until the onions are translucent.

(continued)

2. Add the eggplant, sprinkle with salt, and sauté briefly on low heat, stirring frequently.
3. Add the peppers, tomatoes, juice or water, fennel seed, and dill (if using the dried herb). Reserve the fresh dill. Cover the pot and bring to a simmer, cooking until the eggplant is tender, about 30–40 minutes. Stir frequently.
4. If using fresh dill, add it now along with the lemon juice and optional lemon peel.
5. Stir the uncooked spinach into the stew, turn off the heat, and allow the spinach to wilt from the heat of the stew. We keep the spinach fresh and green over an extended serving period by adding fresh spinach to separate batches of stew as needed.

Servings	Calories	Protein (g)	Fat (g)	Cholesterol (mg)	Carbohydrates (g)	Fiber (g)	Sodium (mg)
1	174	6.4	7.2	17	24.1	3.8	687

Eggplant-Spinach Curry

24 11-oz. Servings

Eggplant dishes are favorites among our customers. Here, eggplant, which absorbs flavors well, is a fine vehicle for a wealth of curry spices. Serve on rice and top with yogurt, toasted cashews, and currants.

Equipment:	2½-gallon stockpot; 4-gallon stockpot
Preparation Time:	40 minutes
Cooking Time:	1 hour

Ingredients	Volume	Weight
Eggplant, cubed	6 qts.	6 lbs.
Onions, chopped	2 qts.	2 lbs.
Vegetable oil	½ cup	
Ginger root, fresh, grated	¼ cup	
Cumin, ground	3 Tbsp.	
Coriander seed, ground	2 Tbsp.	
Cinnamon, ground	1 Tbsp.	
Turmeric	2 tsp.	
Cayenne	½ tsp.	
Cardamom, ground	½ tsp.	
Salt	1 Tbsp.	
Coconut milk, unsweetened (p. 470) or apple juice, unsweetened	2 cups	14 oz.
Vegetable Stock (p. 63) or water	1 qt.	
Spinach, stemmed and rinsed	4 10-oz bags	2 lbs. 8 oz.
Red peppers, chopped	2 qts.	2 lbs.
Lemon juice, fresh	¼ cup	

Procedure

1. Place the cubed eggplant in a colander, sprinkle with salt, and set aside for 20–30 minutes.

(continued)

2. In a 2½-gallon stockpot, sauté the onions in oil until they are translucent.
3. Add the spices and continue sautéing for 3 minutes, stirring often.
4. Rinse the eggplant and drain.
5. Add it to the onions with the coconut milk or juice and the stock or water. Simmer for 20–30 minutes.
6. In a 4-gallon pot, cook the cleaned spinach in a small amount of water until it just wilts. Drain and chop.
7. Add the red peppers to the curry and simmer for 5 minutes.
8. Stir in the spinach and lemon juice. Simmer a final 4 to 5 minutes or until the peppers are tender but firm.

Servings	Calories	Protein (g)	Fat (g)	Cholesterol (mg)	Carbohydrates (g)	Fiber (g)	Sodium (mg)
1	130	3.2	5.6	0	19.8	5.3	339

French Ragout
24 13-oz. Servings

French Ragout is one of our most time-honored and well-loved stews. It's hearty, it's savory, it's a meal with French bread and brie.

Equipment:	2½-gallon stockpot
Preparation Time:	40 minutes
Cooking Time:	45 minutes

Ingredients	Volume	Weight
Vegetable oil	½ cup	
Garlic, minced or pressed	10 cloves or 3 heaping Tbsp.	
Onions, chopped	2½ qts.	2 lbs. 8 oz.
Bay leaves	10	
Thyme, dried	1 tsp.	
Basil, fresh, chopped	½ cup	
or dried	3 Tbsp.	
Celery, sliced	1¾ qts.	1 lb. 12 oz.
Carrots, cut in 1-in. chunks	2 qts.	2 lbs. 8 oz.
Potatoes, cut in 1-in. cubes	2 qts.	3 lbs.
Red wine, dry	2½ cups	
Vegetable Stock (p. 63) or water	1¼ qts.	
Green beans, stemmed, snapped	2 qts.	2 lbs. 6 oz.
Zucchini, cut in 1-in. chunks	2 qts.	2 lbs. 8 oz.
Mushrooms, halved or whole, if small	2 1/2 qts.	1 lb. 12 oz.
Soy sauce		10 oz.
Tomato paste	1 cup	
Tarragon, fresh, chopped	3 Tbsp.	
or dried	1 Tbsp.	
Dijon mustard	1 Tbsp.	
Vinegar	¼ cup	
Molasses	¼ cup	
Salt and black pepper to taste		

(continued)

Procedure

1. In a 2½-gallon stockpot, sauté the onions and garlic until the onions are translucent.
2. Add dried herbs, except for the tarragon. Reserve fresh herbs and tarragon. Stir in the celery and carrots and sauté for an additional 5–10 minutes.
3. Add the potatoes, red wine, and stock or water. Bring the vegetables and herbs to a boil, reduce to a simmer, and cook, stirring often, for 10 minutes.
4. Add the green beans and continue to simmer for 5 minutes.
5. Add the zucchini, mushrooms, soy sauce, and tomato paste. Simmer until the vegetables are tender.
6. Stir in the fresh herbs, tarragon, and flavorings. Adjust for salt and black pepper.

Servings	Calories	Protein (g)	Fat (g)	Cholesterol (mg)	Carbohydrates (g)	Fiber (g)	Sodium (mg)
1	215	5.2	5.4	0	36.0	6.3	841

Golden Curry

24 13-oz. Servings

This is a high-protein, low-fat curry that gains its rich taste and golden color from puréed yellow split peas. It is chock-full of nutrients and flavor. If desired, top with yogurt and serve on rice with Oasis Chutney (p. 335) or Peach Chutney (p. 338).

Equipment:	2-gallon stockpot, 2½-gallon stockpot
Preparation Time:	30 minutes
Cooking Time:	1 hour

Ingredients	Volume	Weight
Yellow split peas	1½ qts.	
Water	1 gal.	
Onions, chopped	1 qt.	1 lb.
Chili peppers, fresh, minced	3 sm.	1.5 oz.
Vegetable oil	¼ cup	
Curry powder, mild	3 Tbsp.	
Cumin, ground	1 Tbsp.	
Ginger root, fresh, grated	6 Tbsp.	
Sweet potatoes, peeled, diced	6 qts.	6 lbs.
Water	1½ qts.	
Cauliflower, cut into florets	1 gal.	5 lbs. 8 oz.
Bell peppers, green and/or red, chopped	1½ qts.	1 lb. 8 oz.
Spinach		10 oz.
Lemon juice, fresh	½ cup	
Salt to taste		

Procedure

1. Rinse the split peas, cover with 1 gallon of water, and simmer until soft.
2. While the peas cook, sauté the onions and chili peppers in a 2½-gallon stockpot until the onions are translucent.

(continued)

3. Add the spices and sauté for 2–3 minutes more, stirring continuously to prevent the onions from burning. Turn off the heat.
4. In a separate pot, blanch the sweet potatoes until barely tender.
5. Add the sweet potatoes with 1½ qts. of water (or stock from the sweet potatoes), the cauliflower, and the peppers to the sautéed onions. Simmer until all the vegetables are tender.
6. While the vegetables simmer, purée the cooked split peas and cooking liquid, if any, in a blender until velvety.
7. Rinse, stem, and coarsely chop the spinach.
8. When the vegetables are done, stir in the purée, the spinach, lemon juice, and salt. Simmer until the spinach just wilts.

Servings	Calories	Protein (g)	Fat (g)	Cholesterol (mg)	Carbohydrates (g)	Fiber (g)	Sodium (mg)
1	325	14.4	3.9	0	61.6	16.4	64

Green Bean and Fennel
Ragout with Shrimp

24 12-oz. Servings

Inhale the fragrances of the South of France with this aromatic, elegant stew. If you prefer, this stew can also stand on its own without the shrimp. Serve with a crusty bread and a crisp salad.

Equipment:	2½-gallon stockpot
Preparation Time:	30 minutes
Cooking Time:	40 minutes

Ingredients	Volume	Weight
Olive oil	½ cup	
Garlic, pressed or minced	10 med. cloves or 3 Tbsp.	
Onions, chopped	2 qts.	2 lbs.
Potatoes, cut into 1/2-in. cubes	3 qts.	3 lbs.
Tomatoes, canned, undrained and chopped	2½ qts.	4 lb. 8 oz.
Thyme, dried	1 tsp.	
Water	1 qt.	
Green beans, trimmed, snapped	3½ qts.	4 lbs.
Fennel bulb, fresh, sliced in ¼-in. thick slices	2 qts.	2 lbs.
Saffron threads	¼ tsp.	
Orange peel, freshly grated	2 Tbsp.	
Lemon juice, fresh	¼ cup	
Salt and black pepper to taste		
Shrimp, peeled, deveined		4 lbs.

Procedure

1. In a 2½-gallon stockpot, sauté the onions and garlic in olive oil until the onions are translucent.

(continued)

2. Add the potatoes, tomatoes, thyme, and water. Cover, bring to a boil, and then reduce heat to a simmer.
3. Add the beans and fennel bulb to the pot. Stir in the saffron, orange peel, and lemon juice. Simmer for 20 minutes, stirring occasionally, until the potatoes and green beans are tender. Adjust for salt and pepper.
4. Cook shrimp separately and add 2–3 oz. (two or three medium shrimp) to each serving.

Servings	Calories	Protein (g)	Fat (g)	Cholesterol (mg)	Carbohydrates (g)	Fiber (g)	Sodium (mg)
1	227	18.0	6.0	130	27.2	3.6	293

Groundnut Stew

24 10-oz. Servings

This stew is a staple in African households with more versions than can be counted. In this version, vegetables are simmered in a creamy peanut butter sauce, which is offset by pungent ginger and cayenne. We serve this dish on rice topped with wedges of hard-boiled eggs. Garnish the plate with banana, mango, or other fresh fruit slices.

Equipment:	2½-gallon stockpot, 8-oz. ladle
Preparation Time:	30 minutes
Cooking Time:	1 hour

Ingredients	Volume	Weight
Onions, chopped	2 qts.	2 lbs.
Peanut or vegetable oil	¼ cup	
Cayenne	1 tsp.	
Garlic, pressed or minced	6 cloves or 2 Tbsp.	
Cabbage, chopped	3½ qts.	2 lbs. 12 oz.
Sweet potatoes, peeled, cubed	4½ qts.	4 lbs. 8 oz.
Tomato juice	1½ qts.	
Apple juice	3 cups	
Salt	1 Tbsp.	
Ginger root, fresh, grated	2 Tbsp.	
Tomatoes, fresh, chopped	1 qt.	1 lb. 8 oz.
Okra, frozen, sliced	1¾ qts.	2 lbs. 4 oz.
Cilantro, fresh, chopped	3 Tbsp.	
Peanut butter	2½ cups	1 lb. 6 oz.

Procedure

1. Sauté the onions, garlic, and cayenne in oil until the onions are translucent.
2. Add the cabbage and sweet potatoes and sauté until the sweet potatoes begin to brighten.

(continued)

3. Mix in the juices, salt, ginger, and tomatoes. Cover, bring to a boil, and then lower to a simmer and cook until the potatoes are tender.
4. Add the okra and simmer for 10 minutes.
5. Add the cilantro, stir in the peanut butter, and heat gently. Add more juice or water if the stew is too thick.

Servings	Calories	Protein (g)	Fat (g)	Cholesterol (mg)	Carbohydrates (g)	Fiber (g)	Sodium (mg)
1	333	10.4	16.1	0	42.2	6.7	651

Jambalaya

24 14-oz. Servings

This dish is dedicated to vegetarians who love Creole cuisine. The carefully tended roux and smoked cheese topping impart the taste and aroma distinctive to many creole dishes.

Equipment:	2½-gallon stockpot, large skillet
Preparation Time:	20 minutes
Cooking Time:	1 hour

Ingredients	Volume	Weight
Vegetable or olive oil	¼ cup	
Onions, chopped	2 qts.	2 lbs.
Garlic, minced or pressed	10 med. cloves or 3 Tbsp.	
Bay leaves	6	
Carrots, sliced diagonally, ⅛-in. thick	1½ qts.	2 lbs.
Celery, chopped	2 qts.	2 lbs.
Basil, dried	2 Tbsp.	
Thyme, dried	1 Tbsp.	
Oregano, dried	1 Tbsp.	
Peppers, red and green, chopped	3 qts.	3 lbs.
Tomatoes, fresh or canned, coarsely chopped	2½ qts.	3 lbs. 12 oz.
Vegetable Stock (p. 63) or water	3 qts.	
Allspice, ground	1 tsp.	
White pepper	1 tsp.	
Cayenne	½–1 tsp.	
Zucchini or yellow squash, sliced diagonally, ¼-in. thick	1½ qts.	2 lbs.
Okra, fresh or frozen, sliced	2½ qts.	3 lbs.
Salt and black pepper to taste		

Roux

	Volume	
Vegetable oil	¾ cup	
White flour	1 cup	

(continued)

Toppings

Scallions, chopped		8 oz.
Smoked Cheddar or smoked Swiss cheese, grated	2½ qts.	1 lb. 14 oz.

Procedure

1. Sauté onions, garlic, and bay leaves in oil until the onions are translucent.
2. Begin the roux: heat the 3/4 cup of oil in a large, heavy skillet until it is hot but not smoking. Whisk in the flour to form a smooth paste, then lower the heat to a very gentle simmer for 20–30 minutes, stirring frequently to avoid burning. When finished, the roux will be a light coffee color.
3. Return to the stew and add the carrots, celery, basil, thyme, and oregano. Cook for about 10–15 minutes.
4. Add the peppers and cook for 5 minutes more.
5. Add the tomatoes, stock or water, and remaining spices. Cover the pot and bring to a boil.
6. Add the zucchini or yellow squash and okra. Lower to a simmer and cook for about 10 minutes or until the vegetables are tender.
7. When the vegetables are done, stir in the roux and adjust for salt and pepper. Simmer gently for another 5 minutes taking care not to scorch.
8. Serve on rice topped with scallions and smoked cheese.

Servings	Calories	Protein (g)	Fat (g)	Cholesterol (mg)	Carbohydrates (g)	Fiber (g)	Sodium (mg)
1	368	13.8	22.2	37	32.5	7.0	307

Mapo Tofu

24 12-oz Servings

This sweet and sour, rich and spicy mushroom sauce is a perfect medium to flavor tofu. The quickly steamed broccoli spears provide color and contrasting taste and texture.

Equipment:	2½-gallon stockpot or wok
Preparation Time:	30 minutes
Cooking Time:	20 minutes

Ingredients	Volume	Weight
Tofu cakes, pressed (p. 474)		10 lbs. 8 oz. (unpressed weight)

Sauce

Soy sauce	1½ cups	
Sherry, dry	1½ cups	
Vinegar, white or cider	¾ cup	
Ginger root, fresh, grated	½ cup	
Tomato paste	1 cup	
Water	1½ qts.	
Sesame oil, dark (p. 473)	6 Tbsp.	
Chili paste with garlic (p. 469)	½–¾ cup	
or garlic, pressed	18 cloves or 5 Tbsp.	
and cayenne	¼–½ tsp.	

Sauté

Vegetable or peanut oil	¼ cup	
Onions, thinly sliced	3 qts.	3 lbs.
Mushrooms, sliced	1 gal.	3 lbs.
Cornstarch	¾ cup	
Cool water	¾ cup	

(continued)

Topping

Broccoli, cut in 3-in. spears	6 qts.	4 lbs. 8 oz.
Walnuts, toasted, chopped	1 qt.	1 lb.
Scallions, diagonally sliced	1 qt.	10 oz.
Brown rice, cooked (p. 468)	3½ qts.	6 lbs.

Procedure

1. Cut the pressed tofu into 1-in. cubes and set aside.
2. Whisk together the sauce ingredients and set aside.
3. In a wok or 2½-gallon stockpot, sauté the onions in oil until they are translucent.
4. Add the mushrooms and continue to sauté until they soften.
5. Pour in the sauce and add the tofu, mixing gently with a wooden spoon, so as not to break up the tofu. Simmer on low heat until the tofu is heated.
6. Dissolve the cornstarch in the cool water and add to the sauté. Simmer, stirring occasionally, until the sauce thickens.
7. In a separate pot, steam the broccoli spears, in batches as needed.
8. Serve each portion of Mapo Tofu ladled over 4 oz. of rice, top with 1 cup broccoli spears, and garnish with toasted walnuts and scallions.

Servings	Calories	Protein (g)	Fat (g)	Cholesterol (mg)	Carbohydrates (g)	Fiber (g)	Sodium (mg)
1	490	14.1	20.3	0	65.6	5.8	932

Menestra

24 12.5-oz. Servings

A sultry Spanish stew animated by artichoke hearts and green olives. Serve with a coarse-grained bread and a green salad.

Equipment:	2½-gallon stockpot
Preparation Time:	30 minutes
Cooking Time:	45 minutes

Ingredients	Volume	Weight
Onions, chopped	2½ qts.	2 lbs. 8 oz.
Garlic, minced or pressed	12 cloves or 3 heaping Tbsp.	
Olive oil	¼ cup	
Carrots, cut in 1-in. chunks	2 qts.	2 lbs. 10 oz.
Potatoes, cut in 1-in. cubes	3 qts.	3 lbs.
Paprika	¼ cup	
Bay leaves	6	
Cayenne	⅛ tsp.	
Hot water (1 cup could be reserved liquid from artichoke hearts)	2 qts.	
Sherry	1½ cups	
Salt	2 tsp.	
Mushrooms, halved		3 lbs.
Peppers, red or green, chopped	1½ qts.	1 lb. 8 oz.
Artichoke hearts, halved (reserve liquid from canned artichokes)	5¼ cups	1 lb. 8 oz.
Green peas, frozen, slightly thawed	1 qt.	1 lb. 4 oz.

Garnish

Eggs, hard-boiled (optional)	12 to 24	
Spanish olives, chopped	1½ cups	

(continued)

Stews and Sautés

Procedure

1. Sauté the onions and garlic in olive oil until the onions are translucent.
2. Add the carrots, potatoes, and spices and sauté a minute or two, stirring frequently.
3. Add water, sherry, and salt. Bring to a boil and then simmer, covered, until the potatoes are barely tender.
4. Stir in the mushrooms and peppers and continue to simmer until the peppers soften.
5. Add the artichoke hearts and green peas and simmer gently to heat through.
6. Garnish with one half to a whole quartered hard-boiled egg, if desired, and/or chopped Spanish olives.

Servings	Calories	Protein (g)	Fat (g)	Cholesterol (mg)	Carbohydrates (g)	Fiber (g)	Sodium (mg)
1	196	5.8	5.6	0	32.0	7.8	748

Mexican Vegetables

24 12-oz. Servings

This stew is an easy way to get your kids (and their parents) to eat their vegetables. It appeals to a wide audience and is great over cornbread.

Equipment:	2½-gallon stockpot
Preparation Time:	20 minutes
Cooking Time:	40 minutes

Ingredients	Volume	Weight
Vegetable oil	¼ cup	
Onions, chopped	2 qts.	2 lbs.
Garlic, minced or pressed	8 cloves or 2 heaping Tbsp.	
Cumin, ground	1½ Tbsp.	
Coriander seed, ground	1½ Tbsp.	
Chili pepper, fresh, minced	4 sm.	2 oz.
or cayenne	¼ tsp.	
Carrots, sliced in 1/2-in. rounds	1½ qts.	2 lbs.
Salt, to taste		
Tomatoes, canned, with juice, crushed	2 qts.	4 lbs.
Peppers, red and/or green, chopped	2 qts.	2 lbs.
Zucchini or yellow squash, sliced in ½-in. rounds	1½ qts.	2 lbs.
Corn, frozen, slightly thawed	2 qts.	4 lbs.
Cilantro, fresh, chopped	½ cup	
Cornbread (p. 323)	24 pieces	3 oz.

Topping

Monterey Jack cheese, grated	3 cups	9 oz.

Procedure

1. Sauté the onions and garlic in vegetable oil until the onions are translucent.
2. Add the cumin, coriander, chilies or cayenne, carrots, and a sprinkling of salt. Sauté a couple of minutes.

(continued)

3. Add the tomatoes and their juice. Simmer, covered, for 5 minutes.
4. Add the peppers and simmer an additional 5 minutes.
5. Stir in the zucchini or squash and simmer until all the vegetables are tender.
6. Add the corn and cilantro and simmer until just heated through.
7. Serve on a 3-oz. piece of split cornbread and top with grated Monterey Jack cheese.

Servings	Calories	Protein (g)	Fat (g)	Cholesterol (mg)	Carbohydrates (g)	Fiber (g)	Sodium (mg)
1	457	14.3	17.0	76	67.4	7.5	669

Mole de Olla

24 12-oz. Servings

The cloves and cinnamon in this Mexican stew guide and surprise the palate away from the better-known Spanish spices. Serve this mole in a bowl topped with grated cheese or a dollop of sour cream, with a square of steaming Cornbread (p. 323) on the side.

Equipment:	2½-gallon stockpot
Preparation Time:	30 minutes
Cooking Time:	45 minutes

Ingredients	Volume	Weight
Onions, chopped	2½ qts.	2 lbs. 8 oz.
Garlic, minced or pressed	6 med. cloves or 2 Tbsp.	
Chili peppers, fresh, seeded, minced	4–6 Tbsp.	1 to 2 oz.
Vegetable oil	¼ cup	
Salt to taste		
Cinnamon, ground	1 Tbsp.	
Cloves, ground	½ tsp.	
Potatoes, cut in 1-in. cubes	2 qts.	2 lbs.
Tomatoes, canned, undrained	3 qts. (1 #10 can)	6 lbs. 6 oz.
Green beans, stemmed, snapped	2 qts.	2 lbs.
Corn, frozen or fresh	1½ qts.	3 lbs.
Zucchini, sliced in rounds	1½ qts.	2 lbs.
Cilantro, fresh, chopped (optional but recommended)	¼ cup	

Toppings

	Volume	Weight
Cheddar cheese, grated	2 qts.	1 lb. 8 oz.
or Sour cream	2 cups	1 lb.

Procedure

1. In a stockpot, sauté the onions, garlic, and chilies in oil until the onions are translucent.

(continued)

2. Add the cinnamon, cloves, and potatoes. Salt lightly and sauté, stirring frequently for about 5 minutes.
3. Add the tomatoes, green beans, and corn, cover the pot, and simmer until the vegetables are just tender.
4. Stir in the zucchini, and cilantro if desired, and continue simmering until all the vegetables are tender.
5. Serve topped with Cheddar cheese or sour cream.

Servings	Calories	Protein (g)	Fat (g)	Cholesterol (mg)	Carbohydrates (g)	Fiber (g)	Sodium (mg)
1	214	5.6	7.2	0	36.3	4.6	199

Stewed Batilgian

24 16-oz. Servings

Pronounced *Bottle-John,* this traditional Armenian dish is intricately and intensely flavorful. Serve, as suggested, over rice with feta cheese or with wedges of warmed pita bread and hard-boiled eggs.

Equipment:	2½-gallon stockpot
Preparation Time:	20 minutes
Cooking Time:	45 minutes

Ingredients	Volume	Weight
Onions, chopped	1½ qts.	1 lb. 8 oz.
Olive oil	¼ cup	
Celery, chopped	3 qts.	3 lbs.
Green beans, stemmed, snapped in half	2 qts.	2 lbs. 6 oz.
Bay leaves	8	
Garlic, minced or pressed	12 cloves or 3½ Tbsp.	
Basil, fresh, chopped	⅓ cup	
or dried	2 Tbsp.	
Eggplant, cubed	1¼ gals.	5 lbs.
Olive oil	¼ cup	
Salt and black pepper to taste		
Tomatoes, canned with juice, crushed	3 qts. (1 #10 can)	6 lbs. 6 oz.
Lemon juice, fresh	⅓–½ cup	
Capers, drained (optional) (p. 469)	½ cup	
Brown rice, cooked (p. 468)	3½ qts.	6 lbs.

Topping

Feta cheese, grated	1½ qts.	1 lb. 8 oz.

(continued)

Procedure

1. Sauté the onions in ¼ cup olive oil until the onions are translucent.
2. Add the celery, green beans, bay leaves, garlic, and basil if using the dried herb. Reserve fresh basil. Cover and cook on medium heat for 5 minutes, stirring occasionally .
3. Place the eggplant on top of the other vegetables, drizzle with the remaining ¼ cup olive oil, and season with salt and pepper. Cover the pot, reduce the heat to low, and cook the eggplant and vegetables for 30 minutes.
4. Add the tomatoes, stir thoroughly, and continue to simmer, stirring often, until all the vegetables are tender.
5. Add the lemon juice, additional salt and pepper, fresh basil, and capers, if desired.
6. Serve each portion on 4 oz. rice, topped with 1 oz. feta cheese. Garnish with a lemon wedge.

Servings	Calories	Protein (g)	Fat (g)	Cholesterol (mg)	Carbohydrates (g)	Fiber (g)	Sodium (mg)
1	334	10.2	11.8	25	49.0	5.2	600

Sweet and Sour Vegetables

24 12-oz. Servings

These Polynesian-style vegetables are delicious alone or spooned over rice. They also become a lovely glazed sauce over either grilled or broiled fish or Tofu–Vegetable Croquettes (p. 225).

Equipment:	2½-gallon stockpot or wok
Preparation Time:	20 minutes
Cooking Time:	30 minutes

Ingredients	Volume	Weight
Vegetable oil	¼ cup	
Onions, chopped	2½ qts.	2 lbs. 8 oz.
Ginger root, fresh, grated	⅓ cup	
Carrots, diagonally sliced	2½ qts.	3 lbs. 5 oz.
Green beans, stemmed, snapped in half	2½ qts.	2 lbs. 12 oz.
Peppers, red or green, cut in long slices	3 qts.	3 lbs.
Zucchini, cut in rounds	3 qts.	4 lbs.

Sauce

Ingredients	Volume	Weight
Pineapple chunks, unsweetened, drained, with juice reserved	1 qt.	1 lb. 10 oz.
Unsweetened pineapple juice and/or apple juice	2 qts. plus 1 cup	
Brown sugar	1½ cups	
White vinegar	2 cups	
Soy sauce	1½ cups	
Garlic, pressed	8 cloves or 2½ heaping Tbsp.	
Tomato paste	½ cup	
Cornstarch	⅔ cup	
Cool water	⅔ cup	

(continued)

Procedure

1. If using a wok, stir-fry each vegetable group separately in a small amount of oil until they're crisp but tender. Cook the ginger root wtih the onions. Remove each group from the wok and keep them warm in a separate pan.
2. If using a stockpot, sauté the vegetables in oil, adding each vegetable group in the sequence listed, going to the next group as the preceding one has begun to soften.
3. In a separate pot, bring sauce ingredients, except cornstarch and water, to a low boil.
4. Dissolve the cornstarch in cool water, add to the sauce, and simmer gently for 3–4 minutes until the sauce thickens.
5. Combine sauce with cooked vegetables.

Servings	Calories	Protein (g)	Fat (g)	Cholesterol (mg)	Carbohydrates (g)	Fiber (g)	Sodium (mg)
1	254	4.3	2.9	0	56.6	5.3	894

Thai Curry

24 10-oz. Servings

The Thais create curries that are citrusy and sweet and often include fresh basil and cilantro. Serve this aromatic and tantalizing dish on rice and garnish with sprigs of fresh basil or cilantro. Increase the protein if desired by serving with Seasoned Tempeh (p. 218) or Seasoned Tofu (p. 220).

Equipment:	2½-gallon stockpot
Preparation Time:	1 hour
Cooking Time:	1 hour

Ingredients	Volume	Weight
Curry Paste		
Garlic, pressed or minced	²/₃ cup	
Chili peppers, chopped	5 sm.	
Ginger root, fresh, grated	½ cup	
Red onion, chopped	2 cups	8 oz.
Cumin, ground	3 Tbsp.	
Brown sugar	¹/₃ cup	
Lemon peel, grated	2 Tbsp.	
Lemon juice, fresh	¼ cup	
Coriander seed, ground	3 Tbsp.	
Basil, fresh, chopped	½ cup	
or dried	2 Tbsp.	
Cilantro, fresh, chopped	³/₄ cup	
Coconut milk, unsweetened (p. 470)		14 oz.
Turmeric	3 Tbsp.	
Salt	1 tsp.	
Vegetable oil	½ cup	
Onions, chopped	2 qts.	2 lbs.
Garlic, pressed or minced	10 cloves or 3 Tbsp.	
Eggplant, peeled and cubed	2 qts.	2 lbs.
Carrots, sliced in half-moons	2 qts.	2 lbs. 10 oz.

(continued)

Potatoes, cubed	2 qts.	2 lbs.
Vegetable Stock (p. 63) or water	2 qts.	
Peppers, chopped	1½ qts.	1 lb. 8 oz.
Green beans, cut in half lengthwise	1½ qts.	1 lb. 10 oz.
Tomatoes, fresh, chopped	2 qts.	3 lbs.

Procedure

1. Purée the curry paste ingredients in the bowl of a food processor. Set aside.
2. Sauté the onions and garlic in oil until the onions are translucent.
3. Add the eggplant, carrots, potatoes, and stock or water. Cover the pot and bring to a boil.
4. Lower the heat to a simmer and add the peppers and green beans. Simmer until the vegetables are barely tender. Add tomatoes and simmer 5 minutes.
5. Stir in the curry paste and simmer gently for an additional 5 minutes.

Servings	Calories	Protein (g)	Fat (g)	Cholesterol (mg)	Carbohydrates (g)	Fiber (g)	Sodium (mg)
1	224	4.9	7.4	0	38.8	7.1	157

Tofu with Vegetable Sauté

24 9-oz. Servings

The Szechuan peppercorns and fennel give this Asian sauté depth and distinction. Serve soon after cooking to retain the vivid colors and varied textures. The baked, spiced tofu in this recipe also works well with simple steamed or roasted vegetables and other vegetable stir-fries.

Equipment:	2½-gallon stockpot or wok
Preparation Time:	20 minutes
Cooking Time:	40 minutes

Ingredients	Volume	Weight
Tofu, pressed (p. 474)		7 lbs. (unpressed weight)

Sauce

Ingredients	Volume	Weight
Soy sauce	1½ cups	
Dry sherry	2 cups	
Orange juice	2 cups	
Ginger root, fresh, grated	¼ cup	
Szechuan peppercorns (p. 473),* toasted, ground	2 tsp.	
Fennel seed, ground*	2 tsp.	
Chili paste (optional) (p. 469)	1 tsp.	
or cayenne (optional)	to taste	
Sesame oil, dark (p. 473)	2 Tbsp.	
Cornstarch	¼ cup	
Cool water	¼ cup	
Vegetable oil	½ cup	
Garlic, minced or pressed	6 med. cloves or 2 Tbsp.	
Carrots, diagonally cut in thin slices	2 qts.	2 lbs. 11 oz.
Bell peppers, red and green, thinly sliced	2 qts.	2 lbs.

*Use 4 tsp. of five-spice powder (p. 471) in place of the fennel and Szechuan peppercorns.

(continued)

| Zucchini, diagonally cut in thin slices | 2 qts. | 3 lbs. |
| Snow peas, trimmed of stem end and strings | 1½ qts. | 1 lb. 8 oz. |

Garnishes

| Roasted peanuts (optional) | 3 cups | 1 lb. |
| Scallions, chopped | 2 cups | 8 oz. |

Procedure

1. Preheat the oven to 400°. Cut the pressed tofu into triangles by slicing each cake horizontally into three even slices and then cutting the stacked slices in half, diagonally. This will yield six triangles per cake of tofu. Spread the triangles in a single layer in shallow baking pans.

2. Mix together the sauce ingredients and marinate the tofu in the sauce for 15 minutes.

3. Pour off the sauce and reserve, leaving a thin layer on the tofu. Bake the tofu at 400° for 30 minutes in a convection oven, if possible. Turn the tofu once or twice.

4. Heat the reserved sauce to a boil.

5. Dissolve the cornstarch in cool water and add to the sauce. Reduce heat and simmer gently, on a flame tamer if possible.

6. Meanwhile, either
   - Sauté the vegetables in oil in a stewpot, in the sequence listed, stirring often and cooking until the vegetables are just tender but still crisp.
   - Stir-fry the vegetables in a large wok or skillet in the sequence listed. Because stir-frying is a high-heat method, carrots will be quickly followed by peppers and zucchini, and the last addition of snow peas will need just 1 or 2 minutes. Stir-frying can be done in separate batches if your wok is not large enough to handle the total volume of vegetables.

7. Pour the sauce into the stewpot or wok with the vegetables and simmer gently for 2–3 minutes.

8. Gently stir in the baked tofu.

9. Serve at once, on rice, topped with scallions and roasted peanuts, if desired.

Servings	Calories	Protein (g)	Fat (g)	Cholesterol (mg)	Carbohydrates (g)	Fiber (g)	Sodium (mg)
1	197	5.4	7.4	0	26.4	3.9	853

Tomatican

24 9-oz. Servings

Easy, economical, and full-flavored, this stew is ready to serve in 45 minutes and is a good candidate for steam table service. Serve in a bowl topped with cheese, over rice, or with Cornbread (p. 323.

Equipment:	2½-gallon stockpot
Preparation Time:	15 minutes
Cooking Time:	30 minutes

Ingredients	Volume	Weight
Olive oil	¼ cup	
Onions, chopped	3 qts.	3 lbs.
Chili peppers, fresh, minced	4–6 (depending on heat)	1½–2 oz.
or cayenne	½ tsp.	
Cumin, ground	3 Tbsp.	
Lima beans, frozen	4½ cups	1 lb. 8 oz.
Tomatoes, canned, with juice, crushed	3 qts. (1 #10 can)	6 lbs. 6 oz.
Water	2 cups	
Corn, frozen or fresh	3 qts	4 lbs. 5 oz.
Cilantro, fresh, chopped	1 cup	1⅓ oz.
Salt to taste		

Topping

Monterey Jack cheese or mild Cheddar, grated	2 qts.	1 lb. 8 oz.

Procedure

1. In the stockpot, sauté the onions and chile peppers or cayenne in oil until the onions are translucent.
2. Add the cumin and lima beans and sauté briefly, stirring continuously.

(continued)

3. Strain the juice from tomatoes into the pot, add the water, and simmer, covered, for 10 minutes.
4. Crush the tomatoes (in the can is easiest!). Then stir tomatoes, corn, and cilantro into the pot. Cover and simmer for another 10 minutes. Adjust for salt.
5. Serve topped with grated Monterey Jack cheese or mild Cheddar cheese.

Servings	Calories	Protein (g)	Fat (g)	Cholesterol (mg)	Carbohydrates (g)	Fiber (g)	Sodium (mg)
1	281	13.2	12.5	25	33.6	2.8	340

Vegetable Pot Pie

24 12-oz. Servings

This is actually a velvety Cheddar–vegetable sauce that we serve over freshly made, split biscuits. It can also fill puff pastry shells or be baked within a double pie crust. Serve with Sweet and Sour Red Cabbage (p. 343) and applesauce.

Equipment:	2½-gallon stockpot, 1 gallon stockpot, 1 gallon saucepan
Preparation and Cooking Time:	1½ hours

Ingredients	Volume	Weight
Onions, chopped	1½ qts.	1 lb. 8 oz.
Vegetable oil	½ cup	
Carrots, diced	1½ qts.	2 lbs.
Salt, to taste		
Potatoes, diced	2 qts.	2 lbs. 4 oz.
Paprika, Hungarian, sweet	1 Tbsp.	
Basil, dried	2 Tbsp.	
Thyme, dried	2 tsp.	
Mushrooms, sliced	2 qts.	1 lb. 8 oz.
Green peas, frozen, slightly thawed	1 qt.	1 lb. 4 oz.
Corn, frozen, slightly thawed	1 qt.	1 lb. 7 oz.
Salt and black pepper to taste		

Cheese Sauce

Ingredients	Volume	Weight
Butter	2 cups	1 lb.
White flour	2 cups	
Milk, warmed	1 gal.	
Dijon mustard	3 Tbsp.	
Nutmeg, ground	1 tsp.	
Cheddar cheese, sharp, grated	2½ qts.	2 lbs.
Salt and black pepper to taste		

(continued)

Stews and Sautés

Procedure

1. Sauté the onions in oil until they are translucent.
2. Add the carrots, sprinkle with salt, cover, and cook on low heat for 5 minutes. Stir occasionally.
3. In a separate pot, boil the potatoes until tender. Drain and set aside.
4. Meanwhile, add the paprika, basil, and thyme to the onions and carrots. Stir in the mushrooms and cook on low heat until the vegetables are tender. Stir occasionally.
5. Prepare the cheese sauce. In a 1-gallon saucepan, melt the butter. Whisk in the flour and simmer, whisking continuously, for about 10 minutes. Gradually add the heated milk and continue whisking until the sauce thickens. Stir in the Cheddar cheese until well melted. Add the Dijon mustard, nutmeg, and salt and pepper.
6. Combine the cooked vegetables, potatoes, green peas, corn, and cheese sauce. Cook until green peas and corn are heated through being careful not to burn the cheese sauce.

Servings	Calories	Protein (g)	Fat (g)	Cholesterol (mg)	Carbohydrates (g)	Fiber (g)	Sodium (mg)
1	546	19.3	36.4	92	38.5	4.8	551

Vegetable Stifado

24 14-oz. Servings

This is a hearty stew flavored with rosemary, lemon, and dill. Serve over couscous or with a hunk of coarse-grained bread and a side of Tzatziki (p. 344).

Equipment:	2½-gallon stockpot	
Preparation Time:	30 minutes	
Cooking Time:	40 minutes	

Ingredients	Volume	Weight
Onions, chopped	2 qts.	2 lbs.
Garlic, minced or pressed	6 cloves or 2 Tbsp.	
Vegetable oil	¼ cup	
Eggplant, cubed	2½ qts.	2 lbs. 8 oz.
Salt	1 Tbsp.	
Potatoes, cubed	2½ qts.	2 lbs. 8 oz.
Tomatoes, canned, with juice, crushed	2 qts.	4 lbs.
Water	1½ qts.	
Rosemary, fresh, finely chopped	1 Tbsp.	
or dried	2 tsp.	
Zucchini or yellow squash, sliced in rounds	2 qts.	2 lbs. 8 oz.
Peppers, red or green, chopped	2 qts.	2 lbs.
Okra, frozen, sliced	1¾ qts.	2 lbs. 4 oz.
Lemon juice	½ cup	
Dill, fresh, chopped	¼ cup	
or dried	1 Tbsp.	
Black pepper and additional salt to taste		

Garnish

Feta cheese, grated	1 qt.	1 lb.

Procedure

1. Sauté the onions and garlic in oil until the onions are translucent.
2. Add the eggplant and salt and cook for 10 more minutes, stirring often.

(continued)

3. Add the potatoes, crushed tomatoes with their juice, water, and rosemary. Bring to a boil, reduce to a simmer, and cook for 15 minutes until the potatoes and eggplant soften.
4. Add the zucchini, peppers, and okra and continue to cook for 5 minutes.
5. Stir in the lemon juice and dill and simmer for 10 minutes more.
6. Add black pepper and salt to taste.
7. Garnish with grated feta cheese.

Servings	Calories	Protein (g)	Fat (g)	Cholesterol (mg)	Carbohydrates (g)	Fiber (g)	Sodium (mg)
1	183	6.3	6.9	17	26.7	4.2	622

Vegetable Tajine

24 10-oz. Servings

This simple Moroccan stew becomes elegant with the inclusion of artichoke hearts, ripe olives, and saffron. Serve on couscous or rice, topped with grated feta cheese if desired.

Equipment:	2½-gallon stockpot
Preparation Time:	30 minutes
Cooking Time:	40 minutes

Ingredients	Volume	Weight
Onions, chopped	2 qts.	2 lbs.
Garlic, pressed or minced	12 cloves or 3 heaping Tbsp.	
Olive oil	½ cup	
Thyme, dried	1 Tbsp.	
Potatoes, cubed	3 qts.	3 lbs.
Green beans, stemmed, snapped	1 qt.	1 lb. 4 oz.
Peppers, red, chopped	1 qt.	1 lb.
Tomatoes, fresh, chopped	2 qts.	3 lbs.
Vegetable Stock (p. 63) or water (and 1 cup reserved artichoke liquid)	1 qt.	
Artichoke hearts, halved (reserve liquid from canned artichokes)	2½ qts.	3 lbs.
Black olives, pitted, halved	2 cups	1 lb. 4 oz.
Saffron	½ tsp.	
Lemon juice, fresh	¼–½ cup	
Parsley, fresh, chopped	1 cup	
Salt and black pepper to taste		

Procedure

1. Sauté the onions and garlic in olive oil until the onions are translucent.
2. Add the thyme, potatoes, green beans, peppers, and tomatoes and cook, stirring

(continued)

continuously, until the color of the green beans deepens and the tomatoes begin to release their juices.

3. Add the stock or water and reserved liquid from artichoke hearts and simmer, covered, until the vegetables are tender.

4. Stir in the artichoke hearts, olives, and saffron. Simmer for 5 minutes. Add the lemon juice, parsley, and salt and pepper to taste.

Servings	Calories	Protein (g)	Fat (g)	Cholesterol (mg)	Carbohydrates (g)	Fiber (g)	Sodium (mg)
1	249	5.3	13.7	0	31.4	6.5	853

Stews and Sautés

Vegetables Rabat

24 11-oz. Servings

North African cooks have a talent for combining fruits, vegetables, and protein into exotic delicacies. In this dish, an array of vegetables is cooked with chick-peas into a golden stew studded with glossy currants.

Equipment:	2½-gallon stockpot
Preparation Time:	30 minutes
Cooking Time:	45 minutes

Ingredients	Volume	Weight
Olive oil	½ cup	
Onions, chopped	2 qts.	2 lbs.
Garlic, minced or pressed	4 cloves or 1 heaping Tbsp.	
Cumin, ground	1 Tbsp.	
Turmeric, ground	2 tsp.	
Cinnamon, ground	1 tsp.	
Cayenne	¼–½ tsp.	
Paprika	1 tsp.	
Salt	1 Tbsp.	
Sweet potatoes, peeled, cubed	2 qts.	2 lbs.
Eggplant, cut in ½-in. cubes	1½ qts.	1 lb. 8 oz.
Carrots, sliced	1 qt.	1 lb. 6 oz.
Vegetable Stock (p. 63), chick-pea cooking liquid, or water	1¼ qts.	
Tomatoes, canned, with juice, crushed	3 qts.(1 #10 can)	6 lbs. 6 oz.
Peppers, chopped	1 qt.	1 lb.
Zucchini, sliced	2 qts.	2 lbs. 12 oz.
Tomato juice (optional)	1 cup	
Chick-peas, cooked, drained, with cooking liquid reserved	1 qt.	
Saffron	¼ tsp.	
Raisins or currants	1 cup	

Garnish

Almonds, toasted, chopped	1½ cups	6 oz.

(continued)

Stews and Sautés

Procedure

1. Sauté the onions in oil for 5 minutes.
2. Add the garlic, spices, and salt and cook on gentle heat, stirring frequently, until the onions are translucent.
3. Add the sweet potatoes, eggplant, carrots, stock or chick-pea liquid or water, and tomatoes with their juices. Bring to a boil and then simmer, covered, for 10 minutes.
4. Stir in the peppers and zucchini. Simmer, covered on low heat, until all the vegetables are tender. If more liquid is needed add 1 cup tomato juice or more stock or chick-pea liquid.
5. Add the chick-peas, saffron, and raisins or currants. Simmer 2 minutes.
6. Serve on couscous, garnished with chopped toasted almonds.

Servings	Calories	Protein (g)	Fat (g)	Cholesterol (mg)	Carbohydrates (g)	Fiber (g)	Sodium (mg)
1	327	9.3	10.3	0	53.6	8.3	527

Winter Vegetable Stew

24 12-oz. Servings

This stew is ideal for a blustery winter day. The ingredients are readily available and inexpensive, and the blend of vegetables and seasonings yields a sweet and savory entrée. Serve with a dark bread and sharp cheese or french bread and Brie.

Equipment:	2½-gallon stockpot
Preparation Time:	30 minutes
Cooking Time:	40 minutes

Ingredients	Volume	Weight
Onions, chopped	2 qts.	2 lbs.
Celery, chopped	2 qts.	2 lbs.
Vegetable oil	½ cup	
Carrots, chopped	2 qts.	2 lbs. 8 oz.
Parsnips, chopped	1½ qts.	2 lbs.
Potatoes, cut into 1-in. cubes	1½ qts.	1 lb. 8 oz.
Green beans, trimmed, cut in half	1½ qts.	1 lb. 12 oz.
Dill, fresh, chopped	¼ cup	
or dried	1 Tbsp.	
Marjoram, dried	2 tsp.	
Beer or ale	2 cups	
Vegetable Stock (p. 63) or water	1 qt.	
Peppers, red or green, chopped	1½ qts.	1 lb. 8 oz.
Mushrooms, sliced	1¼ qts.	1 lb.
Dijon mustard	3 Tbsp.	
Molasses	¼ cup	
Salt and black pepper to taste		

Procedure

1. Sauté the onions and celery in oil until the onions are translucent.
2. Add the carrots, parsnips, potatoes, green beans, herbs, beer, and vegetable stock or water. Bring to a boil and then simmer, covered, about 5 minutes.

(continued)

3. Add the rest of the ingredients and simmer for about 20 minutes or until the potatoes and green beans are tender.

Servings	Calories	Protein (g)	Fat (g)	Cholesterol (mg)	Carbohydrates (g)	Fiber (g)	Sodium (mg)
1	184	3.6	5.4	0	32.1	6.4	104

STUFFED VEGETABLES

Vegetables stuffed with a variety of fillings are traditional festive meal fare throughout the world. They provide a well-balanced, self-contained meal in a unique and lovely presentation. Vegetarian protein sources such as tofu, tempeh, grains, beans, and nuts can be substituted in dishes that standardly use meat. The eclectic combinations of ingredients in many of our recipes provide multicultural results; Chiles en Nogada, a Mexican-style stuffed pepper, uses the Asian staple of tofu. You can also mix and match fillings and "shells" in this section. For example, the rice filling for Eggplant Niçoise could be used to stuff a small winter squash or bell pepper, or the pilaf could be used in Eggplant Marrakech to fill zucchini or tomato shells. Many of these fillings could serve as pilafs or side dishes to accompany other foods. Additionally, the stuffing for Peppers Mexicana or Chiles en Nogoda could be wrapped in tortillas to make burritos or enchiladas.

Chiles en Nogada

24 12-oz. Servings (2 pepper halves per serving)

Tofu is a perfect vehicle to carry the complex flavors that make up a savory vegetable filling. Serve on rice, spooning the pan juices over the peppers.

Equipment:	3 insert pans, 2-in. deep
Preparation Time:	1 hour
Baking Time:	1 hour

Ingredients	Volume	Weight
Onions, chopped	1½ qts.	1 lb. 8 oz.
Garlic, minced or pressed	6 cloves or 2 Tbsp.	
Cinnamon	1 Tbsp.	
Cumin, ground	1½ Tbsp.	
Cayenne	¼ tsp.	
Vegetable oil	⅓ cup	
Tomatoes, canned with juice	4½ cups	2 lb. 4 oz.
Apples, cored, peeled, chopped	3 cups	12 oz.
Raisins	¾ cup	3.75 oz.
Tofu, frozen, thawed, shredded (p. 474)		4 lbs. 8 oz. (weight before freezing)
Almonds, finely chopped	1½ cups	6 oz.
Cider vinegar	3 Tbsp.	
Soy sauce	6 Tbsp.	
Peppers, red and green mixed, if possible	24	
Tomato juice	1 qt.	

Procedure

1. Sauté the onion, garlic, and spices in vegetable oil until the onions are softened.
2. Add the tomatoes, apple, and raisins. Cover the pot and simmer for 5 minutes.

(continued)

3. Stir in the shredded tofu, almonds, vinegar, and soy sauce and simmer for 5 minutes, stirring occasionally. Adjust seasonings and remove from heat.
4. Halve the peppers lengthwise and remove the seeds, leaving the stem end intact to help the peppers hold their shape.
5. Fill each pepper half with 3 oz., or about ½ cup, of filling.
6. Add tomato juice or water to each pan, tightly cover with aluminum foil, and bake at 350° for 30–45 minutes, until the peppers are tender.
7. Serve with rice or Cornbread (p. 323).

Note: This filling can also be used to make cabbage rolls. For 48 rolls, 2 per serving, use 8 heads of napa or Chinese cabbage. Bring a large pot of water to a boil. Reserve the largest and smallest leaves for other purposes. Blanch the medium-sized leaves, a few at a time, for 1 minute. Drain. When the leaves are cool enough to handle, place ½ cup of filling near the base of each leaf. Roll up from the bottom, fold in the sides, continue to roll to close. Place the cabbage rolls in lightly oiled pans and bake at 350° until heated through, about 45 minutes. Serve 2 rolls on a bed of rice topped with Simple Tomato Sauce (p. 251) and garnished with sour cream or yogurt, if desired.

Servings	Calories	Protein (g)	Fat (g)	Cholesterol (mg)	Carbohydrates (g)	Fiber (g)	Sodium (mg)
1	223	6.8	9.7	0	31.0	3.4	383

Dolma

24 14-oz. Servings (1 pepper half and 1 zucchini half per serving)

This hearty dish has its origins in the cuisine of Armenia. It is delicious accompanied by Tzatziki (p. 344).

Equipment:	4 insert pans, 4-in. deep
Preparation Time:	1½ hours including cooking rice
Cooking Time:	45 minutes

Ingredients	Volume	Weight
Brown rice, raw	2¾ qts.	5 lbs.
Olive oil	3 Tbsp.	
Water	3¾ qts.	
Salt	1 Tbsp.	
Olive oil	⅓ cup	
Onions, chopped	2 qts.	2 lbs.
Garlic, pressed or minced	12 cloves or 4 Tbsp.	
Basil, fresh, chopped	2 cups	
or dried	¾ cup	
Marjoram, dried	⅓ cup	
Tomato paste	2⅓ cups	1 lb. 6 oz.
Whole tomatoes, canned with juice, crushed	6 qts. (2 #10 cans)	12 lbs. 12 oz.
Bay leaves	10	
Salt and black pepper to taste		
Zucchini	12 med.	
Bell peppers, green, red, or gold	12 lg.	
Parsley, fresh, chopped	2 cups	
Walnuts, toasted, chopped	2 qts.	2 lbs.
Lemon juice, fresh	⅔ cup	
Salt and black pepper to taste		

(continued)

Stuffed Vegetables

Topping

Yogurt, plain, low-fat or nonfat (optional)   1½ qts.   3 lbs.

Procedure

1. Sauté the rice in 3 Tbsp. olive oil for 3–4 minutes until it begins to smell like popcorn. Stir often to prevent scorching.
2. Add the water and salt, bring to a boil, and then reduce to a simmer and cook covered for 50 minutes.
3. Meanwhile, in the remaining 1/3 cup olive oil, sauté the onions, garlic, and herbs until the onions are softened.
4. Set aside one half of the sautéed onions and herbs for the pilaf.
5. To the remaining half, add the tomato paste, crushed tomatoes and juice, and bay leaves. Simmer for 20 to 30 minutes and add salt and pepper to taste.
6. While the sauce simmers, cut the peppers in half lengthwise and remove the seeds, but leave the stem end intact to hold the stuffing in place. Cut the zucchini in half lengthwise and carefully scoop out the pulp, leaving about ¼ in. of the shell intact. Discard or use the pulp for vegetable stock.
7. In a large bowl, combine the cooked rice with the reserved onions and herbs, parsley, walnuts, lemon juice, salt, and black pepper.
8. Mound the rice pilaf into the vegetable halves and place them in oiled insert pans. Pour one quarter of the tomato sauce in each pan. Tightly cover the pans with aluminum foil and bake for 45–50 minutes at 350°.
9. Serve one pepper half and one zucchini half per serving. Spoon some of the sauce over each and top with yogurt if desired.

Servings	Calories	Protein (g)	Fat (g)	Cholesterol (mg)	Carbohydrates (g)	Fiber (g)	Sodium (mg)
1	625	15.2	30.8	0	79.6	4.7	845

Eggplant Bombay

24 18-oz. Stuffed Eggplant Halves

This dish juxtaposes the full bouquet of curry spices with the comforting quality of creamy mashed potatoes. Serve with Oasis Chutney with Coconut and Dates (p. 335) as a garnish or small side dish.

Equipment:	4 insert pans, 4-in. deep
Preparation Time:	1 hour
Cooking Time:	40 minutes

Ingredients	Volume	Weight
Eggplants	12 med.	
Potatoes (peeled if thick-skinned), cubed	1½ gals.	6 lbs.
Neufchâtel or cream cheese		3 lbs.
Vegetable oil	½ cup	
Onions, chopped	3 qts.	3 lbs.
Cumin, ground	5 Tbsp.	
Coriander, ground	5 Tbsp.	
Turmeric	3 Tbsp.	
Cayenne	¼ tsp.	
or Chili peppers, minced	4 to 6 sm.	
Cloves, ground	½ tsp.	
Cardamom, ground	1 tsp.	
Ginger root, fresh, grated	⅓ cup	
Garlic, minced or pressed	12 cloves or 4 Tbsp.	
Carrots, diced	1½ qts.	2 lbs.
Peppers, green or red, diced	1½ qts.	1 lb. 8 oz.
Green peas, frozen	1½ qts.	2 lbs.
Tomatoes, fresh, diced (optional)	1 qt.	1 lb. 8 oz.
Lemon juice, fresh	¾ cup	

Procedure

1. Slice the eggplants in half lengthwise, leaving the stems on. Arrange them, cut side down, in lightly oiled insert pans. Tightly cover with aluminum foil and bake at 375° until tender, about 40–50 minutes.

(continued)

2. While the eggplant bakes, boil the potatoes until tender. Drain, transfer to a mixing bowl, and mash with the cheese.
3. Sauté the onions and ground spices in oil for a couple of minutes, stirring continuously to prevent sticking.
4. Add the ginger and garlic and continue to cook on low heat until the onions are translucent.
5. Add the carrots and sauté for 10 minutes.
6. Add the peppers and cook until the vegetables are tender.
7. Stir in the peas, tomatoes, and lemon juice.
8. Combine the vegetables and mashed potatoes.
9. Invert the baked eggplant halves in the pans. Mash the pulp a bit with a fork and gently push it to the sides of the eggplant.
10. Fill the hollow of each eggplant half with a heaping cup of the potato mixture. Bake, covered, at 350° for 15 minutes and then uncovered for 15–20 minutes.

Servings	Calories	Protein (g)	Fat (g)	Cholesterol (mg)	Carbohydrates (g)	Fiber (g)	Sodium (mg)
1	435	13.3	19.5	43	57.1	12.0	300

Eggplant Marrakech

24 12-oz. Stuffed Eggplant Halves

This dish has a Moroccan-style filling with aromatic spices and the tart-sweet combination of lemon and currants. Serve with Carrot Salad (p. 321) or Fassoulia (p. 325).

Equipment:	4 insert pans, 4-in. deep	
Preparation Time:	1½ hours	
Baking Time:	30 minutes	

Ingredients	Volume	Weight
Eggplants, whole	12 med.	
Onions, finely chopped	1 qt.	1 lb.
Garlic, minced or pressed	12 cloves or 4 Tbsp.	
Cayenne	¼ tsp.	
Paprika, Hungarian	2 Tbsp.	
Cumin, ground	2 Tbsp.	
Olive oil	½ cup	
Tomatoes, fresh, chopped	2 qts.	3 lbs.
Brown rice, cooked (p. 468)	1½ qts.	2 lbs. 8 oz.
Chick-peas, cooked (p. 467) or canned	1½ qts.	2 lbs. 3 oz.
Currants or raisins	3 cups	14 oz.
Lemon juice, fresh	1 cup plus 2 Tbsp.	
Parsley, fresh, chopped	1½ cups	2 oz.
Salt and black pepper to taste		

Garnishes

Feta cheese, grated	3 cups	12 oz.
Pimiento strips (optional)		

Procedure

1. Leaving the stems on, slice the eggplant in half lengthwise. Place them cut side down in oiled baking pans. Cover the pans tightly and bake at 375° for about 45 minutes or until tender.

(continued)

2. Meanwhile, sauté the onions, garlic, and spices in oil until the onions soften. Stir often to prevent the spices from burning.
3. Add the tomatoes and simmer, covered, for 15 minutes.
4. In a large mixing bowl, combine the sauté with the rice, chick-peas, currants or raisins, lemon juice, parsley, salt, and pepper.
5. Invert the baked eggplant halves in the baking pans. Mash the pulp with a fork, taking care not to break the skins. Push the pulp to the sides, creating a hollow in the center of each eggplant half. Mound one cup of filling in each hollow.
6. Bake, covered, at 375° for 30 minutes.
7. Serve each eggplant half topped with feta cheese and garnished with a pimiento strip, minced parsley, or scallion curls.

Servings	Calories	Protein (g)	Fat (g)	Cholesterol (mg)	Carbohydrates (g)	Fiber (g)	Sodium (mg)
1	319	8.9	9.7	13	54.3	9.6	310

Eggplant Niçoise

24 18-oz. Stuffed Eggplant Halves

Fragrant with saffron, this eggplant stuffing is a vegetable-studded rice pilaf. Serve with Marinated Vegetables (p. 333) or Artichoke Heart–Tomato Salad (p. 313).

Equipment:	4 insert pans, 4-in. deep
Preparation Time:	1 hour for the rice plus 1 hour
Baking Time:	30 minutes

Ingredients	Volume	Weight
Brown rice, raw	1½ qts.	2 lbs. 6 oz.
Olive oil	¼ cup	
Saffron	1 tsp.	
Water	2½ qts.	
Salt	1 Tbsp.	
Eggplants, halved lengthwise	12 med.	
Water	2 cups	
Dry sherry	2 cups	
Olive oil	¼ cup	
Onions, diced	3 qts.	3 lbs.
Peppers, green or red, finely diced	3 qts.	3 lbs.
Dry sherry	¼ cup	
Cayenne (optional)	¼ tsp.	
Tomatoes, fresh, chopped	1½ qts.	2 lbs. 4 oz.
Currants, dried	2 cups	8 oz.
Parsley, fresh, chopped	2 cups	2½ oz.
Black pepper	1 tsp.	
Tomato juice or water	3 cups	

Garnish

Almonds, toasted, slivered	2 cups	8 oz.

(continued)

Procedure

The Rice

1. Sauté the rice briefly in olive oil.
2. Crumble in the saffron and add the water and salt. Bring to a boil and then reduce to a low simmer and cook, tightly covered, for 50–60 minutes. Use a heat diffuser to prevent scorching.

Note: For a more economical dish, substitute 1 Tbsp. ground turmeric for the saffron.

The Eggplant

3. Place the eggplants, cut side down, in four 4-in. deep insert pans. Combine the 2 cups water and the 2 cups dry sherry and add 1 cup of this mixture to each pan. Cover tightly with foil and bake at 375° until tender, about 45 minutes.
4. While the eggplants bake, sauté the onions in oil until they are translucent.
5. Add the peppers, sherry, and optional cayenne. Cover the pot and cook for 10–15 minutes.
6. Add the tomatoes, currants, parsley, and black pepper. Cover and cook just until the tomatoes get juicy.
7. Combine with the cooked rice.
8. Invert the baked eggplant halves and gently mash the pulp with a fork. Push the pulp to the sides, creating a central hollow for the stuffing. Mound ⅔ cup of filling for each eggplant half. Pour ¾ cup tomato juice or water into each insert pan. Cover the pan tightly and bake at 350° for 20–30 minutes, until heated through.
9. Top each serving with a garnish of toasted almonds.

Servings	Calories	Protein (g)	Fat (g)	Cholesterol (mg)	Carbohydrates (g)	Fiber (g)	Sodium (mg)
1	365	8.2	11.3	0	59.9	9.1	418

Holiday Stuffed Squash
with Ginger–Orange Sauce

24 16-oz. Stuffed Squash Halves

Appealing enough for special occasions, this festive dish is nicely accompanied by apple or cranberry sauce.

Equipment:	4 insert pans, 4-in. deep
Preparation Time:	2½ hours
Baking Time:	30 minutes

Ingredients	Volume	Weight
Winter squash (acorn, buttercup, delicata), halved and seeded	12 med.	
Tofu, pressed (p. 474) and cut into small cubes		3 lbs. (unpressed weight)
Soy sauce	⅔ cup	
Sherry, dry	⅔ cup	
Bread, cubed	3 qts.	
Vegetable oil	¼ cup	
Onions, chopped	2 qts.	2 lbs.
Celery, diced	3 cups	12 oz.
Mushrooms, sliced	3 qts.	2 lbs. 8 oz.
Marjoram, dried	1 Tbsp.	
Thyme, dried	1½ tsp.	
Vegetable Stock (p. 63) or water	1½ cups	
Pecans, toasted and chopped	3 cups	12 oz.
Lemon juice, fresh	½ cup	

Ginger–Orange Sauce

Orange juice	1 qt.	
Ginger root, fresh, grated	2 Tbsp.	
Vegetable oil	2 Tbsp.	
Thyme, dried	1 tsp.	
Soy sauce	2 tsp.	
Cornstarch, dissolved in	2 Tbsp.	
Cool water	4 Tbsp.	

(continued)

Procedure

1. Place the squash halves cut side down in oiled baking pans. Add about ½ in. of water to the pan, cover tightly with foil, and bake at 375° for 40 minutes or until the squash is tender.
2. While the squash bakes, marinate the tofu in soy sauce and sherry. Toast the bread cubes.
3. In a wide-bottomed stockpot, sauté the onions and celery in oil until the onions are translucent.
4. Add the mushrooms, herbs, and stock or water and simmer on low heat, covered, for 15 minutes.
5. Stir in the tofu and marinade and the bread cubes. Cook for another 5 minutes, adjust the seasonings, and remove from the heat.
6. Stir in the pecans and lemon juice.
7. Invert the baked squash and mound 1 cup of filling in each squash half. Cover the pans and bake at 350° for 25 minutes, until heated through.
8. Meanwhile, prepare the Ginger–Orange Sauce. In a saucepan, heat all the ingredients, except the dissolved cornstarch. Bring the orange juice mixture to a boil and whisk in the cornstarch mixture. Reduce heat to low and simmer for a few minutes until the sauce thickens.
9. Top each squash half with 2 oz. of sauce.

Servings	Calories	Protein (g)	Fat (g)	Cholesterol (mg)	Carbohydrates (g)	Fiber (g)	Sodium (mg)
1	411	9.4	15.7	0	64.0	3.4	561

Stuffed Vegetables

Stuffed Peppers Mexicana

24 14-oz. Servings (2 pepper halves per serving)

A medley of ingredients common to Mexican cuisine is combined with tempeh, a protein-rich soy product with roots in Indonesia.

Equipment:	2 insert pans, 2-in. deep
Preparation Time:	1 hour
Baking Time:	45 minutes

Ingredients	Volume	Weight
Vegetable oil	½ cup	
Onions, chopped	2 qts.	2 lbs.
Garlic, minced or pressed	12 cloves or 4 Tbsp.	
Tempeh (p. 474), cut in ½-in. cubes		2 lbs.
Tomatoes, fresh, chopped	2 qts.	3 lbs.
or 1 #10 can, drained and chopped	2 qts.	4 lbs. 12 oz.
Corn, frozen, thawed	2 qts.	4 lbs.
Cumin, ground	1½ Tbsp.	
Coriander seeds, ground	2 Tbsp.	
Kidney or pinto beans, cooked or canned, drained, slightly mashed	3 qts. (1 #10 can)	4 lbs. 6 oz.
Spanish olives, chopped (optional)	2 cups	12 oz.
Soy sauce	½ cup	
Salt and black pepper to taste		
Peppers, red, green, or half and half	24 whole	
Tomato juice or water		
Hot sauce (p. 263)	3 cups	1 lb. 8 oz.
Sour cream (optional)	3 cups	1 lb. 8 oz.

Procedure

1. In a large, heavy skillet or stainless steel pot, sauté the onions and garlic in oil until they soften.

(continued)

Stuffed Vegetables

2. Add the tempeh with more oil, if necessary, and continue to sauté until it is browned.
3. Add the tomatoes, corn, and spices and cook, covered, until the vegetables are heated.
4. Transfer the skillet contents to a large bowl. Mix in the cooked beans, olives, soy sauce, salt, and pepper.
5. Cut the peppers in half lengthwise, leaving the stems on. Remove the seeds and membranes and fill each half with about ⅔ cup of filling.
6. Place peppers in lightly oiled pans with ½ in. of tomato juice or water. Bake, tightly covered, at 375° for 40–50 minutes.
7. Serve topped with hot sauce and the optional sour cream.

Servings	Calories	Protein (g)	Fat (g)	Cholesterol (mg)	Carbohydrates (g)	Fiber (g)	Sodium (mg)
1	386	20.7	9.9	0	62.0	5.2	339

Stuffed Vegetables

Stuffed Zucchini Alsace

24 12-oz. Servings (2 zucchini halves per serving)

Zucchini transcends its mundane image with a creamy, herb-and-garlic-infused filling. Serve on a bed of Golden Orzo (p. 328) or rice.

Equipment:	4 insert pans, 4-in. deep, plus 1 half-size insert pan, 4-in. deep
Preparation Time:	1 hour with precooked beans
Cooking Time:	50 minutes

Ingredients	Volume	Weight
Olive oil	¼ cup	
Onions, chopped	1½ qts.	1 lb. 8 oz.
Carrots, diced	3 cups	1 lb.
Celery, diced	3 cups	12 oz.
Salt	1 Tbsp.	
Black pepper to taste		
Tarragon, dried	2 Tbsp.	
Dill, dried	1 Tbsp.	
Bay leaves	2 leaves	
Green pepper, diced	3 cups	12 oz.
Butter	¼ cup	
Garlic, pressed	10 cloves or 3 Tbsp.	
Neufchâtel (p. 472) or cream cheese, cubed		12 oz.
Lemon juice, fresh	2 Tbsp.	
Tabasco	1 tsp.	
Navy beans, dried, cooked and drained, (p. 467), liquid reserved	3½ cups 2¼ qts.	1 lb. 8 oz. 3 lbs. 10 oz.
Liquid from cooked or canned beans, Vegetable Stock (p. 63), or water	1½ cups	
Zucchini, whole	24 med.	

Garnish

Parsley, fresh, chopped	1½ cups	

(continued)

Procedure

1. If using dried beans, soak the beans in water to cover overnight, or for at least 3 hours, or bring to a boil, remove from the heat, and soak for 1 hour. After soaking, drain the beans and cook in 1 gallon of water until tender for 30–45 minutes.
2. Sauté the onions in olive oil for 5 minutes.
3. Stir in the carrots, celery, herbs, and seasonings and sauté for another 10 minutes.
4. Stir in the green peppers and simmer, covered, until the vegetables are tender. Discard the bay leaves.
5. In a small skillet, sauté the garlic in butter until golden.
6. In a large bowl, gently combine the cubed cheese with the lemon juice, Tabasco, and cooked vegetables.
7. Purée 3 cups of beans in a blender or food processor with the reserved 1½ cups of liquid.
8. Combine the purée and the remaining beans with the sautéed garlic and vegetable–cheese mixture. Adjust the seasonings.
9. Slice the zucchini in half lengthwise. Carefully scoop out the middle of each half leaving about ¼ in. of the shell intact. Discard the pulp or use in vegetable stock.
10. Spoon ½ cup of the bean and vegetable mixture into each zucchini half. Pack the filled halves into baking pans. Add ½ in. of water to the bottom of the pans, cover tightly with aluminum foil, and bake at 350° for 45 minutes.
11. Serve topped with chopped parsley.

Servings	Calories	Protein (g)	Fat (g)	Cholesterol (mg)	Carbohydrates (g)	Fiber (g)	Sodium (mg)
1	233	9.6	8.3	16	33.0	4.5	410

DESSERTS

Whether it's a simple, fruit-based dish or a richly indulgent cake, desserts are a compelling part of the meal for many diners. We have noticed that many of our customers decide which dessert to order before making their main dish selection.

The recipes that follow are, to a great extent, home-style, uncomplicated desserts. Most are quite versatile and will fit a wide range of menus. Some of the recipes were developed for our Sunday ethnic nights at the restaurant. For example, Apricot Almond Baklava was for a Middle Eastern menu and Tira Misu was for an Italian night. They have since joined our general repertoire and appear on daily menus in a rotation that depends on the season and the whim of our dessert chefs.

Our baked goods are fairly sturdy and our recipes do not require a knowledge of chemistry to execute. We give both volume and weight measurements, but in the Moosewood kitchen have consistently achieved good results using volume measurements only. We use unbleached white pastry flour for all our cakes.

In keeping with our restaurant tradition of home-style portions, dessert servings are generous, so we expect that these recipes could easily serve more than indicated in those institutions that normally serve smaller quantities.

Apricot Almond Baklava

35 4¹/₂-oz. Servings

We've never seen a baklava like this in traditional Greek cookery, but it seems to us to be a natural flavor combination. The custard-like apricot layer is a delicious surprise sandwiched in the middle of the crisp, honey-drenched pastry. Garnish with fresh orange slices, if desired, and serve with coffee or mint tea.

Equipment:	18¹/₂ × 12¹/₂ x 2-in. baking pan, pastry brush
Preparation Time:	40 minutes
Baking Time:	40 minutes

Ingredients	Volume	Weight
Apricots, dried	1 qt./ 1 L	2 lbs./900 g
Apricot juice	1 qt./ 1 L	36 oz./1 kg
Eggs	6 lg., 1¹/₂ cups/ 350 ml	12 oz./340 g
Butter, melted	2 cups/475 ml	1 lb./450 g
Filo pastry leaves	2 pkgs., approx. 50 leaves	2 lbs./900 g
Almonds, toasted, coarsely chopped	1³/₄ qts./1.75 L	2 lbs. 4 oz./1 kg
Honey	2 cups/ 475 ml	22 oz./625 g

Procedure

1. Simmer the apricots in the juice for 20–30 minutes, until quite soft. Cool.
2. Purée the cooled apricot mixture with the eggs.
3. Preheat the oven to 375° F (190° C).
4. Brush butter on the bottom and sides of the baking pan.
5. Unroll 1 package (approx. 25 leaves) of filo. Place three filo leaves flat in the baking pan, brush with butter, and sprinkle with chopped almonds. Repeat this procedure until the first package of filo leaves is used.

(continued)

6. Spread the apricot purée evenly over the stack of filo.
7. Layer the second package of filo as in step 4, ending with a buttered leaf of filo sprinkled with almonds.
8. Score the top of the baklava, cutting through the top few layers, but not as deep as the apricot filling, into 35 squares (in a 5 piece x 7 piece grid pattern).
9. Bake for 35–40 minutes, until the top is golden brown. Cool on a rack for about 20 minutes.
10. Cut all the way through the scoring and, while the baklava is still warm, drizzle the honey over the entire pastry so that it will soak into the scoring. Store well covered and refrigerated.
11. Serve at room temperature.

Variations:
- Substitute dried peaches or dates for the apricots.
- Substitute pistachios for the almonds.

Note: One-pound packages of commercially prepared filo come in slightly varying dimensions and numbers of sheets. In this recipe, these differences are not significant.

Servings	Calories	Protein (g)	Fat (g)	Cholesterol (mg)	Carbohydrates (g)	Fiber (g)	Sodium (mg)
1	485	9.1	32.6	74	45.8	5.5	165

Butter Almond Pound Cake

16–24 Servings

This rich pound cake with a heady fragrance can be served unadorned or simply coated with a thin glaze of melted chocolate or a glaze of confectioners' sugar mixed with a little amaretto. It is especially delicious dusted with confectioners' sugar.

Equipment:	10-in. Bundt pan
Preparation Time:	20 minutes
Baking Time:	1 hour 15 minutes

Ingredients	Volume	Weight
Butter	2 cups/475 ml	1 lb./450 g
Sugar	3 cups/700 ml	1 lb. 8 oz./680 g
Eggs	6 lg. or 1½ cups/ 350 ml	12 oz./ 340 g
Almond extract	2 tsp./10 ml	
Almonds, toasted, ground	1 cup/235 ml	6 oz./170 g
Pastry flour	3½ cups/825 ml	1 lb. 2 oz./500 g
Milk or half-and-half	½ cup/125 ml	4 oz./115 g
Baking powder	2 tsp./10 ml	
Amaretto or other almond liqueur	½ cup/125 ml	4 oz./115 g

Procedure

1. Preheat the oven to 350° F (180° C).
2. Generously butter the Bundt pan. Dust it with flour and tap out the excess.
3. Cream the butter and sugar. Add each of the following ingredients in turn, beating well after each addition: the eggs and almond extract, the ground almonds and half of the flour, the milk or half-and-half, the baking powder and remaining flour.
4. Pour the batter into the prepared Bundt pan and bake immediately for 1 hour

(continued)

and 15 minutes to 1 hour and 30 minutes, until the cake is firm and golden and a pick tests clean.

5. Cool the cake in the pan on a rack for 10 minutes.
6. Slowly pour the amaretto over the warm cake and allow it to soak in.
7. Invert the cake onto a serving platter, leaving the pan in place over the cake until cool.

Servings	Calories	Protein (g)	Fat (g)	Cholesterol (mg)	Carbohydrates (g)	Fiber (g)	Sodium (mg)
1	428	5.4	21.0	108	53.7	1.1	206

Desserts

Cayuga Mud Cake
32 Servings

With strong hints of coffee and brandy, this dark, not-too-sweet cake is very moist as a result of its long, slow baking at a low temperature. Serve plain or topped with whipped cream.

Equipment:	2 10-in. Bundt pans
Preparation Time:	20 minutes
Baking Time:	1½ hours

Ingredients	Volume	Weight
Butter	3 Tbsp./45 ml	½ oz./15 g
Cocoa powder	2 Tbsp./30 ml	½ oz./15 g
Coffee, strong, freshly brewed	3½ cups/825 ml	28 oz./800 g
Brandy, bourbon, or a coffee, chocolate, or mocha liqueur	½ cup/125 ml	4 oz./115 g
Butter	2 cups/475 ml	1 lb./450 g
Unsweetened (bakers') chocolate	10 naps	10 oz./300 g
Sugar	1qt./1 L	2 lbs./900 g
Pastry flour	1qt./1 L	1 lb. 4 oz./565 g
Salt	½ tsp./2.5 ml	
Baking soda	2 tsp./10 ml	
Vanilla extract	2 tsp./10 ml	
Eggs, beaten	4 lg., 1 cup/240 ml	8 oz./225 g

Procedure

1. Preheat the oven to 275° F (140° C).
2. Generously butter two 10-in. Bundt pans. Dust the pans with cocoa.
3. Heat the coffee, brandy, butter, and chocolate until the butter and chocolate have melted.

(continued)

4. Stir in the sugar and transfer to a mixer bowl.
5. Beat in the flour, salt, baking soda, and vanilla.
6. Add the eggs and beat until the batter is smooth and evenly colored.
7. Pour the batter into the prepared Bundt pans.
8. Bake for about 1½ hours until the cakes pull away from the sides of the pans and the middles spring back when touched.
9. Cool in the pans for 10 minutes. Invert the cakes onto serving plates, leaving the pans in place over the cakes, until the cakes are cool.

Variations

- Dress up the cakes with a simple glossy glaze (3 ounces bittersweet chocolate melted with 2 tablespoons water or coffee).
- For Mandarin Chocolate Cake, replace the coffee with orange juice and the brandy with an orange liqueur, such as Grand Marnier (which could also replace the water, if you make the suggested glaze).

Servings	Calories	Protein (g)	Fat (g)	Cholesterol (mg)	Carbohydrates (g)	Fiber (g)	Sodium (mg)
1	393	4.5	16.9	67	55.5	0.9	205

Chinese Almond Cookies

24 Servings (72 cookies)

These cookies are the quintessential Chinese–American, neighborhood restaurant dessert offering. They are golden-glazed and subtly sweet. Serve with Chinese tea.

Equipment:	baking sheets
Preparation Time:	20 minutes
Baking Time:	20 minutes

Ingredients	Volume	Weight
Pastry flour	5½ cups/1.3 L	1 lb. 12 oz./800 g
Sugar	2 cups/475 ml	1 lb./450 g
Baking soda	1 tsp./5 ml	
Salt	½ tsp./2.5 ml	
Butter	2 cups/475 ml	1 lb./450 g
Eggs, lightly beaten	4 lg. or 1 cup/240 ml	8 oz./225 g
Almond extract	1 Tbsp./15 ml	
Whole almonds	72, about ⅔ cup/160 ml	4 oz./115 g

Glaze

	Volume	Weight
Egg	1 lg., ¼ cup/60 ml	2 oz./55 g
Water	1 Tbsp./15 ml	

Procedure

1. Preheat the oven to 325° F (160° C).
2. Combine the dry ingredients.
3. Cut in the butter until mixture is crumbly.
4. Stir in the eggs and almond extract to form a stiff dough.

(continued)

5. Portion the dough by dividing it into 6 pieces and then cutting each piece into 12 pieces. Roll each small piece of dough between your palms to form 1½-in. balls. Place the balls 3 in. apart on an ungreased baking sheet.
6. Press an almond firmly into the center of the top of each cookie.
7. Lightly beat the glaze ingredients.
8. Brush each cookie with the glaze.
9. Bake for 15–20 minutes, until the bottoms have just begun to brown.

Servings	Calories	Protein (g)	Fat (g)	Cholesterol (mg)	Carbohydrates (g)	Fiber (g)	Sodium (mg)
1	379	6.2	19.5	96	45.5	1.6	242

Chocolate Ricotta

24 1-cup (6-oz.) Servings
($\frac{1}{2}$ cup (4 oz.) chocolate ricotta topped with
$\frac{1}{2}$ cup (2 oz.) whipped cream)

Quick and foolproof to prepare, this pudding-type dessert is rich, velvety smooth, and delicious. It is one of our most often requested recipes. Serve in 6- or 8-oz. dessert cups or glasses. Mound the whipped cream on top of the chocolate ricotta and garnish with shaved chocolate, strawberries, or raspberries, if desired.

Preparation Time: 20 minutes

Ingredients	Volume	Weight
Unsweetened (bakers') chocolate, melted	18 naps, 2½ cups melted	18 oz.
Ricotta cheese	2¾ qts.	6 lbs.
Vanilla extract	4 tsp.	
Honey (more to taste)	1½ cups	1 lb.
Heavy cream, well chilled	1½ qts.	
Vanilla extract	1 Tbsp.	
Honey	⅓ cup	6 oz.
or Confectioners' sugar	1 cup	4½ oz.

Procedure

1. In a blender or food processor, process the melted chocolate, ricotta, vanilla extract, and honey until evenly colored and very smooth. Hold covered and refrigerated until ready to assemble.
2. Whip the heavy cream, vanilla, and honey until softly stiff. Refrigerate.
3. At serving time, spoon the chocolate ricotta into dessert cups and top with whipped cream.

Servings	Calories	Protein (g)	Fat (g)	Cholesterol (mg)	Carbohydrates (g)	Fiber (g)	Sodium (mg)
1	543	15.0	37.5	113	41.4	0.1	164

Classic Poached Pear

24 6- to 8-oz. Servings

This light, elegant dessert has Mediterranean origins, but it is not out of place in a New England Harvest Feast or as the finish of an Asian meal. Any variety of pears is fine, but choose large, well-shaped pears that are not fully ripe and still firm. For an attractive presentation, serve each pear upright on a bed of stiffly whipped, sweetened cream, with a tablespoon of poaching liquid poured over it.

Equipment:	large (3- or 4-gallon) nonreactive stockpot
Preparation Time:	20 minutes
Cooking Time:	45 minutes

Ingredients	Volume	Weight
Pears, whole, fresh, peeled, with stems intact	24	about 12 lbs.

Poaching Liquid

Red wine and/or fruit juice (pear, apple, apricot) in any proportion	4 qts.	8 lbs.
Maple syrup	2 cups	1 lb.
Cinnamon sticks	2	
Oranges, fresh, sliced	2	
Cloves, whole	½ Tbsp.	
Allspice, whole	½ tsp.	

Procedure

1. Bring to a boil the wine and/or fruit juice, maple syrup, cinnamon sticks, and orange slices. Place the whole cloves and allspice in cheesecloth or a tea ball and add to the poaching liquid.
2. Add the pears, lower the heat, and simmer for 30–45 minutes, until the pears are tender, but still firm (the time will depend upon the variety, size, and ripeness of the pears).
3. Remove the pears from the poaching liquid, place in insert pans and refrigerate.
4. When the pears are cool, add poaching liquid to about 1 inch deep. Store refrigerated.

Note: The remaining poaching liquid can be strained and then refrigerated for up to 2 weeks for use in another batch of pears or to cook a dried fruit compote.

Servings	Calories	Protein (g)	Fat (g)	Cholesterol (mg)	Carbohydrates (g)	Fiber (g)	Sodium (mg)
1	161	0.9	0.9	0	38.0	5.2	2

Coconut Pound Cake
16–24 Servings

Creamy white frosting atop this dense, golden cake makes an attractive sweet offering that is especially welcome following a light Indian, Southeast Asian, or Caribbean meal. Serve with orange spice tea or limeade. Garnish with a few fresh orange or kiwi slices, if desired.

Equipment:	10-in. Bundt pan
Preparation Time:	20 minutes
Baking Time:	1 hour

Ingredients	Volume	Weight
Cake		
Butter	2 cups/475 ml	1 lb./450 g
Sugar	3 cups/700 ml	1 lb. 8 oz./680 g
Eggs	6 lg. or 1½ cups/ 350 ml	12 oz./340 g
Coconut extract	2 tsp./10 ml	
Pastry flour	1qt./1 L	1 lb. 4 oz./565 g
Coconut milk, unsweetened (p. 470), milk, or cream	½ cup/125 ml	4 oz./115 g
Baking powder	2 tsp./10 ml	
Frosting		
Neufchâtel or cream cheese	½ cup/ 125 ml.	4 oz./115 g
Butter, softened	½ cup/125 ml	4 oz./115 g
Confectioners' sugar	3 cups/700 ml	14 oz./400 g
Coconut extract	1 tsp./5 ml	
Shredded coconut, unsweetened	½ cup/125 ml	2.25 oz./65 g

Procedure

Cake

1. Preheat the oven to 350° F (180° C).
2. Generously butter the Bundt pan. Dust it with flour and tap out the excess.
3. Cream the butter and sugar.
4. Add each of the following ingredients in turn, beating well after each addition: the eggs and coconut extract; half the flour; the coconut milk, milk, or cream; the remaining flour and the baking powder.
5. Pour the batter into the prepared Bundt pan and bake immediately for 1 hour to 1 hour and 15 minutes, until the cake is firm and golden and a pick tests clean.
6. Cool the cake in the pan on a rack for 10 minutes.
7. Invert the cake onto a serving platter, leaving the pan in place over the cake until cool.

Frosting

8. Beat together the Neufchâtel cheese, butter, confectioners' sugar, and coconut extract until smooth and fluffy.
9. Spread the frosting on the cooled Coconut Pound Cake and immediately dust with the shredded coconut.

Servings	Calories	Protein (g)	Fat (g)	Cholesterol (mg)	Carbohydrates (g)	Fiber (g)	Sodium (mg)
1	488	4.8	23.1	121	66.8	0.5	266

Cornmeal Pound Cake

24 4-oz. Servings

The golden color and natural sweetness of cornmeal are celebrated in this simple but rich pound cake.

Equipment:	4 8-in. loaf pans or 3 saddle pans
Preparation Time:	20 minutes
Baking Time:	1 hour

Ingredients	Volume	Weight
Butter	2 cups/475 ml	1 lb./450 g
Sugar	3 cups/700 ml	1 lb. 8 oz./680 g
Eggs	6 lg., 1½ cups/ 350 ml	12 oz./340 g
Vanilla extract	2 tsp./10 ml	
Milk	1 cup/240 ml	8 oz./225 g
Pastry flour	3 cups/700 ml	15 oz./425 g
Baking powder	2 tsp./10 ml	
Cornmeal	2 cups/475 ml	14 oz./400 g
Confectioners' sugar	½ cup/125 ml	2½ oz./65 g

Procedure

1. Preheat the oven to 350° F (180° C).
2. Generously butter the loaf pans. Dust with flour and tap out the excess.
3. Cream the butter and sugar.
4. Add the eggs and vanilla and beat well.
5. Blend in the milk.
6. In a separate bowl, combine the dry ingredients.
7. Add to the wet ingredients and beat until well blended.
8. Pour the batter into the prepared loaf pans and bake for about 1 hour, until a pick tests clean.
9. Cool on a rack.
10. When cool, dust with confectioners' sugar.

Servings	Calories	Protein (g)	Fat (g)	Cholesterol (mg)	Carbohydrates (g)	Fiber (g)	Sodium (mg)
1	411	5.3	17.6	108	58.7	1.5	208

Cranberry Apple Crisp
24 1-cup Servings

This bright red, festive crisp has a tart-sweet flavor. Serve hot, at room temperature, or cold; plain or topped with whipped cream, vanilla ice cream, or frozen yogurt. Store refrigerated.

Serving Utensil or Equipment:	nonreactive pot, 1 half-size insert pan 4-in. deep, 24 8-oz. dessert cups
Preparation Time:	25 minutes if using whole apples
Baking Time:	1½ hours

Ingredients	Volume	Weight
Cooking apples, whole	12–14 lg.	7 lbs./3.2 kg
or prepared apple slices	1 gal./3.75 L	5 lbs./2.25 kg
Cranberries, whole, fresh or frozen	3 qts./2.85 L	3 lbs./1.35 kg
Apple cider or apple juice	3 cups/700 ml	24 oz./682 g
Maple syrup	2 cups/475 ml	22 oz./625 g
Butter	1 cup/240 ml	8 oz./225 g
Honey	1 cup/240 ml	11 oz./310 g
Cinnamon	1 Tbsp./15 ml	
Nutmeg	1 tsp./5 ml	
Rolled oats	1¼ qts./120 ml	1 lb./450 g

Procedure

1. Preheat the oven to 375° F (190° C).
2. If using fresh apples, peel, core, and slice the apples. Place the apple slices in the unoiled insert pan.
3. In a nonreactive pot, bring the cranberries, apple cider or juice, and maple syrup to a boil. Simmer for about 5 minutes, until most of the cranberries have popped open.
4. Pour the cranberry mixture over the apples.
5. Heat the butter and honey until the butter has melted.
6. Stir in the cinnamon, nutmeg, and oats, until the oats are evenly coated.
7. Spread the oat mixture on top of the cranberries and tamp down firmly.
8. Bake for 1 hour and 15 minutes to 1 hour and 30 minutes, until the apples are tender and the topping is golden.

Servings	Calories	Protein (g)	Fat (g)	Cholesterol (mg)	Carbohydrates (g)	Fiber (g)	Sodium (mg)
1	351	3.6	9.5	21	67.4	7.4	83

Desserts

Favorite Fudge Brownie

24 3″ × 3″ Servings

This has been the most popular and best-selling dessert at Moosewood Restaurant for the past 20 years. Serve at room temperature, plain or topped with ice cream or whipped cream. Store refrigerated.

Equipment: 18½ × 12½ × 2 baking pan
Preparation Time: 10 minutes
Baking Time: 30 minutes

Ingredients	Volume	Weight
Butter	2 cups/475 ml	1 lb./450 g
Unsweetened (bakers') chocolate	11 squares	11 oz./310 g
Brown sugar	1 qt./1 L	2 lbs./900 g
Vanilla extract	2 tsp./10 ml	
Eggs	10 lg. or 2½ cups/600 ml	1 lb. 4 oz./565 g
Pastry flour	2 cups/475 ml	10 oz./300 g

Procedure

1. Preheat the oven to 350° F (180°C).
2. Melt the butter and chocolate.
3. Combine the melted butter and chocolate, brown sugar, and vanilla extract and beat well.
4. Add the eggs and beat well.
5. Add the flour and beat until the batter is smooth.
6. Pour the batter into the buttered baking pan and bake for 25–30 minutes, until the brownie is just beginning to pull away from the sides of the pan and the center is set, but still moist. For more cake-like brownies, bake for an additional 5 minutes.
7. Cool completely before cutting in the pan.

Note: Leftovers can be crumbled and frozen and then served as a sundae topping.

Servings	Calories	Protein (g)	Fat (g)	Cholesterol (mg)	Carbohydrates (g)	Fiber (g)	Sodium (mg)
1	432	5.0	22.8	152	54.7	0.2	204

Fresh Orange Compote
24 5-oz. Servings

Here is all the refreshing goodness of oranges zapped with an unexpected flavor boost. We prefer Robertson's Golden Shred or Thick Cut Orange Marmalade. Fresh Orange Compote is an appealing wintertime dessert. Any time of year it has a place in North African or Middle Eastern cuisines, and it may be especially appreciated as a low-fat treat after a rich meal.

   Serve, chilled, in individual 6-oz. cups. Serve with shortbread or a chocolate wafer cookie on the side, if desired. Fresh Orange Compote is also good served on vanilla ice cream or stirred into plain yogurt.

Preparation Time: 30 minutes

Ingredients	Volume	Weight
Seedless oranges	24 lg. (88s)	
or orange sections	1 gal.	7 lbs.
Orange marmalade	1 cup	12 oz.
Orange liqueur (such as Grand Marnier)	½ cup	4 oz.

Procedure

1. Peel the oranges, removing all the white pith. Cut each orange lengthwise into halves. Cut each half crosswise into ½-in. half-rounds.
2. Stir together the marmalade and liqueur to make a thick sauce.
3. Stir the sauce into the cut oranges. Refrigerate.

Servings	Calories	Protein (g)	Fat (g)	Cholesterol (mg)	Carbohydrates (g)	Fiber (g)	Sodium (mg)
1	101	0.9	0.1	0	24.0	1.0	15

Fruit Ricotta Mousse

24 4-oz. Servings

This creamy, wholesome, high-protein pudding is a perennial favorite among our customers. Garnish with pieces of fresh fruit, if desired.

Preparation Time: 10 minutes

Ingredients	Volume	Weight
Ricotta cheese	5½ cups	3 lbs.
100% fruit spread	2 cups	1 lb. 4 oz.
Fruit, fresh, prepared (raspberries, blueberries, cherries, or strawberries)	2 qts.	(weight varies according to fruit)
or frozen (raspberries, blueberries, or cherries)	(volume varies according to fruit used)	2 lbs.
Heavy cream	1 qt.	2 lb.

Note: Use fruit spread made of the same or a compatible fruit as the fresh or frozen fruit used. We do not recommend using frozen strawberries in this dish, because their texture breaks down after freezing.

Procedure

1. Whip the ricotta for about 3 minutes, until very smooth.
2. Fold in the fruit spread and the fruit.
3. Hold covered and refrigerated until ready to serve.
4. When ready to serve, whip the heavy cream until quite stiff.
5. Fold the whipped cream into the ricotta mixture.
6. Serve immediately or store covered and refrigerated.

Note: Fruit Ricotta Mousse is most light and fluffy when the whipped cream is folded in just before serving. When fully prepared, it can be held for 2 days, but it will become more dense.

Servings	Calories	Protein (g)	Fat (g)	Cholesterol (mg)	Carbohydrates (g)	Fiber (g)	Sodium (mg)
1	245	7.6	18.7	69	12.8	2.7	92

Fruit Shakes

24 Servings

Simple, healthful fruit shakes are quickly prepared and are refreshing after a spicy Mexican, Indian, or Caribbean meal. They are excellent breakfast or brunch items. Serve chilled in glasses or stemware and garnished perhaps with orange, lime, or peach slices or whole berries.

Preparation Time: 5 minutes

Ingredients	Volume	Weight
Strawberry Shake		
Strawberries, fresh, rinsed, stemmed	9 pts.	6 lbs.
or frozen	3½ qts.	6 lbs.
Yogurt: plain, vanilla, or lemon	2 qts.	4 lbs.
Maple syrup	1 cup	11 oz.
Peach Shake		
Peaches, fresh, peeled, pitted, sliced	24 lg.	4 lbs.
	sliced, 3 qts.	
or frozen, sliced	3 qts.	4 lbs.
Yogurt: plain or vanilla	2 qts.	4 lbs.
Fruit juice: peach or apricot	1 qt.	2 lbs. 4 oz.
Mango Shake		
Mangoes, fresh, pitted, peeled, cubed	12 whole	11 lbs.
	cubed, 4 qts.	6 lbs. 8 oz.
Frozen limeade concentrate	¾ cup	7 oz.
Pineapple juice or milk or a combination	3 qts.	6 lbs. 12 oz.
Banana Shake		
Bananas, peeled, sliced	18 whole	5 lbs.
	sliced, 1½ qts.	3 lbs.
Yogurt: plain or vanilla	3 qts.	6 lbs.
Orange juice	1½ qts.	3 lbs. 6 oz.

(continued)

Procedure

1. In a blender, purée all the ingredients until smooth.

Banana Shake

Servings	Calories	Protein (g)	Fat (g)	Cholesterol (mg)	Carbohydrates (g)	Fiber (g)	Sodium (mg)
1	151	6.9	2.1	7	27.6	1.5	81

Mango Shake

Servings	Calories	Protein (g)	Fat (g)	Cholesterol (mg)	Carbohydrates (g)	Fiber (g)	Sodium (mg)
1	161	1.0	0.4	0	41.3	2.2	4

Peach Shake

Servings	Calories	Protein (g)	Fat (g)	Cholesterol (mg)	Carbohydrates (g)	Fiber (g)	Sodium (mg)
1	103	4.6	1.2	5	19.6	1.8	56

Strawberry Shake

Servings	Calories	Protein (g)	Fat (g)	Cholesterol (mg)	Carbohydrates (g)	Fiber (g)	Sodium (mg)
1	116	4.7	1.6	5	22.0	2.6	55

Ginger Apple Crisp
24 1-cup Servings

This apple crisp is enhanced by the spicy bite of ginger delivered in a triple whammy. We use Robertson's brand ginger preserves in this recipe. Serve hot, at room temperature, or cold. Serve plain or topped with whipped cream, ice cream, or frozen yogurt. Store refrigerated.

Serving Utensil or Equipment:	1 4-in. deep half-size insert pan,	
	24 8-oz. dessert cups	
Preparation Time:	20 minutes	
Baking Time:	1½ hours	

Ingredients	Volume	Weight
Whole cooking apples	18 lg.	10 lbs./4.5 kg
or apple slices, prepared	1 gal. (16 cups)/ 3.8 L	7 lbs./3 kg
Apple cider or apple juice	½ cup/125 ml	4 oz./115 g
Maple syrup	½ cup/125 ml	6 oz./170 g
Ginger preserves	1½ cups/350 ml	12 oz./340 g
Butter	1 cup/240 ml	8 oz./225 g
Honey	1 cup/240 ml	11 oz./310 g
Cinnamon	1½ tsp./8 ml	
Nutmeg	1 tsp./5 ml	
Ground ginger	1 tsp./5 ml	
Gingersnap cookie crumbs	2 cups/475 ml	8 oz./225 g
Rolled oats	1 qt./1 L	13 oz./370 g

Procedure

1. Preheat the oven to 375° (190° C).
2. If using fresh apples, peel, core, and slice the apples. Place the apple slices in the unoiled insert pan.

(continued)

3. Add the apple cider or apple juice, maple syrup, and ginger preserves and toss gently until well mixed.
4. Heat the butter and honey until the butter has melted.
5. Add the spices and stir well.
6. Add the gingersnap cookie crumbs and the oats and stir to coat evenly.
7. Spread the oats mixture on top of the apples and tamp down firmly.
8. Bake for 1 hour and 15 minutes to 1 hour and 30 minutes, until the apples are tender and the topping is crisp.

Servings	Calories	Protein (g)	Fat (g)	Cholesterol (mg)	Carbohydrates (g)	Fiber (g)	Sodium (mg)
1	351	3.6	10.4	21	65.6	7.3	142

Gingered Plum Sauce

24 5-oz. Servings

This beautiful burgundy-colored sauce is tart-sweet. Serve it warm or chilled on vanilla ice cream, lemon sherbet, or tapioca. Or serve it as a kissel, topped with whipped cream. It's also excellent at breakfast on pancakes, waffles, or oatmeal. Thin slices of green apple are a good garnish.

Equipment:	nonreactive pot
Preparation Time:	20 minutes

Ingredients	Volume	Weight
Plums, fresh, pitted, sliced	3 qts.	6 lbs.
Maple syrup	1½ cups	1 lb.
Ginger, ground	1½ tsp.	
Cornstarch	2 Tbsp.	
Lemon juice, fresh	⅔ cup	5½ oz.

Procedure

1. In a nonreactive pot, heat the plums, maple syrup, and ginger, stirring frequently, until the plums are still firm but are beginning to release juice.
2. Stir the cornstarch into the lemon juice.
3. Add the cornstarch mixture to the plums and bring to a boil. Cook, stirring frequently, until the liquid thickens and clears.
4. Serve warm or chilled.

Servings	Calories	Protein (g)	Fat (g)	Cholesterol (mg)	Carbohydrates (g)	Fiber (g)	Sodium (mg)
1	117	0.9	0.8	0	28.8	1.8	2

Hazelnut Orange Pound Cake

16 6-oz. or 24 4-oz. Servings

This impressively lofty pound cake is full of flavor. Although the skins of hazelnuts are most often removed in dessert-making, we find that including the ground skins is perfectly acceptable, and possibly preferable, adding color and texture; it certainly saves effort.

Equipment:	10-in. Bundt pan
Preparation Time:	20 minutes
Baking Time:	1 hour

Ingredients	Volume	Weight
Hazelnuts, whole	1½ cups/350 ml	6 oz./170 g
Butter	2 cups/475 ml	1 lb./450 g
Sugar	3 cups/700 ml	1 lb. 8 oz./680 g
Eggs	6 lg. or 1½ cups/ 350 ml	12 oz./340 g
Vanilla extract	1 tsp./5 ml	
Orange extract	1 tsp./5 ml	
Pastry flour	1 qt./1 L	1 lb. 4 oz./565 g
Orange juice concentrate and/or Grand Marnier or other orange liqueur	⅓ cup/80 ml	
Milk	⅓ cup/80 ml	
Baking powder	2 tsp./10 ml	

Confectioners' sugar for dusting the cake

Procedure

1. Preheat the oven to 350° F (180° C).
2. Generously butter the Bundt pan. Dust it with flour and tap out the excess.
3. Toast the hazelnuts until browned and fragrant. Without removing the skins, chop the nuts in a food processor until finely ground but not clumping together, yielding about 2 cups.
4. Cream the butter and sugar.
5. Add the eggs and the vanilla and orange extracts and beat well.
6. Add each of the following ingredients in turn, mixing at low speed until well combined: half of the flour, the orange juice concentrate and/or liqueur and the milk, the remaining flour and the baking powder, the ground hazelnuts.
7. Spoon the batter into the prepared Bundt pan and bake immediately for 1 hour to 1 hour and 15 minutes, until the cake is firm and golden and a pick tests clean.
8. Cool the cake in the pan on a rack for 10 minutes. Invert the cake onto a serving platter, leaving the pan in place over the cake until cool.
9. When the cake is cool, dust it with confectioners' sugar.

Servings	Calories	Protein (g)	Fat (g)	Cholesterol (mg)	Carbohydrates (g)	Fiber (g)	Sodium (mg)
1	434	5.4	23.5	108	52.0	0.5	205

LD's Mango–Yogurt Dessert

24 ¹/₂-cup Servings

This Indian-inspired treat makes a luscious and cooling finish for a spicy meal. We've discovered that maple syrup nicely complements the flavor of mangoes, so we call for it here. However, a different sweetener could be used. Garnish individual servings, if desired, with fresh mint leaves or a sprinkling of chopped pistachios or walnuts.

Preparation Time: 30 minutes
Chilling Time: 30 minutes

Ingredients

Ingredients	Volume	Weight
Mangoes, peeled, cubed or sliced	2¹/₄ qts.	4 lbs.
Yogurt, plain	1¹/₂ qts.	3 lbs.
Cardamom, ground	1 tsp.	
Maple syrup	¹/₃ to ¹/₂ cup	3–5 oz.

Procedure

1. Stir together the mango cubes or slices (with juice), yogurt, and cardamom.
2. Add maple syrup to taste (depending on the sweetness of the mangoes used).
3. Chill for at least 30 minutes, to allow the flavors to blend, before serving.

Servings	Calories	Protein (g)	Fat (g)	Cholesterol (mg)	Carbohydrates (g)	Fiber (g)	Sodium (mg)
1	84	3.3	1.1	3	16.6	1.1	41

Lemon Yogurt Grapes
24 6-oz. Servings

Very cooling and refreshing, this can serve as a dessert, a side dish, or an attractive brunch item, piled into melon wedges. Lemon Yogurt Grapes complements rich or spicy-hot entrées, particularly Middle Eastern or Indian. Lemon Yogurt Grapes couldn't be faster or easier to make. Serve garnished with fresh mint leaves, if desired, to accent the frosty pale good looks of this simple dish.

Preparation Time: 10 minutes

Ingredients	Volume	Weight
Seedless grapes, stemmed, rinsed	4½ qts.	6 lbs.
Lemon-flavored yogurt	1½ qts.	3 lbs.

Procedure

1. Gently stir the grapes into the yogurt, until well coated.
2. Serve immediately or chill.

Variations
*   Use both seedless grapes and melon balls.
*   Thicken and intensify the yogurt by draining it in paper coffee filters or several layers of cheesecloth for several hours, until 2 or 3 cups of whey have been removed.

Servings	Calories	Protein (g)	Fat (g)	Cholesterol (mg)	Carbohydrates (g)	Fiber (g)	Sodium (mg)
1	120	3.5	1.1	3	27.3	1.4	40

Lemon Custard Cake

24 4¹/₂-oz. Servings

This favorite old-fashioned dessert separates into layers during baking—a tart-sweet pudding on the bottom and a light, spongy cake on top. Serve plain or garnished with fresh berries for color.

Equipment:	24 8-ounce ramekins or oven proof custard cups, 1 flat-bottomed insert pan
Preparation Time:	15 minutes
Baking Time:	50 minutes

Ingredients	Volume	Weight
Pastry flour	2 cups/475 ml	10 oz./300 g
Baking powder	2 tsp./10 ml	
Sugar	3 cups/700 ml	1 lb. 8 oz./680 g
Buttermilk	1¹/₂ qts./1.4 L	3 lbs./1.36 kg
Lemon juice	2 cups/475 ml	1 lb. 2 oz./500 g
Egg yolks, beaten	8 lg., ³/₄ cup/ 180 ml	6 oz./170 g
Lemon peel, grated (optional)	2 Tbsp./30 ml	
Egg whites	16 lg., 2¹/₂ cups/ 600 ml	1 lb. 4 oz./565 g
Salt	¹/₂ tsp./2.25 ml	
Sugar	2 cups/475 ml	1 lb./450 g
Boiling water		

Procedure

1. Preheat the oven to 350° F (180° C).
2. Prepare the ramekins or custard cups with a light coating of oil or cooking spray.
3. Combine the flour, baking powder, and 3 cups of sugar.
4. Add the buttermilk, lemon juice, egg yolks, and optional lemon peel. Mix until well blended.
5. Beat the egg whites and salt until stiff.
6. Beat in 2 cups of sugar.
7. Fold the egg whites into the batter.
8. Distribute the batter evenly among the ramekins, 3/4–1 cup per ramekin.
9. Place the ramekins into flat insert pans or baking pans. Pour boiling water into the pans to halfway up the sides of the ramekins.
10. Bake for 50–55 minutes, until puffy and golden.
11. Serve warm or chilled.

Servings	Calories	Protein (g)	Fat (g)	Cholesterol (mg)	Carbohydrates (g)	Fiber (g)	Sodium (mg)
1	300	7.4	3.0	102	62.3	0.5	183

Desserts

Maple Nut Pie

24 Servings (3 10-in. pies)

Our customers swoon over the silky richness of this delicious pie. Maple syrup adds a new flavor dimension to classic Southern pecan pie. We use walnuts just as often as pecans, and we also like a combination. We usually use Grade A or Grade B dark amber maple syrup, finding it not only less expensive but also darker and more flavorful than the fancier grades.

Maple Nut Pie is a suitable finish to a meal of traditional Southern foods or a New England harvest meal. Serve plain or with a dollop of whipped cream or vanilla ice cream and with apple or pear slices.

Equipment:	3 10-in. pie pans
Preparation Time:	25 minutes
Baking Time:	1 hour

Ingredients	Volume	Weight
Pie shells, unbaked (see p. 451)	3 10-in.	
Walnut or pecan halves or large pieces	1½ qts./1.4 L	12 oz./500 g
Butter, melted	1 cup/240 ml	8 oz./225 g
Pastry flour	½ cup/125 ml	3 oz./85 g
Vanilla extract	1 Tbsp./15 ml	
Salt	2 tsp./10 ml	
Eggs	12 lg., 3 cups/ 700 ml	1 lb. 8 oz./680 g
Maple syrup	1 qt./1 L	2 lbs.13 oz./1.25 kg
Heavy cream or half-and-half	1 qt./1 L	2 lbs.1 oz./930 g

Procedure

1. Preheat the oven to 375° F (190° C).
2. Spread the nuts evenly across the bottoms of the pie shells.
3. Beat the butter, flour, vanilla extract, and salt until smooth.
4. Add the eggs, maple syrup, and heavy cream or half-and-half and beat well.
5. Pour the liquid mixture into the pie shells. Push the floating nuts down into the liquid to coat them, to prevent burning during baking.
6. Bake for about 60 minutes, until the crusts have browned and the filling is set.
7. Chill before slicing. Store refrigerated.

Servings	Calories	Protein (g)	Fat (g)	Cholesterol (mg)	Carbohydrates (g)	Fiber (g)	Sodium (mg)
1	537	8.5	32.6	167	54.8	0.8	501

Desserts

Peach Parfait with Amaretto Cream

24 6-oz. Servings

Peaches and cream is classic; the addition of amaretto and amaretti is inspired. This is an ideal dessert to showcase fresh, perfectly ripe peaches, but during most of the year, when good peaches are unavailable, frozen peach slices work quite well. The creamy richness of Peach Parfait with Amaretto Cream is best appreciated following a light, piquant entrée. Top each parfait, if desired, with a toasted almond or a strawberry or raspberry.

Equipment: 24 8-oz. parfait glasses or wine glasses
Preparation Time: 30 minutes

Ingredients	Volume	Weight
Heavy cream, well chilled	1½ qts.	3 lbs.
Amaretto (almond liqueur)	¾ cup	6 oz.
Confectioners' sugar	1 cup	4½ oz.
Amaretti (crisp macaroons), crumbled	3 cups	10 oz.
Peaches, fresh, peeled, pitted, sliced	4½ qts.	6 lbs.
or defrosted frozen	4½ qts.	6 lbs.

Procedure

1. Whip the heavy cream until soft peaks form.
2. Add the amaretto and confectioners' sugar and whip until stiff.
3. Chill until ready to assemble the individual parfaits.
4. Arrange the parfait or wine glasses and bowls of whipped cream, crumbled amaretti, and peach slices, for assembly of individual servings. In each of the parfait glasses, layer in the following order: 1/4 cup peaches, 1 Tbsp. amaretti, 1/4 cup whipped cream. Repeat.
5. Serve immediately or chill for up to 3 hours before serving.

Variations
- Replace the peaches with sliced strawberries or pitted sweet cherries.
- Replace up to half of the peaches with raspberries or blueberries.
- Replace the amaretti with crisp sugar cookies or gingersnaps, and, in the whipped cream, substitute 1 Tbsp. vanilla extract for the amaretto.

Servings	Calories	Protein (g)	Fat (g)	Cholesterol (mg)	Carbohydrates (g)	Fiber (g)	Sodium (mg)
1	339	2.4	22.6	78	30.9	2.3	51

Desserts

Peppermint Butter Wafers
24 Servings (48 cookies)

These wafers are thin, crisp, and refreshing. We serve them as "a little something" dessert or with ice cream or tea.

Equipment:	baking trays
Preparation Time:	15 minutes plus 30 minutes standing time
Baking Time:	10 minutes

Ingredients	Volume	Weight
Butter	1 cup/240 ml	8 oz./225 g
Peppermint leaves, fresh, finely chopped	½ cup/125 ml	1 oz./30 g
Sugar	1 cup/240 ml	8 oz./225 g
Eggs, beaten	2 lg., ½ cup/ 125 ml	4 oz./115 g
Salt	⅛ tsp./1 ml	
Pastry flour, white or whole wheat	1½ cups/350 ml	8 oz./225 g

Procedure

1. Preheat the oven to 375° F (190° C).
2. Cream the butter, mint, and sugar.
3. Let stand at room temperature for 30 minutes to suffuse the butter with mint flavor.
4. Add the eggs and mix until well blended.
5. Add the salt and flour and mix just until the batter is smooth.
6. Drop rounded teaspoons of batter, 2 in. apart, onto lightly oiled baking trays.
7. Bake for 10–15 minutes, until the edges are light brown.
8. Remove the cookies from the baking tray while still hot.

Variation
- Place a semisweet chocolate drop or chunk in the center of each unbaked wafer for that classic chocolate–mint combination.

Servings	Calories	Protein (g)	Fat (g)	Cholesterol (mg)	Carbohydrates (g)	Fiber (g)	Sodium (mg)
1	147	1.5	8.3	43	17.0	0.2	98

Pie Shells

3 10-in. Pie Shells

This is not the flakiest pie crust, but it's tasty and is not fragile. It cuts well and holds a filling without breaking, and the edges don't crumble easily. The dough rolls out with ease and handles well without tearing. We don't follow any finicky pie crust rules—we usually cut the butter into the flour simply by rubbing it between fingers, and we don't chill the dough before rolling it.

Add the optional sugar and vanilla when preparing pie shells for a dessert pie; omit them for a savory pie.

Equipment:	3 10-in. pie pans
Preparation Time:	20 minutes

Ingredients	Volume	Weight
Pastry flour	3 cups/700 ml	15 oz./425 g
Sugar (optional)	3 Tbsp./45 ml	1½ oz./40 g
Butter	1 cup/240 ml	8 oz./225 g
Water, buttermilk, or fruit juice	about 6 Tbsp./ 90 ml	3 oz./85 g
Vanilla extract (optional)	1 tsp./5 ml	

Procedure

1. Mix together the flour and optional sugar.
2. Cut the butter into the flour.
3. Sprinkle 4 Tbsp. of the water or other liquid over the flour and stir, adding more if needed to form a stiff dough that holds together.
4. Divide the dough into three equal pieces.
5. Roll out each piece of dough, fit it into a pie plate, and crimp or flute the edges. Chill until ready to use. If stacking, separate with sheets of waxed paper. If storing for more than a couple of hours, wrap in plastic.

Servings	Calories	Protein (g)	Fat (g)	Cholesterol (mg)	Carbohydrates (g)	Fiber (g)	Sodium (mg)
1	132	1.9	7.8	21	13.5	0.6	78

Prune and Armagnac Cake

32 5½-oz. Servings

This glossy, dark, very moist, and spicy cake makes the most of the special affinity between prunes and Armagnac. Serve with whipped cream or vanilla ice cream.

Serving Utensil or Equipment:	2 10-in. Bundt pans
Preparation Time:	40 minutes
Baking Time:	1 hour

Ingredients	Volume	Weight
Prunes, pitted	1 qt./1 L	2 lbs. 12 oz./1.25 kg
Armagnac or cognac	½ cup/125 ml	3 oz./90 g
Water	1 qt./1 L	2 lbs./900 g
Vegetable oil	2 cups/475 ml	15 oz./425 g
Brown sugar	1 qt./1 L	2 lbs./900 g
Eggs	10 lg., 2½ cups/ 600 ml	1 lb. 4 oz./565 g
Vanilla extract	2 Tbsp./30 ml	
Pastry flour	1½ qts./1.4 L	1 lb. 14 oz./850 g
Baking soda	2 Tbsp./30 ml	
Salt	2 tsp./10 ml	
Allspice, ground	1 tsp./5 ml	
Nutmeg, ground	2 tsp./10 ml	
Cloves, ground	2 tsp./10 ml	
Cardamom, ground	1 tsp./5 ml	
Cinnamon, ground	4 tsp./20 ml	
Buttermilk	3 cups/700 ml	1 lb. 8 oz./680 g

Glaze

Ingredients	Volume	Weight
Sugar	2 cups/475 ml	1 lb./900 g
Lemon juice	4 Tbsp./60 ml	2 oz./55 g
Armagnac or cognac	½ cup/125 ml	3.5 oz./100 g
Reserved prune cooking liquid	½ cup/125 ml	5 oz./140 g

Procedure

1. Preheat the oven to 350° F (180° C).
2. Generously butter the Bundt pans. Dust them with flour and tap out the excess.
3. Simmer the prunes, Armagnac, and water for 20–25 minutes, until the prunes are tender. Drain, reserving the liquid.
4. Coarsely chop the prunes.
5. Cream the oil and sugar.
6. Add the eggs and vanilla extract and beat well.
7. Combine the dry ingredients.
8. Add the dry ingredients to the wet ingredients and mix until well blended.
9. Add the buttermilk and beat just until the batter is smooth.
10. Fold in the chopped prunes.
11. Pour the batter into the prepared Bundt pans and bake for 1 hour to 1 hour and 10 minutes, until a pick tests clean.
12. Cool the cakes in the pans on a rack for 10 minutes.
13. Invert the cakes onto serving platters, leaving the pans in place over the cakes for 15 minutes.
14. Bring to a boil all the glaze ingredients and boil for 2 minutes, stirring continually.
15. Pierce the cakes with a toothpick or skewer. Slowly pour the glaze over the cakes, allowing it to soak in.

Servings	Calories	Protein (g)	Fat (g)	Cholesterol (mg)	Carbohydrates (g)	Fiber (g)	Sodium (mg)
1	485	5.8	16.0	83	77.6	2.2	293

Desserts

Pumpkin Pear Pie

24 Servings (3 10-inch pies)

The spicy richness of pumpkin and the bland sweetness of fresh pears are well paired. Serve cold. Small bunches of fresh grapes are lovely garnishes in autumn.

Equipment:	3 10-in. pie pans
Preparation Time:	35 minutes
Baking Time:	1 hour

Ingredients	Volume	Weight
Pie shells, unbaked (see p. 451)	3 10-in.	
Pumpkin, puréed, cooked	1½ qts./1.4 L	3 lbs./1.36 kg
Eggs	9 lg., 2¼ cups/ 530 ml	1 lb. 2 oz./500 g
Brown sugar	1½ cups/350 ml	12 oz./340 g
Ginger, ground	1½ tsp./8 ml	
Salt	1 tsp./5 ml	
Pears, whole, fresh	15	5 lbs./2.25 kg
Cinnamon	1½ tsp./8 ml	
Nutmeg	1½ tsp./8 ml	
Sugar	⅓ cup/80 ml	

Procedure

1. Preheat the oven to 400° F (200° C).
2. Prick the bottom and sides of each unbaked pie shell with a fork. Bake for 10 minutes. Set aside to cool.
3. Reduce the oven to 375° F (190° C).
4. Mix together the pumpkin, eggs, brown sugar, ginger, and salt until well blended.
5. Peel and core the pears. Cut them lengthwise into ⅛-in. slices.
6. Combine the cinnamon, nutmeg, and sugar.
7. Arrange the pear slices in the cooled pie shells. Sprinkle the pears with the cinnamon–sugar mixture. Pour the pumpkin mixture over the pears and smooth it with a spatula.
8. Bake for 50–60 minutes, until the crust has browned and the filling is set.
9. Cool at room temperature. Store refrigerated.

Servings	Calories	Protein (g)	Fat (g)	Cholesterol (mg)	Carbohydrates (g)	Fiber (g)	Sodium (mg)
1	347	6.1	14.8	130	50.0	2.9	388

Desserts

Sara's Fresh Apple Cake
24 5½-oz. Servings

This easy, moist cake, filled with chunks of fresh apples, has a lot of homey appeal. We've found that most cakes, and this one in particular, bake best in pans made of a material that conducts heat more slowly, such as aluminum, rather than a quicker conductor, such as stainless steel. Dust with confectioners' sugar or top with whipped cream or vanilla custard sauce.

Equipment:	18½ x 12½ x 2-in. baking pan
Preparation Time:	20 minutes
Baking Time:	1 hour

Ingredients	Volume	Weight
Butter	1 Tbsp./15 ml	
Sesame seeds	½ cup/125 ml	3 oz./85 g
Vegetable oil	2 cups/475 ml	15 oz./425 g
Brown sugar	1 qt./1 L	2 lbs./900 g
Eggs	6 lg., 1½ cups/ 350 ml	12 oz./340 g
Apple juice, milk, or water	½ cup/125 ml	4 oz./115 g
Vanilla extract	1 Tbsp./15 ml	
Pastry flour	1½ qts./1.4 ml	1 lb. 14 oz./850 g
Cardamom, ground	½ tsp./2.5 ml	
Cinnamon	2 tsp./10 ml	
Baking powder	2 tsp./10 ml	
Baking soda	1 tsp./5 ml	
Apples, fresh, peeled, cored, and chopped	1½ qts./1.4 L	2 lbs./900 g
Nuts, chopped: walnuts, pecans, or almonds	2 cups/475 ml	8 oz./225 g

Procedure

1. Preheat the oven to 350° F (180° C).
2. Butter the baking pan and sprinkle the bottom with the sesame seeds.
3. Beat the oil, brown sugar, and eggs until creamy.
4. Add the apple juice and vanilla extract and mix until well blended.
5. In a separate bowl, stir together the flour, cardamom, cinnamon, baking powder, and baking soda.
6. Stir the dry ingredients into the wet ingredients. The batter will be stiff.
7. Fold in the apples and nuts.
8. Bake in the prepared pan for about 1 hour, until a knife inserted in the center comes out clean.

Servings	Calories	Protein (g)	Fat (g)	Cholesterol (mg)	Carbohydrates (g)	Fiber (g)	Sodium (mg)
1	572	7.9	28.7	67	73.6	3.2	87

Scandinavian Dried Fruit Pudding

24 5½-oz. Servings

A wholesome but flavorful dessert. For visual appeal, we suggest serving it layered with whipped cream, in tall, clear glass dessert cups.

Equipment:	large nonreactive pot
Preparation Time:	1 hour (includes 30 minutes cooking time)

Ingredients	Volume	Weight
Dried fruit, mixed: apricots, prunes, pears, apples	2 qts.	about 2½ lbs.
Fruit juice: cranberry, apple, pear, apricot, prune, or a mix	3 qts.	6 lbs. 10 oz.
Nutmeg	2 tsp.	
Cinnamon	1 Tbsp.	
Cloves, ground	½ tsp.	
Tapioca, quick-cooking	¾ cup	4 oz.

Note: The weight of dried fruits varies considerably (a 2-cup measure of apples = 6 oz., pears = 8 oz., apricots = 12 oz., pitted prunes = 13 oz.); the weight we give for dried fruit is based on equal amounts of each of the suggested fruits.

Procedure

1. In an uncovered nonreactive pot, simmer the dried fruit, juice, nutmeg, cinnamon, and cloves for 30 minutes. Drain, reserving the fruit and liquid separately.
2. If necessary, add water to the liquid to make 8 cups. Stir the tapioca into the liquid and let stand for 5 minutes.
3. Bring to a boil and then cook, stirring continuously, for 3 minutes. Let stand for 20 minutes.
4. Combine the tapioca pudding and the cooked fruit.
5. Chill.

Servings	Calories	Protein (g)	Fat (g)	Cholesterol (mg)	Carbohydrates (g)	Fiber (g)	Sodium (mg)
1	121	0.5	0.6	0	30.2	2.1	7

Sour Cream Gingerbread

24 Servings

Yielding generous, high portions, this is an exceptionally moist and rich gingerbread. Serve unadorned, dusted with confectioners' sugar, or topped with whipped cream and fresh apple slices, chunky applesauce or pear sauce, vanilla or lemon custard sauce, or lemon sauce.

Equipment:	18½ x 12½ x 2-in. baking pan
Preparation Time:	20 minutes
Baking Time:	35 minutes

Ingredients	Volume	Weight
Eggs	7 lg. or 1¾ cups/415 ml	14 oz./400 g
Sour cream	1¾ cups/415 ml	14 oz./400 g
Molasses	1¾ cups/415 ml	14 oz./400 g
Brown sugar	1¾ cups/415 ml	14 oz./400 g
Pastry flour	1¼ qts./1.2 L	1 lb. 9 oz./700 g
Salt	1 tsp./5 ml	
Ginger, ground	1 Tbsp./15 ml	
Baking soda	4 tsp./20 ml	
Butter, melted	1½ cups/350 ml	12 oz./340 g

Procedure

1. Preheat the oven to 350° F (180° C).
2. Lightly beat the eggs.
3. Mix in the sour cream and molasses.
4. Combine the dry ingredients.
5. Add the dry ingredients to the wet ingredients, beating until smooth.
6. Add the melted butter, mixing just until well blended.
7. Pour the batter into an oiled baking pan and bake for about 35 minutes, until the center springs back and a pick tests clean.

Servings	Calories	Protein (g)	Fat (g)	Cholesterol (mg)	Carbohydrates (g)	Fiber (g)	Sodium (mg)
1	393	5.7	17.2	116	54.5	0.6	336

Sour Cream Raisin
Pound Cake

16 6-oz. or 24 4-oz. Servings

This cake is a very satisfying offering for afternoon tea. Dust with confectioners' sugar and garnish with fresh peach slices or some other fresh fruit.

Serving Utensil or Equipment:	10-in. Bundt pan
Preparation Time:	30 minutes
Baking Time:	1 hour

Ingredients	Volume	Weight
Raisins	1 cup/235 ml	6 oz./170 g
Brandy	½ cup/125 ml	3½ oz./100 g
Butter	2 cups/475 ml	1 lb./450 g
Sugar	3 cups/700 ml	1 lb. 8 oz./680 g
Eggs	6 lg., 1½ cups/ 350 ml	12 oz./340 g
Vanilla extract	2 tsp./10 ml	
Sour cream	½ cup/125 ml	3½ oz./100 g
Pastry flour	1 qt./1 L	1 lb. 4 oz./565 g
Baking powder	2 tsp./10 ml	
Nutmeg, ground	½ tsp./2.5 ml	

Procedure

1. Soak the raisins in the brandy for at least 10 minutes. Drain, reserving the brandy.
2. Preheat the oven to 350° F (180° C).
3. Generously butter the Bundt pan. Dust it with flour and tap out the excess.
4. Cream the butter and sugar.
5. Add the eggs and vanilla extract and beat well.
6. Add the reserved brandy and the sour cream and beat well.
7. Combine the flour, baking powder, and nutmeg.
8. Add the dry ingredients to the wet ingredients and beat well.
9. Fold in the drained raisins.
10. Pour the batter into the prepared Bundt pan and bake for about 1 hour, until the cake pulls away from the sides of the pan and a pick tests clean.
11. Cool the cake in the pan on a rack for 10 minutes.
12. Invert the cake onto a serving platter, leaving the pan in place until cool.

Variations

- Substitute brown sugar for white sugar.
- Substitute whiskey for brandy.
- Substitute yogurt for sour cream.
- Substitute dried cranberries for raisins.

Servings	Calories	Protein (g)	Fat (g)	Cholesterol (mg)	Carbohydrates (g)	Fiber (g)	Sodium (mg)
1	398	4.4	18.1	109	53.0	0.7	206

Tira Misu
24 8-oz. Servings

Our version of Tira Misu is very easy to prepare and is lighter than the traditional offering, which is made with mascarpone cheese and egg yolks. We use Bistefani brand lady fingers (aka Savoiardi). Serve chilled and garnish, if desired, with chocolate-covered coffee beans or fresh fruit, such as raspberries or sliced oranges or strawberries. Tira Misu looks its best when served not more than a few hours after it was assembled.

Equipment:	24 8- to 10-oz. dessert cups	
Preparation Time:	25 minutes	

Ingredients	Volume	Weight
Coffee, freshly brewed, cooled	1 qt.	2 lbs.
Coffee or mocha liqueur, brandy, or marsala	¼ cup	2 oz.
Ladyfingers	48	14 oz.
Cream cheese or Neufchâtel, at room temperature		3 lbs.
Confectioners' sugar		2 lbs.
Instant coffee granules	½ cup	¾ oz.
Cocoa powder, unsweetened	¼ cup	
Vanilla extract	2 tsp.	
Heavy cream, whipped until stiff	1 qt. (unwhipped)	
Semisweet chocolate, grated	1 cup	4 oz.

Procedure

1. Arrange the dessert cups on trays for easy assembly of individual servings.
2. Combine the brewed coffee and the liqueur in a wide shallow bowl and place it near the dessert cups.
3. Break a ladyfinger into halves, dip the halves into the coffee for just a second until moistened but not falling apart, and drop them into a dessert cup. Repeat this process, placing two moistened ladyfinger halves in each cup. Reserve the coffee mixture and the remaining 24 ladyfingers.
4. Beat the cream cheese, confectioners' sugar, instant coffee, cocoa, and vanilla extract until evenly colored and fluffy.
5. Fold in the stiffly whipped cream.
6. Spoon the cream cheese mixture into the dessert cups.
7. Moisten each of the remaining ladyfingers, following the procedure described in Step 3. Into each dessert cup, push two halves down along the sides of the cup into the cream cheese mixture.
8. Sprinkle grated chocolate over each Tira Misu.
9. Refrigerate.

Servings	Calories	Protein (g)	Fat (g)	Cholesterol (mg)	Carbohydrates (g)	Fiber (g)	Sodium (mg)
1	572	7.3	36.9	174	54.9	0.3	208

Desserts

Triple Pear Crisp

24 8-oz. Servings

This wholesome and popular crisp retains the juiciness of fresh pears intensified by the concentrated sweetness of dried pears. Serve warm or chilled, with vanilla ice cream, whipped cream, or custard sauce.

Equipment:	4-in. deep half-size insert pan
Preparation Time:	25 minutes
Baking Time:	1½ hours

Ingredients	Volume	Weight
Pears, dried, stemmed, chopped	1 qt./1 L	1 lb. 4 oz./565 g
Pear juice	1 qt./1 L	2 lbs. 3 oz./1 kg
Butter, melted	2 cups/475 ml	1 lb./450 g
Maple syrup	1 cup/240 ml	11 oz./310 g
Cinnamon, ground	1 Tbsp./15 ml	
Nutmeg, ground	2 tsp./10 ml	
Rolled oats	2 qts./1.9 L	1 lb. 12 oz./800 g
Pears, fresh, stemmed, cored, chopped	1 gal. (16 cups)/ 3.8 L	7 lbs./3 kg

Procedure

1. Preheat the oven to 375° F (190° C).
2. Simmer the dried pears and the pear juice for about 10 minutes, until the pears are tender.
3. Meanwhile, stir the melted butter, maple syrup, cinnamon, and nutmeg until the spices are evenly distributed.
4. Stir in the oats.
5. Combine the simmered dried pears and juice with the fresh pears.
6. Spread out the combined pears in the insert pan and top with the oat mixture.
7. Bake for about 1½ hours, until the fresh pears are tender and the topping is browned and crisp.

Variation
- Peel the fresh pears. Add ½ cup pear liqueur, such as Poire William. Replace half of the oats with amaretti (crisp Italian-style macaroons).

Servings	Calories	Protein (g)	Fat (g)	Cholesterol (mg)	Carbohydrates (g)	Fiber (g)	Sodium (mg)
1	351	2.0	16.4	41	54.0	5.5	161

Tropical Fruit Salad

24 1-cup Servings

The ginger-and-lime dressing turns simple fresh fruit salad into an enticing dessert, side dish, or brunch item. The proportions of various fruits are not critical—include whatever ripe and colorful fruit is available.

Preparation Time: 30 minutes

Ingredients	Volume	Weight
Fruit, mixed fresh, prepared: pineapple, cantaloupe, honeydew, mango, strawberries, kiwi, oranges, grapefruit, star fruit, bananas	6 qts.	

Dressing

Honey	½ cup	5½ oz.
Ginger, ground	1 Tbsp.	
Lime juice	1½ cups	14 oz.

Procedure

1. Stir the honey and ginger until well mixed.
2. Mix in the lime juice.
3. Pour the dressing over the fruit and stir well.
4. Serve at room temperature or chilled.

Note: This salad stores well, covered and refrigerated, for several hours.

Note: Add bananas just before serving.

Servings	Calories	Protein (g)	Fat (g)	Cholesterol (mg)	Carbohydrates (g)	Fiber (g)	Sodium (mg)
1	124	1.5	0.7	0	31.8	2.5	8

Guide to Ingredients

Anise: This licorice flavored spice is generally sold as seeds and is best when ground right before using. Anise is not a spice to be typecast, it can be found in dishes and pastries from eastern Europe and the Mediterranean to China. It is available from spice suppliers, gourmet food suppliers, and many supermarkets.

Annatto Seed (achiote seed): This small, red seed is used as a subtle flavoring and vivid coloring agent in Latin American dishes. At Moosewood, we prize annatto for its coloring property, which gives grains, sauces, and stews a brilliant yellow-orange color. We achieve this with "annato oil" which we prepare just before sautéing. *To make ¼ cup of oil, swirl 1 Tbsp. of seeds into 4 Tbsp. of vegetable oil. Cook for 5 minutes on medium-low heat, or until the oil turns a deep red-orange. Strain the seeds. The oil is ready for use in cooking.* Annatto can be purchased at stores that sell Latin American ingredients and at some specialty spice shops.

Annatto Oil: See Annatto.

Beans, dried: When possible, we would rather cook dried beans from scratch than use canned beans. Canned beans have a good amount of added salt and, often, additives and preservatives. There are those times, however, when canned beans seem like a gift from the gods, so we give them a good rinse, and carry on. Sahadi, Goya, Eden, Westbrae, and Randall are brands that offer some types of beans without additives or preservatives, although often only in quantities smaller than #10 cans.

Most dried beans need to be softened by soaking before they are cooked. This is not true for small, soft beans (lentils or split peas) or even some larger, softer types (lima beans). To prepare any bean, however, the first step is to spread the beans out on a flat tray and sort through them for stones and shriveled or discolored beans. After you have sorted the beans, immerse them in cool water both to rinse them of dust and to allow loose hulls and harvesting debris to float to the surface. Pour off this water and refill the pot, covering the beans with fresh water. The beans are now ready to be soaked. Either soak them overnight in a cool spot to avoid fermentation (a cooler won't inhibit the softening process) or bring the beans to a boil, turning off the heat and letting them sit for 1 hour. After soaking, drain the beans and discard the soaking water. The soaking process helps extract the sugars that can cause digestive problems for some people. Cover the beans with fresh water for cooking. The following chart lists the water-to-bean ratio for specific beans. Bring the water to a boil, reduce it to a simmer, and cook, checking periodically that the beans are always covered with water. Replenish the water if the level drops below the surface of the beans and continue simmering until the beans are thoroughly cooked.

(continued)

Variety	Water–Bean Ratio	Cooking Time After Soaking	Cooked Quantity of 1 cup Dried Beans
Black-eyed peas	3:1	30 minutes	2½ cups
Black turtle	5:1	1 hour	3 cups
Chick-peas (garbanzos)	6:1	1–1½ hours	3 cups
Lentils	3:1	30 minutes	3 cups
Lima beans	3:1	1 hour	3 cups
Mung beans	4:1	45 minutes	3 cups
Navy pea	3:1	1 hour	2¾ cups
Pinto	3:1	45 minutes	3¼ cups
Red kidney	3:1	1–1½ hours	2¾ cups
Red lentils	2:1	15–20 minutes	3 cups
Soy beans	5:1	2 hours	2¾ cups
Split peas (green)	3:1	45 minutes–1 hour	1¾ cups
Split peas (yellow)	3:1	30 minutes	2¼ cups

Bread Crumbs: When we call for fresh bread crumbs, we are simply referring to day-old bread (whole wheat, white, or rye), finely crumbled in the bowl of a food processor.

Brown Rice: A nutritious, flavorful grain that our customers literally eat up. It is available in short, medium, and long grain varieties. The longer the grain the fluffier the rice, so we tend to use the medium and long grains for pilafs, stuffed vegetables, and soups. The virtues of short grain rice are its flavor and substance. It provides a good bed for richly seasoned stews and saucy fish dishes.

To prepare brown rice in large quantities (8 cups or more of uncooked rice), rinse the rice and drain well. Heat a small amount of oil in a stockpot and sauté the rice quickly, stirring continuously to avoid scorching. This quick sauté yields a cooked rice that is fluffy and distinct. When the rice releases a nutty aroma, add an equal amount of water to rice plus an additional 2–3 cups. Long grain or Basmati brown rice requires an additional 1 cup of water. Add water, cover the pot, and bring to a boil. Then, reduce the heat to low and simmer on a heat diffuser for 30–40 minutes. Resist stirring the rice while it cooks.

Bulghur (cracked wheat): A quick-cooking wheat product (steamed, dried, and cracked wheat berries), available in coarse, medium, and fine grades. The finer the grade, the lighter (both in color and texture), the bulghur. *To cook bulghur, add an equal amount of boiling water, cover, and soak for about 20 minutes. Fluff with a fork, and, if the grains are still crunchy, sprinkle with a little more hot water and cover for another 10 minutes.* It is available through natural food distributors and natural food stores and in the ethnic section of some supermarkets.

Calamata: This smooth-skinned, eggplant-colored Greek olive has a pulp that is both salty and sweet. Calamatas can be used as either salad olives or as an ingredient in cooking. For cooking, the pits can be easily extracted by pressing against the olive with the flat of a broad-bladed knife. Calamata olives are available from gourmet, Greek, and Middle Eastern food suppliers.

Capers: These small, green, pickled buds are coveted for their tangy, salty, distinctive taste. They particularly complement fish and serve as an interesting counterpoint to creamy or acidic sauces. The harvesting and importing of the tiny, Mediterranean capers account for their high price. However, because of their strong taste, a little goes a long way. They are available from gourmet food distributors and at the supermarket. Refrigerate after opening; they keep indefinitely.

Chili Oil: A hot oil used as a seasoning in Asian cooking. Chili oil can be found in Asian food stores and the ethnic section of some supermarkets.

Chili Paste with Garlic: A commercial Asian product made of chili peppers, salt, oil, and garlic. This condiment is used as a flavoring and a hot seasoning. Chili paste with garlic is available at Asian food stores and in the Asian section of some supermarkets.

Chinese Fermented Black Beans (salted black beans; Chinese black beans): These black soybeans have been steamed, fermented, seasoned, and salted to yield an intensely salty and tasty flavoring. Because of their strength, usually a small amount of beans is called for in a given recipe. Dried black turtle beans cannot be substituted. Fermented black beans have a distinctive taste that particularly enhances fish and seafood dishes. To use, rinse the beans briefly in cold water, drain, and mix with other seasonings. Sometimes the beans are mashed before the seasonings are added. Fermented black beans are available at Asian food stores, through Asian and gourmet food distributors, and in the ethnic section of some supermarkets. They can be stored indefinitely in a tightly lidded jar at room temperature. Over time, white crystals may form on the beans, but they are still usable.

Chinese Rice Vinegar: This rice wine vinegar is milder and sweeter than Western vinegars. It is available in three strengths—white, red, and black, from mildest to sharpest. The rice vinegar called for in our recipes refers to the white, the mildest. Small amounts of distilled white vinegar or cider vinegar can be substituted. Sometimes labeled rice wine vinegar, this product is available at Asian groceries, through Asian and gourmet food distributors, and in the ethnic section of many supermarkets. It will keep indefinitely at room temperature.

Chinese Rice Wine: This cooking wine of China is a flavorful wine that is somewhat lighter than the dry white wines used for cooking in the West. If unavailable, substitute vermouth or sake, a Japanese rice wine. Rice wine can be purchased at Asian food stores, through Asian and gourmet food suppliers, and in the ethnic section of some supermarkets. It keeps well under refrigeration.

Cilantro: This fresh herb, the green leaves of the coriander plant, resembles flat leaf parsley and has a fan club that encircles the globe. One eminent food authority says that if all the other herbs used worldwide were stacked against the amount of cilantro used, you would see a molehill next to a mountain. Cilantro has its devotees and its antagonists, but conversions to cilantro occur constantly. We always use it fresh, adding it at the last minute, primarily in Latin American, Indian, African, and Southeast Asian dishes. We purchase it through our produce or fresh herb suppliers.

Coconut Milk, Unsweetened: The coconut milk called for in our recipes is pure, unsweetened coconut milk. It should not be confused with the sweetened variety often intended for use in mixed drinks. Brands free of additives and preservatives are on the market, and we have been able to procure them in bulk through our natural foods supplier. Individual cans are available at some natural foods stores. Unsweetened coconut milk (often with preservatives) can often be found in Asian food stores and in Hispanic, Asian, and Indian sections of some large supermarkets.

Coconut milk can also be made from scratch. *To make 1 cup of milk, combine 1 cup of unsweetened shredded coconut with 1½ cups of hot tap water and let stand for 5 minutes. Pureé in a blender; then pour the puree through a strainer into a bowl. Press as much coconut milk as possible out of the coconut pulp. Strain the milk a second time through a fine mesh strainer.* Freshly made coconut milk will keep for 3 days if tightly covered and refrigerated. It will keep indefinitely if frozen.

Couscous: Fluffy and grainlike, couscous is made of finely milled semolina wheat. Central to the cuisines of North Africa and the Middle East, it is used as a bed for rich stews and in stuffings. We use a quick-cooking variety that can be ready in 10 minutes, employing an off-the-stove steaming method. *Using a 1⅓:1 water to couscous ratio, combine the couscous, boiling water, a little salt, and 1 tsp. of oil. Cover tightly and let steam for 10 minutes. Fluff with a fork.* Couscous can be purchased at many supermarkets and Middle Eastern groceries and through gourmet food distributors. It is often available in whole wheat form from natural food sources.

Currants: The currants referred to in our recipes are a variety of extra small raisins imported primarily from Greece. The name derives from Corinth, their place of origin. These currants are unrelated to the tart red or black currants grown in more northern climates that are used in jellies and preserves. We often choose currants instead of standard raisins because currants maintain their glossy color when cooked, contributing a lovely jeweled effect to a dish. Their tiny size also adds sweetness without dominating texture. We procure currants through our natural food supplier and specialty foods purveyor. They are often available at the supermarket where dried fruit and nuts are stocked.

Fish Sauce: This staple flavoring ingredient of Southeast Asia is made of salted, fermented fish. Westerners often find its strong smell overwhelming, but once cooked, the smell dissipates and its flavor is quite mild. Fish Sauce is available at Asian food stores and through Asian food suppliers. It will keep indefinitely, bottled and capped, at room temperature.

Five-Spice Powder: A Chinese spice combination composed of the following ground spices: star anise, Szechuan peppercorns, fennel or anise seed, cloves, and cinnamon. Five-spice powder is available at Asian food stores, through Asian and gourmet food suppliers, and in the ethnic section of some supermarkets. It will keep for months stored in a tightly lidded glass jar.

Ginger Root: Fresh ginger is a knobby root with a paper-thin, light bronze skin. It is used throughout Asia, offering a refreshing and spicy accent to stocks, sautés, marinades, and sauces. Dried ground ginger, in general, cannot be substituted for fresh ginger root. If the skin is smooth and unscarred, with a nice sheen, simply scrub ginger root with a vegetable brush to clean, and finely grate. If the skin is tough or beginning to shrivel, peel before grating. Ginger root is available through most produce suppliers, in the produce section of many supermarkets, and at Asian food stores. It can be stored in a plastic bag or glass jar for about 2 weeks if refrigerated, or indefinitely if frozen.

Haas Avocado: We mention this variety of avocado because we're happiest with its buttery taste, creamy texture, and lovely two-tone color. Haas are usually grown in California. They are recognizable by their pear shape and dark green, lizardy skin. The smooth-skinned Florida varieties we've tried, although larger, may be less flavorful and sometimes have a stringy texture. Haas are available through wholesale produce suppliers and supermarkets.

Hoisin Sauce: A thick, reddish-brown, sweet, and spicy paste used as a glaze or dipping sauce in Chinese cooking. Hoisin is a commercial product made of fermented soybeans, flour, salt, sugar, vinegar, chili peppers, and spices. It can be purchased from Asian and gourmet food suppliers and in the ethnic section of many supermarkets. For a dipping sauce or light sauce, hoisin can be thinned with water, stock, or fruit juice. Hoisin is available in glass jars or cans. Once opened, transfer any leftover canned hoisin to a glass jar. It will keep for many months refrigerated.

Horseradish, Prepared: This pungent condiment is often used to offset rich meat and fish dishes or as an ingredient that gives zest to creamy sauces and dressings. It is made of finely ground fresh horseradish root, vinegar, and salt. Horseradish is commercially available, bottled, in white or red form. Beet juice has been added to the red variety for color and sweetness. Prepared horseradish can be purchased from wholesale distributors and supermarkets. Keep refrigerated once opened.

Matzo Meal: A course meal ground from matzo, a Middle Eastern unleavened cracker bread. Matzo meal is available in boxes in the kosher food section of many supermarkets.

Mirin: A very sweet Japanese rice wine used exclusively for cooking. In the absence of mirin, 2/3 cup of dry sherry and 1/3 cup of sugar can be substituted for 1 cup of mirin; or 3/4 cup of sherry and 1/4 cup of honey. Mirin can be purchased at Asian food stores, in the macrobiotic section of some natural food stores, and in the ethnic section of some supermarkets. Mirin will keep for months in a cool, dry place.

Miso: A distinctively flavored, rich, salty, fermented soybean-and-grain paste, originating in Japan. We use miso in soups, stews, dressings, spreads, and sauces. Usually, we use mild, light rice miso and less often, dark soy miso or barley miso. Miso is available from natural food suppliers, Asian food sources, and the Asian section of many supermarkets.

Neufchâtel: A soft, creamy cheese, lower in fat than cream cheese, that can successfully replace cream cheese in many of our recipes. We purchase Neufchâtel in bulk through our cheese supplier; it is also available in 8-oz. packages in many supermarkets.

Old Bay Seasoning: This spice blend from the areas around the Chesapeake Bay is used primarily on fish and seafood, most frequently (and most liberally) as a seasoning for steamed crabs. An interesting blend of spices, Old Bay has found its way into some of our egg salads, mayonnaise dipping sauces, and dressings. Old Bay can be found in the spice or seafood section of many supermarkets. If it is unavailable, consider ordering it from The Baltimore Spice Co., Baltimore, Md. 21208.

Orzo (rosamarina): A small, rice-shaped pasta that cooks quickly, so can be added raw to simmering soups and stews. Orzo provides a good bed for roasted vegetables, stews, and intensely seasoned fish or seafood platters. It is available from wholesale food distributors, Italian or Greek food suppliers, and gourmet food suppliers and can be found in the ethnic section of many supermarkets.

Polenta: We serve this Italian cornmeal "pudding" beneath Italian or Latin American stews and vegetable dishes. *The simplest version requires water and cornmeal in a 3:1 ratio cooked with salt for 30 minutes. Richer versions include butter or olive oil and Parmesan or Cheddar cheese. We often serve polenta cutlets: Pour out hot polenta in a thin layer on a baking sheet and refrigerate. Within an hour it will have stiffened and can be cut into pieces. Cut the chilled polenta into triangles and then dip the cutlets into egg, bread crumbs, and Parmesan cheese. Next, bake until crisp and serve topped with a favorite tomato sauce.*

Rosamarina: The Italian word for *orzo* (see above).

Seitan (wheat gluten): Used throughout Asia as a meat substitute, this low-fat, protein-rich, chewy, flavor-absorbing wheat by-product is becoming increasingly popular among consumers who are yearning for the texture of meat without the cholesterol or moral conflict. Seitan is a commercial product available at Asian food stores and, increasingly, in natural food stores. Although seitan or wheat gluten originates in Asian cuisines, we've discovered that it can be borrowed to "beef up" other ethnic dishes as well. Refrigerate after opening; it will keep for 1 week.

Sesame Oil, Dark: When our recipes call for sesame oil, we are referring to the dark, aromatic variety extracted from roasted sesame seeds. Dark sesame oil is amber in color and its flavor adds warmth and depth to many Asian dishes. Its flavor is strong, so use sparingly. Light sesame oil has a very different taste and cannot be substituted. Dark sesame oil can be purchased through Asian food distributors and in Asian food stores and the ethnic section of many supermarkets. To prevent rancidity, store in a cool place. Caution: dark sesame oil scorches easily so it should be used as a flavoring, not as a cooking oil.

Shiitake Mushrooms: Fresh or dried, this unusually flavored Japanese mushroom can richly flavor broths and sauces. Shiitakes are expensive, but only a small quantity are needed to add their distinctive flavor. Additionally, the liquid remaining from softening the dried mushrooms carries their essence and can be used as an ingredient. Shiitakes are available at Asian food stores and through specialty foods suppliers.

Soy Sauce: This Asian liquid condiment is used as a flavoring and source of sodium. Because soy sauce is intensely salty, use less salt if supplementing with soy sauce for its flavoring properties. We use soy sauce in most of our Asian dishes and have also discovered that it adds depth, flavor, and sweetness to many of our soups, stews, and bean dishes, regardless of their ethnicity. We prefer additive- and preservative-free soy sauces and have found them to be of superior quality. Soy sauce can be obtained from Asian foods distributors and supermarkets. It is often available in bulk at Asian food stores, natural food stores, and from natural food suppliers. There are low-sodium varieties of soy sauce available.

Star Anise: This Chinese spice, named for its eight-pointed star shape, is used whole or ground. Star anise has a mild licorice flavor that intensifies with cooking. It is available at Asian food stores, through Asian and gourmet food distributors, and at some specialty spice shops. Whole Star Anise will keep for months when stored in a tightly lidded glass jar in a cool, dry place. Grind right before using for the best flavor.

Sun-dried Tomatoes: This tart-sweet form of tomatoes, like olives or capers, adds a rich and sharp surprise of concentrated flavor. We use sun-dried tomatoes in our pita sandwich fillings, with very mild cheeses, and in rich sauces. They can also be a delicious component of a grilled vegetable platter. As with most dried foods, the flavor of sun-dried tomatoes is intense and the cost is high. But because of the concentrated flavor, a few go far. Sun-dried tomatoes are sold dried, vacuum-packed, and oil-packed. Soak sun-dried tomatoes in hot water for about 20 minutes to soften and plump before adding to a dish. The vacuum-packed and oil-packed tomatoes are ready for immediate use. We have found that the vacuum-packed tomatoes are less salty and superior in taste. Sun-dried tomatoes are available at Italian markets and gourmet food stores, through specialty food suppliers, and in the Italian foods section of some supermarkets.

Szechuan Peppercorns: These reddish-brown, split-husk peppercorns have a mild peppery flavor and release a distinctive aroma when toasted. Toast in a dry skillet until the peppercorns begin to smoke. Crush to a fine powder in a spice grinder or with a mortar and pestle. Szechuan peppercorns are available from Asian grocers and Asian and gourmet food suppliers and in the ethnic section of some supermarkets. Store whole and untoasted in a tightly lidded jar.

Tahini: This light, pourable paste is made from unroasted, hulled, and ground sesame seeds. It has a creamy texture and a beige color and is primarily used in Mediterranean and Middle Eastern dishes. It should not be confused with the sesame paste found in certain natural food stores and Asian groceries, which is darker, stiffer, much stronger tasting, and usually called sesame paste. Tahini is available from natural food distributors and in the ethnic section of many supermarkets.

Tamarind Concentrate: This brown, glossy paste with a sour and distinctive taste is sold in small jars, and is used as a flavoring in Indian and East African cooking. It is made from the seeds of a small tropical tree native to those regions. Tamarind concentrate can be added directly to a dish or dissolved first in hot water. It can be purchased at Indian and Asian food stores.

Tempeh: A cultured soybean product that is an important source of protein in Indonesia. Tempeh absorbs flavors well and has a chewy, meaty quality. We most often sauté it with onions and spices or crisp-fry it. Tempeh usually comes frozen. It is most easily handled if semithawed and then cut into cubes before cooking. It is available at natural food stores and through natural food distributors.

Tofu (bean curd): This soybean product is produced in white cakes of varying weights. Tofu has little taste on its own, and its culinary value lies in its ability to absorb seasonings readily while contributing protein and substance to a meal. Tofu is a popular source of protein in Asian cuisines, but we use it globally. See Tofu Burgers (p. 223), Tofu Burritos (p. 303), and Delancey St. Pita (p. 74).

> *Pressing Tofu:* This process extracts water from tofu, giving it a chewier texture and allowing it to absorb flavors more intensely. Arrange the tofu on a baking sheet, rest another baking sheet on top of the cakes, and balance a weight on the top sheet. The weight can be a stack of books or plates. Press the tofu for 30 minutes, remove the

weight, and drain off the water that has been pressed out. The tofu is now ready to be sliced.

Freezing Tofu: This treatment of tofu yields a drier product that we crumble or shred and use to lend a meatlike texture to burritos, stuffed cabbage, borekas, and chili. To freeze tofu, arrange the number of cakes needed on a baking sheet. Freeze for at least 4 hours; then thaw overnight in a cooler. Once thawed, squeeze the tofu like a sponge, removing as much water as possible. The tofu is now ready to be crumbled or shredded for cooking.

Tortillas: Tortillas are most familiar to us in Mexican and Latin American dishes: tostados, enchiladas, and burritos. We've also found them to be a convenient and versatile substitute for the traditional wrappers of other cuisines. See, for example, Mu Shu Vegetables (p. 285) and Roti (p. 293). Wheat tortillas range in size from 6 inches in diameter and up; corn tortillas are generally small, 4½–6 inches in diameter.

Udon Noodles: The Japanese traditionally use these noodles in their flavorful broths and soups. Udon is a hearty wheat noodle, slightly wider and flatter than linguine. It is available in Asian food stores and where Japanese foods are sold.

Vegan: This form of vegetarianism excludes all animal products, including dairy, eggs, and, at times, even honey.

Approximate Percentage of Edible Portions in Fresh Fruits and Vegetables *

Fruit/Vegetable	Percentage (%) †
Apples	76
Asparagus	56
Avocado	72
Banana	67
Beans, green or wax	88
Beets	76
Blueberries	86
Broccoli	61
Brussels sprouts	74
Cabbage, green	79
Cantaloupe, served without rind	50
Carrots	82
Cauliflower	55
Celery	75
Chard	77
Cherries, pitted	89
Cranberries	97
Cucumbers, unpared	95
pared	73
Eggplant	81
Endive, chicory, escarole	74
Grapefruit, sections	47
Grapes, seedless	95
Honeydew melon, without rind	57

*To find the quantity to purchase, divide the recipe amount by the percentage yield. For example, if a recipe calls for 4 lbs. of apples, peeled and cored, divide 4 by 0.76 to yield 5.26 lbs. to be purchased.

†Percentage is calculated on the basis of 1 pound as purchased.

Adapted from *Food Buying for Type A School Lunches*, U.S. Dept. of Agriculture, PA-270, revised 1972.

Appendix 1 (Continued)

Fruit/Vegetable	Percentage (%) [†]
Kale	74
Lettuce, head	75
Lettuce, leaf	67
Mushrooms	97
Okra	78
Onions	89
Orange sections	56
Parsnips	85
Peaches	76
Pears	78
Peas, green	38
Peppers, green	82
Pineapple	52
Plums	94
Potatoes	81
Potatoes, sweet	80
Rhubarb, partly trimmed	86
Rutabagas	85
Spinach, untrimmed	74
partly trimmed	92
Squash, acorn	88
Squash, Hubbard	66
Squash, zucchini	98
Strawberries	89
Tomatoes	91
Turnips	81

Appendix 2

Volume–Weight Equivalents

One of the most challenging aspects of assembling our recipes is related to establishing a consistency in weights and volumes. Often the size of our eggs in a given week, the way we did or did not pack our grated cheese, down to the size of our florets both differed, at times, from the industry standard, and sometimes even among ourselves.

Ultimately, we found agreement among our testers and decided to reproduce our list for you. When our measurements came close to the industry standard, we used the industry standard. When there was a significant difference, we went with our measures, because they more closely represented the quantity, size, and shapes of the ingredients we use.

Our weights and measures apply to the ingredients we use after they have been prepped for cooking—cleaned, cored, peeled, seeded, and stemmed.

We offer one last word about measuring. With the exception of our desserts, our seasoned cooks never measure ingredients for the dishes in our repertoire. As a result, these dishes rarely look exactly the same twice and often this is how recipes actually improve. We hope we have given you a group of reliable delicious recipes, but we are not possessive and hope that you as professional chefs will feel free to modify and innovate as you see fit or as the spirit moves you. And, please, share your successes with us.

Ingredient	Volume	Weight
Apples, peeled, diced	3⅓ cups	1 lb.
Artichoke hearts	3 cups (12 whole)	1 lb.
Asparagus, sliced	3⅓ cups	1 lb.
Avocados, peeled, pitted, cubed	2 cups	1 lb.
Bananas, sliced	2 cups	1 lb.
Barley, uncooked	2 cups	1 lb.
Beans, fresh, cut	3⅓ cups	1 lb.

(continued)

Ingredient	Volume	Weight
Beans, dried, uncooked (see p. 468 for cooked weights and measurements)		
Black	2½ cups	1 lb.
Chick-peas or garbanzo	2¼ cups	1 lb.
Great Northern	2½ cups	1 lb.
Kidney	2⅔ cups	1 lb.
Lentils	2½ cups	1 lb.
Lima	2⅔ cups	1 lb.
Navy pea	2¼ cups	1 lb.
Pinto	2½ cups	1 lb.
Blueberries, fresh	3½ cups	1 lb.
Bread crumbs, dry	1 qt.	1 lb.
Bread crumbs, fresh	2 qts.	1 lb.
Broccoli, florets	5¼ cups	1 lb.
Bulghur, raw	3 cups	1 lb.
Cabbage, shredded	5⅘ cups	1 lb.
Carrots, raw sliced	3 cups	1 lb.
Cauliflower, coarsely chopped	2½ cups	1 lb.
Celery, chopped	1 qt.	1 lb.
Cheeses, grated		
Bleu	1 cup	4.75 oz.
Cheddar	1 cup	3 oz.
Feta	1 cup	4 oz.
Monterey Jack	1 cup	3 oz.
Mozzarella	1 cup	3 oz.
Parmesan, coarsely grated or shredded	1 cup	4 oz.
Provolone, mild	1 cup	3 oz.
Swiss and Jarlsberg	1 cup	4 oz.
Chili peppers	4 sm.	2 oz.
Coconut, dried, shredded	1 cup	4 oz.
Coconut milk, unsweetened	2 cups	14 oz.
Corn, kernel	2⅔ cups	1 lb.
Cornmeal	3 cups	1 lb.
Couscous, uncooked	2⅓ cups	1 lb.
Cucumbers, seeded, diced	3½ cups	1 lb.

(see p. 468 for cooked weights and measurements)

Ingredient	Volume	Weight
Currants	1 qt.	1 lb.
Egg, large	2 cups	1 lb.
Eggplant, diced	1 qt.	1 lb.
Garlic, peeled	8 cloves	1 oz.
Leeks, chopped	1 qt.	1 lb.
Lemon	1 lemon = 2 Tbsp. juice/ 1 Tbsp. peel	
Mushrooms, sliced	5 cups	1 lb.
chopped	6 cups	1 lb.
Noodles, raw	5⅓ cups	1 lb.
Nuts, chopped	1 qt.	1 lb.
Okra, frozen, chopped	3¼ cups	1 lb.
Olives, chopped	2⅔ cup	1 lb.
whole	1 qt.	1 lb.
Onions, chopped	1 qt.	1 lb.
Parsley, fresh, chopped	3 qts.	1 lb.
Peaches, fresh, sliced	3 cups	1 lb.
Peanut butter	1¾ cups	1 lb.
Peanuts	3¼ cups	1 lb.
Peas, green	3¼ cups	1 lb.
Peppers, bell, chopped	4 med. = 1 qt.	1 lb.
Potatoes, raw, diced	1 qt.	1 lb.
white, cooked	2 cups	1 lb.
sweet, cooked	2 cups	1 lb.
mashed	2½ cups	1 lb.
Raisins	3¼ cups	1 lb.
Rice, brown, raw	2½ cups	1 lb.
cooked	2⅓ cups	1 lb.
Scallions, chopped	1 cup	2.5 oz.
Snow peas, with strings removed	5⅔ cups	1 lb.
Spinach, raw	5 qts.	1 lb.
cooked	2½ cups	1 lb.
frozen	1⅓ cups	1 lb.
Squash, summer and zucchini, diced	3 cups	1 lb.
Squash, winter, peeled, cubed	1 qt.	1 lb.

(continued)

Ingredient	Volume	Weight
baked, mashed	2 cups	1 lb.
Tomatoes, fresh, chopped	2²/₃ cups	1 lb.
canned, with juice, crushed	2 cups	1 lb.
canned, with juice	#10 can/3 qts.	6 lbs. 6 oz.
drained	2 qts.	4 lbs. 12 oz.
sun-dried	1 cup	3 oz.

Vegetarian Pyramid

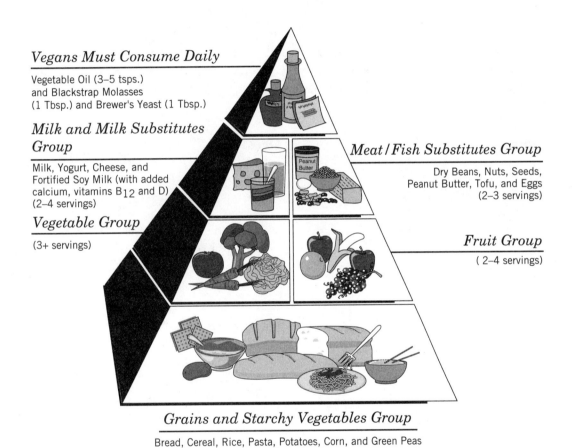

Vegans Must Consume Daily

Vegetable Oil (3–5 tsps.)
and Blackstrap Molasses
(1 Tbsp.) and Brewer's Yeast (1 Tbsp.)

Milk and Milk Substitutes Group

Milk, Yogurt, Cheese, and
Fortified Soy Milk (with added
calcium, vitamins B_{12} and D)
(2–4 servings)

Vegetable Group

(3+ servings)

Meat / Fish Substitutes Group

Dry Beans, Nuts, Seeds,
Peanut Butter, Tofu, and Eggs
(2–3 servings)

Fruit Group

(2–4 servings)

Grains and Starchy Vegetables Group

Bread, Cereal, Rice, Pasta, Potatoes, Corn, and Green Peas
(6–11 servings)

List of Nondairy and Vegan Dishes

All of these recipes are nondairy. Included are compositions in which grated cheese, sour cream, yogurt, or hard-boiled eggs are optional accompaniments but are not essential to the tastiness of the dish. The stews and sautés section also contains recipes not listed here that could be slightly altered to become nondairy dishes. For example, serve Mexican Vegetables without the cheese topping and on a bed of rice, instead of split cornbread. Recipes with an asterisk after them are also vegan—they contain no animal products, including eggs or honey.

Soups

Autumn Gold*
Black Bean*
Budapest Vegetable*
Davina Stein's Vegetable*
Finnish Golden Split Pea*
Gazpacho*
Lebanese Vegetable*
Miso-Vegetable*
Mulligatawny*
North African Split Pea*
Portuguese Kale and White Bean*
Turkish Spinach-Lentil*
West African Peanut*

Sandwiches and Dips

Baba Ganoush*
Delancey St. Pita*
Floating Cloud Pita*
Hummus*
Mockamole*
Monterey Pita*
Olivada*
Roasted Eggplant-Pepper*
White Bean Dip*

Dressings

Honey-Mustard Vinaigrette
Japanese Dressing*
Lemon-Tahini Dressing*
Miso-Ginger Dressing*
Roasted Garlic Dressing*
Tofu Mayonnaise*
Tofu-Basil Dressing*
Vinaigrette Salad Dressing*

Main Dish Salads

Black Bean and Rice Salad*
Couscous with Artichoke Hearts and
    Walnuts*
Rice Salad Provençal*
Russian Salad
Tabouli*
Thai Noodle Salad*
Udon Noodles and Vegetables*
Vegetable-Tofu Almondine*
White Bean and Tomato Salad*

Casseroles

Potato Kugel
Tofu "Meatloaf"

Fish

Caribbean-Style Fish
Chesapeake Catfish
Fish Algiers
Fish Cantonese
Fish Marseilles
Fish West African Style
Fish with Artichoke Hearts and Red
    Peppers
Flounder with Spinach and Almonds
Mediterranean Fish Stew
Patrani Machi
Salmon Teriyaki

Legumes

BBQ Tempeh and Peppers*
Caribbean Black Beans*
Creole Beans and Rice*
East-West Braised Eggplant*
Greek-Style Cannellini and Vegeta-
    bles*
Honolulu Beans*
Jerk Tofu*
Lentil Dhal*
Refritos*
Seasoned Tempeh*
Seasoned Tofu*
Spicy Chick-Peas
Tofu Burgers*
Tofu-Vegetable Croquettes*

Pasta

Pasta e Fagioli*

Sauces and Salsas

Aioli
Asian Marinade*
Avocado Salsa*
Citrus Salsa*

Fennel-Mustard Sauce
Hot Sauce*
Mango Salsa*
Peanut Sauce*
Taratour Sauce*

Side Dishes

Artichoke Heart-Tomato Salad*
Asian Cabbage Slaw*
Asian Greens*
Bulghur Pilaf*
Cantonese Roasted Vegetables*
Carrot Salad*
Easy Artichokes*
Fassoulia*
Golden Orzo*
Golden Spanish Rice*
Greek Roasted Potatoes*
Kasha with Mushrooms
Marinated Vegetables*
Oasis Chutney*
Pasta with Peas and Onions*
Peach Chutney*
Rice Pilaf with Orzo*
Roasted Vegetables*
Sara's Greens*
Sweet and Sour Red Cabbage*

Stews and Sautés

Brunswick Stew*
Caribbean Vegetable Stew*
Eggplant Mykonos*
Eggplant-Spinach Curry*
French Ragout*
Golden Curry*
Green Bean and Fennel Ragout
Groundnut Stew*
Mapo Tofu*
Menestra*
Sweet and Sour Vegetables*

(continued)

Appendix 4   ∾ ∾ ∾ **485**

Thai Curry*
Tofu with Vegetable Sauté*
Vegetable Tajine*
Vegetables Rabat*
Winter Vegetable Stew*

Stuffed Vegetables
Chiles en Nogada*
Dolma*
Eggplant Niçoise*

Holiday Stuffed Squash*
Stuffed Peppers Mexicana*

Desserts
Classic Poached Pear*
Fresh Orange Compote*
Gingered Plum Sauce*
Scandinavian Dried Fruit Pudding*
Tropical Fruit Salad

Index

Index